THE
PERFECTION
DECEPTION

THE
PERFECTION
DECEPTION

Why Trying to Be Perfect Is Sabotaging Your Relationships,
Making You Sick, and Holding Your Happiness Hostage

JANE BLUESTEIN, PhD

Health Communications, Inc.
Deerfield Beach, Florida

www.hcibooks.com

Library of Congress Cataloging-in-Publication Data
is available through the Library of Congress

© 2015 Jane Bluestein, PhD

ISBN-13: 978-07573-1825-2 (Paperback)
ISBN-10: 07573-1825-8 (Paperback)
ISBN-13: 978-07573-1826-9 (ePub)
ISBN-10: 07573-1826-6 (ePub)

Publisher: Health Communications, Inc.
        3201 S.W. 15th Street
        Deerfield Beach, FL 33442–8190

Cover design by Larissa Hise Henoch
Interior design and formatting by Lawna Patterson Oldfield
Author photo by Steve Bercovitch, Distinctive Images, Inc., Delray Beach, Florida

*Dedicated to the healthy pursuit of excellence;
to the right to recognize our beauty, our gifts, and
the power of our spirit; and to the courage
to reclaim what's been lost.*

CONTENTS

ACKNOWLEDGMENTS

During the course of researching this book, I sent out several requests for specific information and experiences. My online network never failed to respond, and their voices are as much a part of this book as any print resource I discovered. I only regret that I could not include all of the contributions in the text of this book.

I wish to express my thanks for the responses, input, validation, inspiration, and encouragement that the following people shared through personal interactions, emails, interviews, conversations, surveys, written correspondence, media clippings, snail mail, phone calls, and posts on social media sites. This list also includes individuals who have provided support, information, guidance, or inspiration at various points during my journey. This book would not be the same without their generous and important contributions.

Sallie Ackley
Miriam Adderholdt
Simone Albert
Titus Alexander
Rudolf Alfano
Mel Alper

Rhea Alper
Marilyn Anderson
Hamidah Bahashwan
Wale Balogun K.
Beth Bauer
Judith Bennett

Peggy Bielen
Garland Blackwell
Irv Bluestein
Steve Bluestein
Sherry Bolinger
Peter Bowman
Roberta Kaplan Braverman
Flo Bry
Glenn Capelli
Betty Carlson
Brynn Carter
Charlene Cheek
Eric Chong
Barb Clark
Lynn Collins
Kimanzi Constable
Cheryl Converse-Rath
Tammy Cox
Lisa Cramer
Todd Daniels
Stan Davis
Veronica de Andres
Jennie de Groat
Olga and Jacques DeQuillien
Dorothy Distel
Deborah Drake
Willie Drinkwater
Lisa Drucker
Renetta DuBose
Bernie Dunham
Gary Dutery
Anissa Emery

Nicola Everitt
Theodora (Teddy) Fakles
Evonne Fisher
Susan Fitzell
Joanna Folino
Jacqueline Fowler
Ken Fraser
David Friedli
Pamela Victoria Garrett
Sally Giannini
Virginia Duran Ginn
Paul Grover
Susannah Grover
Laura Gutman
Tabitha Hall
Betty Hatch
Carol Noel Hawley
Kathleen Hayes
Judy Heck
Mark Justice Hinton
Beti Wyn Holcomb
Marilyn Hosea
Betina Hsieh
Marsha Pomeroy Huff
Victor Allan Caraos Ilagan
Mark Ita
Eric Katz
Martha Kaufeldt
Susan Klebanoff
Nancy Knickerbocker
Hannah Kohl
MaryAnn Kohl

Mary Alyce Lach
Cathy Ladman
Claire Landman
Lynne Lang
Beth Langley
Janessa Leonski
Trudy Ludwig
Margit Crane Luria
Loretta Maase
Karen Manahan
Dave Markowitz
David Marshall
Wendy Marshall
Piero Mattarelli
David Maxwell
Ida Mazzoni
Evelyn Mercur
Marilyn Mercur
Susan J. Miller
Chick Moorman
Robert Morrow
Dennis Mutchler
Kristie Bates Norwood
Matt Orrison
Janice Patton
Morgan Patton
Barbara Pero
Tawnya Perry
Sandra Pokos
Silke Powers
Kay Provolt
Andy Quiñones

Darren Raichart
Cindy Ray
Robert Reasoner
Maurine Renville
Diane Rheos
Ines Rivera
Joi Mushie Nina Robinson
Tom Robinson
Marcia Rosen
Mollie Rosenfield
Marc Rubenstein
"Biker Steve" Saiz
Jo Ann Schaefer
Elizabeth Schoch
Linda Seligson
Will Shank
Mark Sheldon
Sherry Shellenberger
Steven Smiley
Jennifer Smith
Michael Smith
Kayla Chance Snell
Linda Sorenson
Mercedes Stewart
Debra Sugar
Sharon Tandy
Lisa Tannenbaum
Jerry Tereszkiewicz
Paul Tereszkiewicz
Liesel Teversham
Claude Thau
Don Tillman

Michelle Tillman   Jeff Wolfsberg
Aaron Trummer   Carl Young
John Vasconcellos   Karen Young
Kim Weiss   Virginia Zeuli
Mary Sue Williams   Ralph Zotter
Venita Wolfe

PART I

Welcome to Our Perfect World

CHAPTER 1

"What's Wrong with Perfectionism?"

A few weeks after I started work on this project, I ran into a friend I hadn't seen in a while. When he asked what I was up to, I said I was doing research for a book on perfectionism. He just stared at me. "What's wrong with perfectionism?" he asked. Several others have posed similar inquiries, occasionally continuing with a tirade on shoddy workmanship and terrible customer service—as though that were the only alternative. "If you ask me [I didn't], we need a whole lot *more* perfectionism," one individual insisted.

Oh, silly people. Of course we don't. There is a very big difference between striving for excellence and striving for perfection. Dedicating ourselves to doing our best and aiming for continual improvement is healthy and desirable. Hiding our naturally flawed humanness

> There is a very big difference between striving for excellence and striving for perfection.

behind a deceptive image of perfection is stressful, exhausting, and ultimately crazy-making.

Oddly, the literature is all over the place on this topic. I've seen a dozen or so self-assessment quizzes—and at least as many definitions of perfectionism and lists of characteristics of perfectionistic people. Several theories tried to distinguish "healthy perfectionism" from "neurotic perfectionism," often with an inventory of "advantages" of perfectionism thrown in. These comments raised some major red flags for me. Considering the risks of equating our worth and adequacy with our ability to maintain an illusion of perfection, I see this distinction as frankly misleading and dangerous.

So I want to be very clear about the basic premise on which this book is based: Perfectionism is *not* a good thing. I've witnessed (and experienced) its toxic and corrosive effects on our thinking, our bodies, our relationships, our work, and our sense of worth. It's a handy mask for a fear of making mistakes or being on the receiving end of negative judgments and rejection—a disordered adaptation to a need for safety, approval, and a sense of adequacy, driven by a belief system that tells us we're not good enough, don't have enough, or haven't achieved enough. It's the voice of the Inner Critic that screams "failure," "loser," or "fraud," regardless of the authenticity of our efforts, progress, or success.

> Perfectionism is not a good thing. I've witnessed (and experienced) its toxic and corrosive effects on our thinking, our bodies, our relationships, our work, and our sense of worth.

Paul Hewitt, a psychologist who has been researching perfectionism for decades, has little patience "with researchers who argue that perfectionism—the need to be or appear perfect—can sometimes serve as a healthy motivation for reaching ambitious goals." People who make that claim "just ignore the fairly large literature that says that it's a vulnerability factor for unipolar depression, anorexia, and suicide," he says.[1] Hewitt's website includes a quote by poet Alfred de Musset that says, "Perfection does not exist. To understand it is the triumph of human intelligence; the desire to possess it the most dangerous kind of madness."[2]

Happily, the majority of contributors and researchers agree. "Perfectionism is a wound," writes psychologist Thomas Greenspon. "It is never healthy, and it may never heal entirely."[3] Author Anne Lamott calls perfectionism "the voice of the oppressor. It will keep you very scared and restless your entire life if you do not awaken and fight back."[4] Comedian Craig Ferguson observed in a television interview, "I think perfectionism is a manifestation of self-hate."[5] And author and blogger Penelope Trunk finds it "amazing that people admit to being perfectionists. To me, it's a disorder . . . Perfectionism messes you up. It also messes up the people around you."[6]

Theologian F. Forrester Church views perfectionism through the lens of addiction, as dangerous and destructive as any substance or behavior. "Whether it is for riches or thinness, fitness or knowledge or fame, the desire for perfection shuts out all other people and pleasures one by one. It is an addiction like cocaine: even more deadly in proportion to its purity."[7] And sociologist Christine Carter notes that "perfectionism is not a happiness habit . . . As a recovering perfectionist I can testify that perfectionism is the absolute bane of happiness."[8]

So this book is about what happens when our aspirations and self-concepts are defined by something artificial and unrealistic, something outside ourselves, something beside the pure joy of doing, creating, learning, or just being. Because whether perfectionism is motivated by a need for other people's approval, by an ego identification with some socially engineered fad, or as a matter of conditioning that impels us to self-impose expectations that are impossible to reach, the outcomes will invariably show up in a variety of problems based in chronic disappointment—with ourselves and others.

It's Not the Same as Doing Our Best

Few people would argue against the value of precision, care, and attention to detail in the services we receive—especially from people like mechanics, surgeons, or air traffic controllers, where an error could have life-or-death consequences. However, we're looking for ways to aspire to the highest possible levels of performance and being our best that don't conjure all the harmful, stressful, and destructive outcomes we see as tag-alongs to perfectionism.

Weighing its purported usefulness against the hidden costs presumes that perfectionism is driven by a desire for accomplishment. It's not. There are no "two sides" to perfectionism, as one contributor suggested. By its very nature, perfectionism reflects a dysfunction we don't see in even the most intensely disciplined pursuit of goals undertaken for the satisfaction inherent in the process of pursuing them.

> By its very nature, perfectionism reflects a dysfunction we don't see in even the most intensely disciplined pursuit of goals.

Rather, perfectionism is about everything that tells us that who we are is not good enough, along with our willingness to accept that message (consciously or unconsciously), and the lengths to which we go to try to change or compensate for a core belief in our own inadequacy. There are lots of ways perfectionism can express itself, but at its center is fear, fragmentation, and a deep, pervasive sense of emptiness.

I understand that the waters can get kind of murky because we're probably all extra fussy about certain things. But is the fact that my mother would be more likely to leave the house in her underwear than without making her bed an issue of perfectionism, or simply the outcome of a lifelong habit and routine? When a friend assessed her 16-year-old daughter's anger about getting a B+ as an indication of the girl's perfectionism, her daughter's insistence that she had done all the work required for an A suggested a desire for justice and fairness, not an inability to live with an error or a less-than-perfect grade.

Educator Beti Wyn Holcomb shared, "Perfectionism is unattainable, but it's a goal we often strive to achieve." Instead, she recommends setting high standards and taking steps toward success, tackling successive challenges along the way. Effort, progress, and achievements are simply parts of the process of growth and learning, which will invariably involve mistakes, setbacks, and even failure at times.

Perhaps the biggest obstacle to accepting the value of this process is a relentless cultural tendency toward all-or-nothing thinking, which makes it hard to recognize the difference between making a mistake and *being* one. So I can understand how, in this context, someone might hear my insistence on pathologizing perfectionism as a celebration of mediocrity. Please believe me: there is a healthy alternative.

I will always advocate for things like hard work, a desire to do the very best we can do, and a hunger for learning, growing, and continual improvement. But I see nothing remotely positive or wholesome about perfectionism, and believe that the descriptions of what others refer to as "healthy perfectionism" would, in most cases, fall more comfortably under the heading of "healthy striving for excellence" instead.

I also believe that there is a place *beyond* our search for perfection in which we can connect with a deep level of wholeness and authenticity, within ourselves and others—a place where we can appreciate our best efforts, imperfect though they may be. This is no small task, and it will require us to recognize and move beyond the distracting, distorting layers of superficiality and illusion that we encounter everywhere we turn.

CHAPTER 2

The Culture
of Perfectionism

Several years ago, I got a call from a then-popular television talk show, asking if I'd be available to be on a panel about parenting issues. I had done nearly 200 media interviews by then, including prestigious programs on public radio and national television, so I felt quite comfortable agreeing to participate on this show.

When I didn't hear back from them, I called to follow up. My contact confessed that despite my extensive background and proficiency in this field, they were looking for someone "younger and more hip." Well, okay then. I have no idea who they ultimately selected or if they even produced that episode, but clearly for them, young and trendy trumped knowledge and experience, even in recruiting for such a serious topic.

"The media has an aversion to humans in their natural life span," observes mental health worker Rudolf Alfano. In a culture that worships appearance, personality, social status, youth, and financial achievement, a rather narrow definition of good packaging takes on holy grail proportions. "We see the world around us in slices of media definitions of who we might be if we were perfect," says educational administrator, Aaron Trummer. We hear about "the perfect body, the perfect house, the perfect car, the perfect man for you." In fact, he says, we use the word *perfect* so frequently and haphazardly that its meaning "has become hackneyed and meaningless."

Nonetheless, it's hard to argue against the impact of this constant barrage of information about who we are supposed to be. "We're bombarded by messages from advertisers, schools, employers, and friends that we must be the best, look superhuman, smell perfect, and stay young forever," notes author Kimbriel Dean. This information "affects the way we look at ourselves and the world around us."[9]

Messages like these can ultimately condition us to confuse celebrity with significance, valuing superficiality over genuine worth, often at the personal cost of self-confidence and authenticity. Set the bar high enough and nobody can measure up. Even when you're good, someone will find a way to let you know you're not good enough. Product sales and services depend on our insecurities, inviting us to scrutinize every aspect of our lives, constantly searching for signs of lack and imperfection. Measured against artificial, inflated, and distorted standards, few of us have far to look before some item or procedure takes on must-have status.

Even those of us who know better are vulnerable. A number of videos have surfaced to expose how perfectly lovely people are transformed into impossible, unreal images, their hair and faces enhanced by professionals, their images subsequently sculpted with electronic magic to enlarge the eyes, stretch the neck, reshape the body, and conceal any hint of cellulite and blemishes. We *know* it's a lie. The "before" and "after" images prove that even the models don't look like themselves.[10]

"The ideal is based on absolutely flawlessness," claims researcher and filmmaker Jean Kilbourne, adding that "the most important aspect of this flawlessness is that it cannot be achieved." Some celebrities and models are starting to object, in some cases, flat-out refusing to be digitally enhanced. "No one looks like this," Kilbourne says.[11]

Yet my research uncovered story after story of individuals who had been sucked into this airbrushed and Photoshopped version of reality and consistently saw themselves as coming up short. "The message we hear is that average is not okay," claims clinical therapist Monica Ramirez Basco.[12] "There is a reason," writes Laura Willard, "that even when I was in really great shape, wore a size four, and was healthy, it was never good enough for me. All of my logic and intelligence have trouble combatting what I've seen as 'perfect' day after day for my entire life."[13]

And it's not just women who succumb to this pressure. "While most people agree the average woman looks nothing like what we see in fashion magazines and on the runway, rarely do we talk about how men are portrayed in those very same magazines," claims video blogger Franchesca Ramsey. "Turns out we're all affected by those impossibly high beauty standards!"[14]

For example, I discovered a story about a guy who had undergone 113 surgical procedures in order to become a "human Ken doll," his notion of the "the perfect man."[15] Also in the news was a 33-year-old man who had spent $100,000 over the previous five years so he could more closely resemble a popular teen music idol.[16] To what degree do we have to be so troubled by what we see as our imperfections that we willingly put ourselves through the pain, expense, and medical risks involved in making ourselves into the image of a young celebrity, much less a child's toy?

The Pressure to Be Perfect

"Appearance perfectionism"
is only one dimension of a
much larger issue that comes
in many shapes and forms.

Although "appearance perfection-ism" drives some of the most extreme and long-term searches for external and visible proof of worth, and may be the one aspect of perfectionism men-tioned most in the literature and media, it is only one dimension of a much larger issue that comes in many shapes and forms. Whether we're talking about the size of our thighs or absence of six-pack abs, the neatness of our homes, the status of the colleges our children attend, the quality of our sound system, the grades on our tests, or the passion in our relationships, few aspects of our lives can escape this scrutiny, and most of us will forever live in the shadow of what passes for cultural ideals.

All this pressure adds layers of stress to already complex and busy lives, and in a culture in which "we're defined by what we do and how productive we are," as physician Stephan Rechtschaffen states,[17] it's easy to see why overcommitting is so common among perfection-ists. When busyness becomes evidence of our worth, even stress starts looking kind of good. "Stress helps you seem important," says a tongue-in-cheek flyer from the Health Office of De Anza College. "Anyone as stressed as you must be working very hard and, therefore, is probably doing something very crucial."[18] Author Julia Cameron takes a more serious view: "Only recently recognized as an addiction, workaholism still receives a great deal of support in our society. The phrase 'I'm working' has a certain unassailable air of goodness and duty to it."[19]

Most of us have more to do than time to do it. We also live in the most stimulating time in human history, and there are just so many fascinating things to explore, learn, play, make, and do. So yeah, we agree to stuff that ends up demanding more time and energy than we ever expected and we get distracted because sometimes daily life is little more than one interruption after another. This, to me, is not an issue of perfectionism. We may feel just as frazzled, but somehow the dynamic

Perfectionism is the line we cross when we're over our heads because we're constantly trying to prove ourselves—seeing our frantic lives as evidence of our worth—or becoming a moving target to distance ourselves from the real issues we need to address in our lives.

isn't nearly as disordered or harmful. Perfectionism is the line we cross when we're over our heads because we're constantly trying to prove ourselves—seeing our frantic lives as evidence of our worth—or becoming a moving target to distance ourselves from the real issues we need to address in our lives.

Our vulnerability to this pressure is common and pernicious. Author and coach Liesel Teversham was already feeling overwhelmed when an opportunity for more work came in. She was afraid that her colleagues would lose respect for her abilities and capabilities if she "dared turn down this work." She was also concerned that the company offering the work would never ask her again if she declined their offer: "I had the deluded idea that only people who faithfully slaved away serving others could possibly earn respect."[20]

Look at the pressure so many of us put on ourselves to conform to a reality that simply does not suit our schedule, body, personality, income, interests, or situation. For example, how many young people have bought into the idea that they can't possibly succeed without undertaking grueling course loads, some starting as early as middle school? Straight-A, 4.0 grade point averages are no longer enough for some kids, many of whom fill their schedules with Advanced

Placement and Honors courses, shooting for a 5.0 instead—the new perfect.

And what happens when ideals fall beyond our reach? When Elicia Brown's baby refused to nurse, Brown wasn't just disappointed. "I was a failure as a mother," she wrote, noting that it was several months before she "stopped crying about this imperfect beginning" and was able to delight in her growing child.[21] Clinical psychiatrist David Burns talks about athletes and coaches who buy into the idea of that their path to "significant gains in strength and endurance" requires pushing themselves "beyond their natural limits to the point of agony." No pain, no gain, right?[22] Similarly, after neuroscientist Sandra Aamodt stated that 80 percent of ten-year-old girls in the U.S. say they've been on a diet, she concluded, "Our daughters have learned to measure their worth by the wrong scale."[23]

So what is driving these perceptions? Basco suggests that "under every perfectionist schema is a hidden fantasy." Whether this outcome is internal or external, "the fantasy is that some really good thing will come from being perfect."[24] Burns agrees, stating, "The implied promise is that perfectionism brings rewards. Are these rewards real or is the promise false and the allure based on illusion?"[25]

I see his question as rhetorical because no matter how high perfectionists climb, part of being a perfectionist is that we will never reach the top. The day after comedian Robin William's suicide made headlines, an article quoted him saying, "You have an internal critic, an internal drive that says, 'Okay, you can do more.' Maybe that's what keeps you going . . . Some people say, 'It's a muse.' No, it's not a muse! It's a demon!"[26]

The Lure of the Fantasy

With a focus on product and outcome (over process and growth, for example), perfectionism actually seems to create its own illusions. Looking good distracts from whatever lurks behind the curtain. Holcomb offers an example she sees in schools. "There are kids who score high on tests, but they can be lazy, uncaring, and poorly motivated in their day-to-day activities at school," she observes, comparing these students to the ones "who do poorly on tests but in their daily work, they are excited, industrious, great collaborators, involved on all levels, and friendly to boot!" Although high-scoring students look great on paper, the numbers don't always reflect the characteristics that make them great students, much less great friends, colleagues, or neighbors. (Or as another contributor noted, "A perfect golf shot does not necessarily go in the hole.")

This begs the question of intention and brings us back to the point of our pursuits. Educator Jennifer Smith describes perfectionism as "a desire to achieve something that lacks flaws. It is an unobtainable goal that potentially has no end." Yet the notion of perfection is so thoroughly embedded in our culture that we continue to see encouragement for its pursuit. Football coach Vince Lombardi once advised chasing perfectionism to achieve excellence.[27] Honorable intentions aside, I see one serious problem here because perfectionists rarely recognize excellence when we see it or achieve it. We can always do more, always make things better. And so the chase continues.

But what are we really chasing? Actor Jim Carrey wishes that "people could realize all their dreams of wealth and fame . . . so that they can see that it's not where you'll find your sense of completion."[28] Achieving what others might see as a perfect life, perfect body, or perfect income does not guarantee satisfaction or happiness. And how can we appreciate the good in our lives when we are consistently preoccupied with the parts we perceive to be missing, insufficient, or flawed?

Perhaps "perfect" is little more than a construct that only exists—or doesn't—in subjective judgment. Even nature isn't immune. Artist and filmmaker Xiangjun Shi has been enchanted by the idea of perfection since childhood. "However while seeking a rational world, irrationality shadows every step of my journey," she claims.[29] "I'm just dumbstruck by how nature totally enjoys the imperfect and asymmetrical." She ponders "this celebration of irregularity and randomness," describing the character of the world as "wanting to be two opposite things at once." And she closes with a comment that suggests that she has made peace with this dichotomy.[30]

But can the rest of us pull off this feat? Spiritual teacher Osho notes: "Your whole idea about yourself is borrowed . . . from those who have no idea of who they are themselves."[31]

> "Your whole idea about yourself is borrowed . . . from those who have no idea of who they are themselves."

It's not easy to disconnect who we are from the distorted reflections and projections we encounter, much less recognize the perfection in whatever beauty, talents, kindness, or achievements we bring to this life—in whatever state of growth or development we have achieved in this moment. Because it's not specifically the elevation of the superficial that's the problem, but instead, our attachment to the random characteristics assigned to an ever-changing ideal that keeps us feeling empty and broken.

CHAPTER 3

Reality as Defined by the Media

Perfectionistic ideals have been around for a while, certainly since long before television and the Internet. But the messages people received within family, religious, and cultural institutions in previous centuries did not have to compete with a daily deluge of program content, advertisements, product placement, billboards, or website banners and pop-up ads. The sheer volume of information we encounter in an average day has skyrocketed in recent years, with nonstop directives about every aspect of our lives. So of all the influences that encourage tendencies toward perfectionism, the media may be the easiest to target, but it is also the hardest to ignore.

Try this on for a bit of perspective. By 1958, the number of homes in the United States with television had risen to slightly more than 83 percent, up from nearly 56 percent only four years earlier. By 2007, 99 percent of American homes had at least one TV, with an average of 2.24 sets in each home. Globally, a 2011 report shows televisions in 98 percent of homes in industrialized countries and, across what media expert Tomi Ahonen calls the "digital divide," 73 percent of homes in emerging countries have at least one TV.[32]

Of course, we don't just *have* televisions. We watch them. A lot. "The average American over the age of two spends more than thirty-four hours a week watching live television," says David Hinckley, referring to a 2012 report, which adds another three to six hours for watching recorded programs.[33] Advertising aside, the stories, people, and situations we see portrayed in all this content can have a powerful impact on what we believe to be important, or even real.

What We See Versus Who We Are

Early television programming reflected the audience that could afford to buy TVs, although "as the households with TVs multiplied and spread to other segments of society, more varied programming came in."[34] Nonetheless, until fairly recently, there was a remarkable similarity from one program's cast to the next. Day after day, we were exposed to a world in which divorce did not exist, parents never fought with any degree of seriousness or consequence, and with few exceptions, issues like mental illness, addiction, alcoholism, or abuse were not shown or even discussed.

In most shows, even the most serious problems were conveniently resolved by the end of the episode.[35] There were few people of color or people with disabilities, and the closest thing to a nontraditional family might include a widowed sheriff cheerfully raising his son with the help of Aunt Bee. How did our own families stack up to this version of reality?

The content and characters we see in the media provide a window into lifestyles, challenges, and experiences that may look very different from our own. How-to programs feature experts who turn out beautiful recipes, flawless craft projects, and stunning home renovations. They make it look so easy because we rarely get to view the hours of prep or numerous helpers, much less the time in hair and makeup required to present us with this "perfect" package.

Oh, and if you think that whole conformity thing went out in the 1960s, just take a look at news stations these days, where the appearance of so many of the anchors—especially the women— reflect such a remarkable similarity that it can be hard to tell them apart. How many equally qualified or even better-qualified individuals missed the cut only because they didn't fit the networks' narrow appearance specifications? (Veteran news anchor Julie Chen confirmed this experience when she revealed that she was only able to advance her career after getting plastic surgery to make her look "less Chinese."[36])

While television programming has come to reflect a greater range in both diversity and dysfunction, there are still generic ideals in many of these programs, whether implied or blatantly obvious. Even the more relatable characters we watch are generally fit and thin, and often look much younger than their real-world counterparts. They have great hair, can run a mile in five-inch heels without breaking a sweat or smudging their mascara, and live in places with little hint of the piles of bills, dishes, or clothes that clutter ordinary lives.

And everybody is just so . . . pretty! That is, unless an individual is specifically cast to be the non-pretty character. This is especially true for women. "With men, there are some scenarios where it stops mattering how he looks. With women, it always matters," claims writer David Wong. "If the female wacky sidekick isn't attractive . . . then every scene needs to be about how ugly and fat and mannish she is. That has to be the core of her character."[37]

This particular brand of hostility and dismissiveness imparts powerful messages about who is worthy of love and acceptance. If every person who isn't young and thin and elegant and pretty is presented as the butt of a joke (or even a quirky anomaly), what does that say to those of us who look more like *those* characters than the rest of the cast?

Television, movies, advertising, and the Internet offer us a mirror in which we inspect and evaluate ourselves and our lives against the images we encounter. If we rarely see people who look like us, live like us, or struggle with the same issues we face every day—even if those aren't the people or situations we turn to the media to see—the discrepancies can chip away at our sense of adequacy and worth.

And if there's any doubt about the distortion in the media we consume, consider the message people get from watching pornography, which is not only widely accessible but widely *accessed*, and by increasingly younger audiences.[38] "Growing up, watching porn," said one teen in an article on the need for proper sex education, "that's sort of where you get your grasp of what's normal and what's not."[39] See a little problem here? "Yes, pornography is fiction," reported a similar article. "However, there's a risk if young women and men misunderstand sex as a result of a porn-only sex education."[40]

This issue also conveys a warped version of how bodies are supposed to look and work. In terms of the impossible standards, which generally accompany all forms of perfectionism, how will most viewers compare with what they see in an "adult" film? While some effort has been made to compare "real sex" to "porn sex,"[41] this industry has created a huge market for endurance or enlargement products for men and is considered to be a factor in a sharp increase in demand for genital cosmetic surgery for women.[42]

If "regular folks" have a presence anywhere in the media, it is usually on reality shows. The modern equivalent of a gladiator spectacle with a win-at-all-costs mentality, these programs not only lower the value of effort and dignity, but also encourage judgment, criticism, and even humiliation as a legitimate form of entertainment. They rely on flaws, failure, conflict, and drama to sustain audience engagement, legitimizing meanness, even cruelty, in the process. Anything less than someone's idea of perfect is fair game, and the more emotional the reaction the better. To what degree does this attitude give people off-screen the permission and entitlement to judge others and publicly express hurtful opinions or hateful behaviors, compounding the number of not-good-enough messages people are likely to receive?[43]

Advertising for a Perfect Life

Certainly the greatest impact of the media on our values, priorities, and needs has come from advertising. This avalanche of images and messages becomes harder to avoid as ads increasingly encroach on the content we're trying to access.

Example: in the 1950s, commercial time on television accounted for 13 percent of the show, or roughly four minutes for every half hour. Today approximately one-third of programming time on commercial stations is devoted to ads.[44] The movie experience is not much better. Commercials run in between trailers at theaters before and after the advertised start time of movies that captive audiences have paid to see.[45]

Much of our recorded media and downloads also contain ads, and it's getting harder to visit web pages or view videos without having to endure ad banners, pop-ups, or long and frequent commercials. (Even paid subscriptions for some streaming programs include commercials you can't block or skip.) And let's not forget print media. Although subscriptions and advertising have declined in the past few decades, the influence of ads in newspapers and magazines is still considered significant.[46] Print media can get away with the most dramatically deceptive images, and in some cases actually include more advertising than actual content.[47]

Temptation is everywhere we turn. What percentage of snail mail and phone calls turn out to be junk, ads, or solicitations these days? The best spam filters can barely keep our inboxes from being inundated with offers to help us attain the ideals they promote, if only we click this or buy that. So really, short of pulling the plug, stopping our mail, and never leaving the house, we are going to encounter messages that play on fears that we'll never look good, find a mate, perform sexually, sleep well, get over our cold, get where we're going, or be happy in general without salvation from what they have to sell us.

"Ads sell more than products," notes Kilbourne. "They sell values, they sell images, they sell concepts of love and sexuality, of success, and perhaps most important, of normalcy. To a great extent, they tell us who we are and who we should be."[48] But the success of any appeal to make us "better" depends on our willingness to accept the idea that our bodies, clothes, relationships, children, homes, pets, and our lives in general are somehow flawed. "Almost every commercial presupposes the imperfection, inadequacy, and misery of adult human beings," observed perception expert, Alva Noë.[49]

> The success of any appeal to make us "better" depends on our willingness to accept the idea that our bodies, clothes, relationships, children, homes, pets, and our lives in general are somehow flawed.

As a result, we have an overwhelming number of products, services, resources, and forms of entertainment competing for our attention. Perhaps it's understandable that the industry is so willing to play on weaknesses and doubts, turning our vulnerabilities into enticing catchphrases. Feminist activist Gail Dines speculates, "If tomorrow, women woke up and decided they really liked their bodies, just think how many industries would go out of business."[50] Blogger Tess Munster comments on how often we hear that "we aren't good enough if we are overweight or 'curvy.' We are constantly told that the true key to happiness is limited to the size you wear."[51]

David Wong mentions "ad campaigns desperately appealing to males who fear that they've lost their masculinity," implying that using a competitor's product will cost guys their "Man Card."[52] That's right: keep us scared enough and we start reaching for our *credit* cards. Research professor Brené Brown warns that "no one is immune. Trying to avoid media messages is like holding your breath to avoid air pollution—it's not going to happen."[53]

Shaping Young Minds

The media may not be the only thing that feeds the development of perfectionism, but all the messages we receive can have a powerful impact on our expectations and beliefs. I think that this is especially true for young people, who have always been particularly vulnerable to subtleties in advertising, images, and product placement. Sure there's some good stuff out there, including resources to help parents, teachers, and kids themselves develop awareness, discretion, and media savvy.

But content also shapes curiosity, as well as what viewers come to see as how things should be. How accurate, realistic, and influential is the information young people discover in their quests? Going online to learn algebra, for example, is less likely to distort kids' expectations or self-image than, say, going to a porn site to learn about sex. "Information isn't knowledge," claims Noë. "And information that is fast and cheap, like fast, cheap food, isn't nourishing."[54]

Pediatrician Tim Jordan sees the impact of media messages early in children's lives. When he asks middle-school girls to draw and describe their idea of an "ideal woman at 25–30 years of age," the results tend to be fairly consistent across this demographic. "Girls spend most of their time focused on the woman's appearance. Notice the word *perfect* keeps showing up: perfect teeth, boobs, hair, nails, skin, and other features. She got a full scholarship to an Ivy League college, and she's beautiful and popular without trying. This [latest] version has her weighing in at 5'7" and between 100–130 pounds, which incredibly is the most reasonable measurements I've seen yet . . ."[55]

These results probably won't surprise many people. "Girls tend to feel fine about themselves when they're eight, nine, ten years old," reports Kilbourne. "But they hit adolescence and they hit a wall, and certainly part of this wall is this terrible emphasis on physical perfection." The primary message centers on the importance of how we look, teaching us, from a very young age, "that we must spend enormous amounts of time, energy, and above all, money, striving to achieve this look and feeling ashamed and guilty when we fail."[56] Jordan shares that the girls in his studies "are just showing us the unhealthy conditioning they have already absorbed from the culture. Think how much pressure they face every day trying to measure up to this unrealistic, impossible standard. And they are screaming out, loud and clear, for guidance and perspective."[57]

But from where will this leadership come? Even the adults in these kids' lives aren't always reliable arbiters of perspective because they, too, have been subject to the same cultural conditioning and systemic dysfunction, and may not have the tools or even awareness of the problem to create balance and sanity within a system that supports neither.

PART II

Building
a Perfectionist

CHAPTER 4

Risk and Vulnerability

As easy and obvious as it is to look to the media and advertising as a key factor in the development of perfectionism, it turns out to be only one of a bunch of potential ingredients that can put people at risk. Media gives us ideals against which we examine the external features of our bodies, homes, and lifestyles. But what about the internal landscape, the characteristics and beliefs that are put in place before media messages have any possible meaning or influence?

When I first started researching this project, I found that much of the material on perfectionism focused on a very specific population or issue. Giftedness got a lot of attention, as did body image, eating disorders, and to a slightly smaller degree, parenting subjects ranging from buying the right crib to getting kids into the right college. Minorities, addictions, disabilities, and stereotypes came up as well, with contributors from a wide range of religious or ethnic backgrounds each claiming perfectionism as their exclusive birthright. While all of these groups certainly deserve recognition regarding their experiences in this context, it turns out that each represents a rather small slice of a much bigger picture.

One of the more curious comments I found declared perfectionism to be a "uniquely American phenomenon."[58] But interviews and survey responses from individuals on six continents say otherwise. This is a *human* issue. It can look different from one person to another, but it is hardly limited to a single locale. In fact, one contributor who works in several countries outside the United States noted, "I've seen it in just about every culture, though the flavors of it might vary."

Even thinking of perfectionism as a "first world" problem feels like a stretch. This isn't about status or income, nor is it an issue only for people with enough time or money to fret about things like "mommy wars and Pinterest stress,"[59] odd filters for identifying adequacy, to be sure. And yes, there are places on this planet where "toothless women smile with no shame" and "round women are thought to be just as beautiful as thin women,"[60] places where no one is likely to be especially worried about thigh gaps or genital symmetry. But I would imagine that all cultures and micro-societies have some notion of "perfect," and to varying degrees, exert pressure on members of those groups to strive to reach those ideals.

Biology and Temperament

Before we get into cultural and family influences, let's take a moment to talk about the role Nature plays in an individual's tendency toward perfectionism. I'm inclined to focus on the impact of external factors, but it would be unfair to ignore the fact that, as therapist Ann W. Smith observes, for some individuals, perfectionism "is also a part of their DNA, personality, and temperament."[61] But just how big a role do these factors play?

In the usual nature-versus-nurture argument, psychologist and youth development expert Marilyn Price-Mitchell notes that "there is growing evidence in the field of neurobiology that some of us are more hard-wired for perfectionism than others and that this becomes a lifelong personality trait. But we also know that perfectionism is nurtured by life experiences and culture."[62]

In fact, in every resource where inborn factors were mentioned, there was also an acknowledgment of the impact of environment and experiences in and outside the home.[63] Nowhere was there a suggestion that perfectionists are wholly at the mercy of their genetic makeup. This is a good thing. Because although we may not have much control over an innate biological design that predisposes people toward certain perfectionistic traits, being able to recognize cultural traditions, personal behaviors, and interaction patterns that foster these pathological tendencies gives us a good bit of control over our ability to diminish those factors that would otherwise "escalate into a lifetime pattern of perfectionism."[64]

A Word About Fear and the Brain

There's one other bit of biology that bears mention here, and that's about what happens when the brain interprets or anticipates something as a threat. The brain is designed to sort and prioritize information it receives from our environment. Anything that suggests the possibility of danger, whether real or imagined, becomes the brain's highest priority, triggering a fight, flight, or freeze response from the faster-acting limbic system. This emotional impulse generally lacks the benefit of more rational, complex cerebral operations, which pretty much shut down to allow this survival response to occur.[65]

The problem, according to psychologist Daniel Goleman, is that "the human brain hasn't had a hardware upgrade in about 100,000 years."[66] The same biological mechanism that kept our distant ancestors from being eaten by hungry predators kicks in even "when the threat is symbolic," says author Shel Horowitz. So while the point is to ensure our survival, when the limbic system feels threatened, which can happen when we feel angry, frightened, or embarrassed, for example, "it can respond not just irrationally, but destructively."[67]

This fact is important because perfectionism has a lot to do with fear. It's often linked to a fear of failure, rejection, abandonment, or intimacy, as well as risk to our basic needs for things like love, acceptance, belonging, success, dignity, and control in our lives. Being "good enough" takes on survival proportions when these needs feel threatened. This fear can actually be bigger than our most primal needs for physical safety, and sadly, even our strongest survival instincts don't always override the fears associated with perfectionism. Unrealistic expectations (from self or others) do not mix well with a fear of failure, a pattern that may explain an increased risk of suicide among perfectionists.[68]

> Being "good enough" takes on survival proportions when these needs feel threatened. This fear can actually be bigger than our most primal needs for physical safety, and sadly, even our strongest survival instincts don't always override the fears associated with perfectionism.

The compensations we choose—whether deliberate or (more likely) unconscious—are simply attempts to guarantee our seat at the table of our choosing. Understanding the ways in which our brain has interpreted our experiences as potential threats can help us face, and ultimately change, the destructive behaviors and beliefs that developed as a result of those experiences. Further, this awareness can help prevent us from contributing to someone else's sense of inadequacy, perhaps curtailing a vulnerability to perfectionism before it ever has a chance to take hold.

CHAPTER 5

Safe and Secure

I f you've ever taken a basic psychology course, you've probably heard about a guy named Abraham Maslow. Back in 1943, Maslow published a book about what motivates human behavior. Although many have since challenged his original hierarchy (which proposed that higher-level needs were dependent on the satisfaction of more basic needs), you'll be hard-pressed to find an alternative that does not include the need for safety and security.[69] A responsive and caring parent, friend, or partner can help us feel safe, as can a sense of confidence in our competence, persistence, and resilience. Lacking these assets (and assuming that our physiological needs for air, food, sleep, etc. have been met), our attention shifts its focus to our emotional and social survival.

I believe that perfectionism grows out of a desire to create feelings of safety, belonging, and worth, in part by insulating ourselves from things like criticism, humiliation, rejection, and abandonment. When these needs are not adequately met, we tend to compensate in order to survive, and the results aren't always pretty.

Attachment and Safety

From the moment of birth, babies need adults with whom they can connect and on whom they can depend. "Human beings are hardwired to attach," says Ann Smith. "Our survival depends on it."[70] Although the need for attachment continues throughout our lives, it is especially important during those first helpless and vulnerable years. The more constant and reliable this bond, the safer and more secure we feel. "When caregivers respond quickly and consistently, children learn that they can depend on the people who are responsible for their care, which is the essential foundation for attachment," reports educator Kendra Cherry.[71]

These early attachments are critical to our development. "Our earliest relationships actually build the brain structures we use for relating lifelong," explains therapist Linda Graham.[72] Further, "children who are securely attached as infants tend to develop stronger self-esteem and better self-reliance as they grow older," says Cherry. "These children also tend to be more independent, perform better in school, have successful social relationships, and experience less depression and anxiety."[73]

But here's the thing. Sometimes, the grown-ups don't have it together to be there for their kids in a way that makes this secure attachment happen. Adults dealing with a lack of skill, poor parenting models, prior or current abuse, physical or mental health issues, excessive work demands, relationship conflicts or divorce, financial stresses, grief or loss, or simple feelings of overwhelm may find bonding and caregiving difficult, even with the best intentions.

"The interruption of attachment is a universal experience for human beings dealing with stress of any kind early in life," says Ann Smith.[74] And kids whose parents are not sensitive to their children's needs, or who are unavailable physically or emotionally, may end up with "inse-cure forms of attachment style" and can be at risk for certain behav-ioral or mental health problems as a result.[75] Authors Melinda Smith, Joanna Saisan, and Jeanne Segal advise that a spectrum of attachment disorders can result from "negative experiences in this early relation-ship. If young children feel repeatedly abandoned, isolated, power-less, or uncared for—for whatever reason—they will learn that they can't depend on others and the world is a dangerous and frightening place."[76] Even very young children can pick up on a parental discon-nect and lack of response, and will immediately exhibit physical and emotional distress if their efforts to reconnect are unsuccessful.[77]

Because this attachment is critical regardless of circumstance, "chil-dren will do whatever is necessary for attachment, connection, and attention, regardless of circumstance," says Ann Smith. "While our little bodies are developing, our minds are busy reading body language and interpreting facial expressions, touch, and tone of voice in order to figure out what is needed for us to get the attention we must have for survival." When we sense our caregivers are unavailable or unrespon-sive, "our anxiety sets off an alarm in our unconscious that propels us toward action . . . to work out the best way to draw in a parent, upstage a sibling, calm the situation, or make someone happy with us."[78] Not surprisingly, some of the creative strategies we come up with look a whole lot like the characteristics we see among perfectionists.

When Parents Go to the Opposite Extreme

A few days ago, a friend posted the following quote on her social media page: "A hazard is something a child does not see. A risk is a challenge a child can see and chooses to undertake or not. Eliminat-ing risk leads to a child's inability to assess danger."[79] As a longtime

---

Eliminating risk leads to a child's inability to assess danger.

---

proponent of helping kids develop a sense of responsibility and self-management skills, this message spoke to my experiences as a teacher and as a volunteer in a health clinic years ago. In both environments, I encountered scores of young people who had such limited experience in facing challenges or making decisions that they tended to either make reckless choices, defer to peer pressure, or freeze in the absence of immediate adult guidance and supervision. Often, their experience included well-meaning, but overprotective, parents—adults who gave their kids few opportunities to explore available options, evaluate possible outcomes, or develop much confidence in their ability to handle problems.[80]

"I've seen dysfunction bred from over-attachment and from under-attachment, both of which can make a child feel inadequate and insecure," notes teacher Susannah Grover. Certainly there is a fine line between the two, and coming to a common-sense middle ground can be a challenge. Of course we want kids to feel safe, but securely attached is not the same as smothered, and many of the issues perfectionists describe can trace their roots back to a bubble-wrapped childhood.

"We owe our children love and protection," writes pediatrician Perri Klass. "We also owe them a certain amount of wisdom as they grow. It's not our job to protect them so completely that they grow up without knowing disappointment, pain, fear, or frustration."[81] Author Anna Quindlen agrees that this level of involvement isn't particularly good for kids. "If your mother has been micromanaging your homework since you were six, it's hard to feel any pride of ownership when you do well. You can't learn from mistakes and disappointments if your childhood is engineered so there aren't any."[82]

Parental worries, whether "realistic or implausible," inspire attempts to control and protect, often taking responsibility for choices children should be learning to make themselves, while also conveying a message that the world is not a particularly safe place. The adult's anxiety can compromise a child's independence and self-management. In the process, "many children begin to overestimate threat, just like their parents, and begin to view objects or situations in a fearful manner," observes psychologist L. Kevin Chapman.[83]

And although it may seem like the most logical, loving thing to do, anxiety experts Reid Wilson and Lynn Lyons have discovered that constantly reassuring kids or allowing them to avoid stressful or uncomfortable situations actually *increases* a child's anxiety and makes their world smaller as they become increasingly likely to avoid stressful interactions or situations. "Parents shouldn't take hurdles down to protect kids from insecurities," they advise. "They need to help them jump over the hurdles."[84]

For those of us who grew up in a different world—where parents weren't constantly hovering (much less joined at the hip) and where we could go off with our bikes or friends until dinner without the need for GPS tracking—the new extremes can seem a bit bizarre. But I would hardly recommend pretending that it's still 1960 because, for better or worse, it's not. Klass dismisses any nostalgia for those often-romanticized times as well. "I don't for a minute long for the dear old adventurous days before car seats, bike helmets, or childproof caps on medication bottles," she writes. "On the other hand, I think there are times when we extend our desire to protect our children from harm past all reason, sense, or hope of success."[85]

Klass acknowledges the potential for extreme risk management to create risks of its own, leaving kids "without the skills, experiences, and minor life lessons that they'll need to handle the big challenges as they grow up."[86] Authors Miriam Adderholdt and Jan Goldberg agree. "Parents who protect their children too much are depriving them of the opportunity to learn from their mistakes. They teach their children that errors are unacceptable, and that it's more important to succeed than to enjoy and learn from an experience."[87]

While I understand how headlines and current events can incline parents to err on the side of caution, I think that much of the worry and overinvolvement in kids' lives goes beyond their children's safety. For far too many parents, I believe there are also issues of identity and adequacy involved. And yes, perfectionism, too.

Being the Perfect Parent

If you're wondering why it's gotten so hard to run down the middle between attachment extremes, consider the amount of pressure so many parents—especially moms—express about their role. A 2005 issue of *Newsweek* took a look at "how today's perfectionist mothers are driving themselves and their kids crazy with the pressure to be the ideal mother, while still being fit, sociable, and sexy."[88] Quindlen, one of the contributors to that magazine, noted in an article about how hard it's become to be a good-enough mother that "we live in a perfection society now. We believe in the illusion of control, and nowhere has that become more powerful—and more pernicious— than in the phenomenon of manic motherhood."[89]

A brief aside here: it is worth noting that the majority of articles and survey responses that came up in my research focused on women, despite the fact that men are also susceptible to perfectionism. As men increasingly assume the role of primary caregiver, the "experience of hands-on parenting can configure a caregiver's brain in the same way that pregnancy and childbirth do."[90] So it's likely that this trend will continue to broaden across genders.

Quindlen was also one of millions of other baby boomers who counted herself "part of the first generation of women who took for granted that we would work throughout our lifetime, and like most pioneers, we made it up as we went along." These options came at a cost, however. If women chose to give up their work opportunities, "then the tending of kids needed to be made into an all-encompassing job." Mothers who worked outside the home felt the need to show that this choice wasn't going to mess up the kids, and approached parenting with the same seriousness as deal making.[91]

Swamped with a deluge of expert advice on baby care as well as "videos, computer software, smart baby toys, or audiotapes to advance brain development," many women reported an "overwhelming pressure of trying to orchestrate an ideal upbringing," says author Judith Warner, noting this trend among moms (especially middle- and upper-middle-class professional women) who have "gone off the deep end trying to do everything right." Not only does this approach create problems for kids, but practicing what she calls "hyperintensive mothering" puts an awful lot of stress on adults, leaving women exhausted, messing up marriages, spoiling children, and creating "a widespread, choking cocktail of guilt and anxiety and resentment and regret."[92]

In the process, parenting became a hypercompetitive sport. "Keeping up with the Joneses turned into keeping up with the Joneses' kids," says Quindlen.[93] But even if buying the right stroller or getting the child into some prestigious, expensive private school is indeed in the best interests of the child, staking our adequacy on our kids' accomplishments—much less accessories—is not a particularly healthy way for parents to satisfy their own needs for identity, value, and self-worth.

When the Boundaries Blur

In November 2009, psychologist and TV host Phil McGraw broadcast a show featuring parents of talented athletes, adults whose ambitions for their children crossed beyond encouragement into abusive, even criminal territory. These parents were "in it to win," pushing their kids past physical and emotional endurance, berating them for mistakes, and in one case, even injecting the child with steroids to increase his chance of success.[94]

"It is really important to me that my daughter be a winner," said one of the guests on the show. But clearly this was not about the kids. "We have to ask ourselves as parents when we're pushing our children, whose agenda are we running?" queried McGraw. "Is it [the child] that really wants this thing you're after, or is it you?"[95] Coach and youth sports expert John O'Sullivan describes a similar "race to nowhere" in which "an adult-driven, hypercompetitive race to the top in both academics and athletics . . . serves the needs of the adults, but rarely the kids."

> "We have to ask ourselves as parents when we're pushing our children, whose agenda are we running?"

He notes that "the course is littered with the scarred psyches of its participants," describing "a generation of children that have been pushed to achieve parental dreams instead of their own, and prodded to do more, more, more and better, better, better." As was the case with the young people on McGraw's show, O'Sullivan cautioned that instead of producing better athletes, this approach created bitter, burned out, and resentful young people who often quit sports altogether.[96]

Certainly, this situation is not limited to sports. Frustrated educators frequently complain of seeing parents' input stamped on the reports and projects kids turn in, far too complex and sophisticated for the children to have done on their own. This is about more than wanting children to succeed. Sharon Tandy, a speech and language pathologist, claimed that when students at her school are tested for admission into gifted programs and don't make the cut, the parents take it harder than the kids. She mentioned parents "who get their kids tested every six months for the gifted program," aiming for the bragging rights they associate with this placement.

Likewise, the pressure goes beyond academic or athletic achievement. "I gained a lot of weight in high school," shared another contributor. "No one bothered to ask what was going on with me on the inside. It was all about how being fat was an embarrassment to my mom. My fat was *her* failure, *her* shame," she added. And how many people have pursued the career or mate their parents desired for them, regardless of compatibility with their true interests, talents, or desires? (I've worked with quite a few parents who insist that they want their children to be happy, but who also hold very narrow and specific parameters for the choices the parents deemed acceptable.)[97]

"Some parents try to relive their own lives through their children's accomplishments," write Adderholdt and Goldberg. "They see their children as giving them a second chance to do all the things they never got around to when they were younger." They cite examples of parents who sign their kids up for piano lessons or insist that their children go to a particular college because these are things that the parents never got to do.[98] Or in the (slightly paraphrased) words of Carl Jung: "Nothing affects the life of a child so much as the unlived life of its parent."[99]

So it should come as no surprise that a list of family patterns and adult behaviors common among children at risk would include the pressure kids can experience from the adults' dependence on the kid's "appearance, achievement, or performance to give a sense of worth to the family."[100] That's an awful lot to put on a child, yet the practice of "turning tots into trophies" to satisfy the psychological needs of adults "seeking status in the achievements of their children" is widespread and apparently on the increase.[101] Separating ourselves from our loved ones, especially our children, can be an enormous challenge. It requires a great deal of mindfulness and confidence to avoid crossing those boundaries.

"Of course, parents have always been proud of their children's accomplishments," writes journalist Hara Estroff Marano. "But now children's achievements have become a marker of how their mothers and fathers are doing in the increasingly prominent job of parenting . . . In a novel twist on the age-old status dynamic, parents now rely on their offspring's competitive performance in athletics and, especially, academics for their own inner sense of security and social approval." In the process, Marano adds, "adults are creating a new kind of child labor that may be at least as unhealthy and onerous as the old. Kids no longer have to till fields from dawn to dusk or toil in sooty factories, but more and more, they are handed the burden of power-lifting their parents' sense of self." In the same article, Marano quotes author and history professor Steven Mintz, who targets the "violence of raised expectations" as a dangerous trend in child-rearing. "More than in the past, children are viewed as a project by perfectionistic parents," he contends.[102]

Alva Noë would seem to agree. "We don't have kids anymore," he says. "We *parent*. That is, we work hard to produce perfect children."[103] But to what end? And at what cost? Fusing one's identity to another person is always a risky endeavor. What will serve us far better is our ability to see and respect our kids as separate, individual beings with their own needs and their own paths to follow, as well as a healthy sense of self, *regardless* of the choices they make along the way. Because counting on kids to give us something we lack can create a perfect storm, not only for being continually disappointed and unfulfilled, but also for projecting our agendas

> Fusing one's identity to another person is always a risky endeavor. What will serve us far better is our ability to see and respect our kids as separate, individual beings with their own needs and their own paths to follow.

and neediness onto children who will either spend their lives scrambling to get our approval, or simply giving up when the task seems impossible to accomplish.

CHAPTER 6

Shaping Our Reality

The adjectives start early. From the moment of our birth, we are: beautiful, scrawny, smart, difficult, strong. Pick one. At one time or another, we've probably heard them all. And these labels are just the beginning. Add in what we learn from how people interact with us, plus the expressed or implied rules that exist in every family system or organization, and it's clear that we receive a steady stream of messages, expectations, and judgments throughout our lives. This information shapes our sense of who we are as well as the tools we use to navigate various relationships and systems.

These communications can be tangible and direct: a compliment, grade, or spoken threat, for example. But they can also be much more subtle: a smile, a nod, a raised eyebrow, or a sigh of disappointment. Regardless of how these signals are communicated, when the messages are predominantly negative or threatening, we respond with whatever we believe will make things better so we can maintain our sense of connection and safety. This can happen at any age and in any relationship, but the messages have their greatest impact when we are young and at our most vulnerable.

Seeking Safety, Earning Love

Educator Darren Raichart recalls, "As a teenager, I strove for perfection. Most of my drive came from wanting to please my dad, who
was a perfectionist. Other people told me I didn't need to be perfect,
but I tuned them out because the person I admired most expected
perfection." Turns out, Raichart is in good company. "While culture forms the social context,"
Thomas Greenspon writes, "the family is where
perfectionism is generated."[104] Many contributors agree, confirming the origins of their perfectionism in their attempts to get their parents' approval.

"The family is where
perfectionism is
generated."

In other stories, early behavior patterns emerged as more of a
pursuit of sanctuary from stressful or painful family dynamics. "Few
things were as important to my father as education and the expression
of creative talent," one contributor shared. "To his credit, he sup-
ported and encouraged my interests, especially in art or music. Sadly,
he also had a quick temper and would usually take it out on anyone
handy. But I noticed that he would pretty much leave me alone if I
was studying, practicing the piano, or down in the basement painting. So guess how I spent a whole lot of my childhood?"

"Every family is tribe, and therefore every family has its own
moral and cultural code—its own guidelines that signal: *This is how
we do things around here*," observes author Elizabeth Gilbert. "In order
to remain safe and accepted within the boundaries of the tribe, you
must follow these rules." Of course many people grow up with per-
sonalities and aspirations that don't fit the mold, and these differences can evoke threats of shame and exclusion, so it's natural that
we would do whatever it takes to adhere to the tribe's expectations.
"It's exceedingly rare for a tribe of origin to celebrate the departure

of one of its members. They really don't like it when you break the rules. Remember—those tribal rules are *sacred*. Even when the rules are totally dysfunctional and dark and insane, those rules are still *sacred*. Adherence to those rules determines cohesion, and cohesion determines survival—so nothing less than life itself is at stake here!"[105]

It doesn't take long for even very young children to figure out how to get on Mommy and Daddy's good side—or at least keep the wolves at bay. In our efforts to please, we learn to define and navigate our reality according to the signals we get from others. We hone our people-pleasing skills to earn love we're not sure we deserve.

> In our efforts to please, we learn to define and navigate our reality according to the signals we get from others.

And as clinical psychologist Andra Brosh notes, we trust that if we are "nice enough, accommodating enough, easy enough, quiet enough, supportive enough, agreeable enough, and available enough, then the people in [our] life won't leave."[106] Sure, our survival responses can produce positive outcomes, including great learning and achievement. But as Greenspon observes, "Environments of non-approval, inconsistent approval, or even conditional positive approval by adult caregivers lead to children's feelings that they can never be good enough."[107]

As long as we believe that the love and acceptance we receive is conditional, there will always be a bit of dysfunction in our compensation. "Perfectionism is an expression of a mental takeover, where the mind is trying to fill in for the missing guidance and unconditional acceptance that, in a perfect world, would be there," says Susannah Grover. "But the mental takeover is very black and white and driven by a harsh superego—the internalized critical parent—with its ever-ready devices of shame, blame, and grandiose ideas about what is achievable and reasonable to expect from oneself." She notes that this process ignores our actual developmental capabilities, "with a replacement tendency towards precociousness, driven by the perfectionistic ideation. It's crazy-making."

The Culture of Conformity

Artist Silke Powers clearly remembers her failed attempts to cut out a perfect circle in kindergarten. "I would cut on the line and then again off the line . . . I still remember everything about that day, including the look of disappointment on my teacher's face." Elementary school wasn't much better. "I could never do the art assignments right, so I was told I just wasn't good at art. I could never write essays the way our teacher thought they needed to be written, and I was told I wasn't good at writing." Although her favorite activities today involve "art—including coloring outside the lines—writing, and anything else creative, that whole part of my life was put on hold because I believed that if you don't do things the way they are 'supposed to be done,' you are doing them wrong, you have no talent, and you might as well stop trying."

Powers's experience reflects a common thread running through the fabric of our culture—the idea that there is one right way to do something and one way only, very black and white. "I firmly believe that these early messages were crucial in sending me on my path to perfectionism," she shares. "They happened at a time in my life when I didn't know better. Whatever adults said was law. And I believed every word of it."

Conformity is always based in fear. "Any tribe can turn against an individual who dares to step out of line, or who dares to question the rules, or who dares to ascend beyond what is expected or allowed," says Gilbert. "And the stakes are always the

> Conformity is always based in fear.

same: Conform, or you will be eternally punished."[108] Of course! We are conditioned by the reinforcement we get for doing as we're told, and doing it the *way* we're told. Challenge the established order and we put our sense of belonging, acceptance, and safety in jeopardy.

Structure and guidance provide a sense of security, especially when we're younger. This only becomes problematic when our beliefs, behaviors, or desires fall outside the expectations and conventions that govern our families, schools, religious organizations, or social milieu. "Conformity can be comforting," writes psychologist James T. Webb. "Being an individual, particularly if one is challenging traditions, is often uncomfortable."[109]

No doubt. But conformity comes at a cost, not just to individuals, but to our culture and economy as well, which need people who are willing to take risks and stretch the limits of the status quo. "Creativity is one of the most important economic resources of the twenty-first century," maintains Gary Gute, director of the Creative Life Research Center at the University of Northern Iowa. He notes the demand "for people to think more creatively, not only to solve problems but also to identify problems that need to be solved."[110]

Jean Van't Hut, who calls herself a "children's art enabler," agrees with the need for outside-the-box thinking. "If children are allowed, even encouraged, to experiment (and to fail), they are more likely to grow creatively. If they hear that there is just one right way to do something, they're less likely to try other things."[111] And the more often children get that message, the more intractable that belief becomes.

Kids who will jump into activities in preschool or kindergarten will, in very short time, become much more cautious about taking initiative, making decisions, investigating, and experimenting in the presence of adults. "I see that as kids get older, they stop trusting the dreaming, doodling part of their brain and start looking for the 'right' answer," says creative writing coach Karen Benke. "It takes a lot of courage to look at the world and experience things with our own eyes and ears and taste buds and fingertips and not just go along with the crowd."[112]

But being a perfectionist is often about being the best. So where does conformity come in? How do we reconcile the desire to stand out with the need to fit in? I think that the real issue is about *where* and *how* we fit in, and where we look to define what "right" or "good enough" really means. To what are we actually conforming? Are we chasing someone else's idea of what defines value, or are we seeking congruence with the needs and desires of our authentic self? What happens when we color outside the lines, and are we willing to live with those consequences, good or bad?[113]

"Just when the world requires flexibility and comfort with ambiguity, perfectionism creates rigidity," cautions Marano.[114] Perfectionism will always stand at odds with creativity because innovation involves trial and error, which generally means making mistakes along the way. But if originality and imagination consistently invite criticism, anger, ridicule, or disappointment, we will keep making the sky blue and the sun yellow, never daring to reach for a different crayon.

> Perfectionism will always stand at odds with creativity because innovation involves trial and error, which generally means making mistakes along the way.

Learning from Our Role Models

Blogger Sarah Koppelkam offers some advice about how to talk to your daughter about her body. "Don't," she says, other than teaching her how it works. She cautions against commenting on weight—gained *or* lost—and focusing positive feedback on strength, health, or happiness instead. "Better yet, compliment her on something that has nothing to do with her body," she writes. Koppelkam also advises against making comments on other women's bodies (nice or mean), and firmly adds, "Don't you dare talk about how much you hate your body in front of your daughter."[115]

Parents can be powerful models for growing perfectionists. Their guidance helps shape our ideas of acceptability and worth. The messages come in many forms, with many lessons learned from the behavior and beliefs our parents express about themselves. With body image showing up so frequently in the literature about perfectionism, I wasn't surprised at the number of contributors (mostly women, but not exclusively) who have struggled with eating disorders and related body issues. Many of these individuals also mentioned parents (mostly mothers but not exclusively) who were rather judgmental about how other people looked, and in many cases, had struggled with similar problems themselves.

"My mom was always very slender and fashionable," one contributor recalls. "When she gave up cigarettes, she put on a few pounds. I was pretty young then and happy she had quit smoking. But I remember how disgusted she'd be when she would see herself in the mirror. To pick up on her self-loathing left a very deep groove in my psyche." Adequately primed, her mother's subsequent projections, "scrutinizing what I ate, commenting when my clothes were tight, and worse, constantly praising me when I lost weight (like if she says it enough, I won't gain it back), or trying to force me to eat when she thought I was too thin," led this young woman to a lifelong mistrust of her appetite and a chronic dissatisfaction with her appearance. "Even as an adult, it was just as bad being thin as it was being fat. It's like you just can't [expletive] win."

Not all of the stories were about food or weight. Retired teacher Roberta Braverman describes how many of the parents of her gifted students could be so hard on themselves, modeling perfectionism for their children without even realizing it. "When they get something wrong, they're not willing to laugh it off. They're very self-critical, so the children become very severe with themselves." How our parents respond to the mistakes they make, whether berating themselves or projecting their anger and shame onto others, conveys very strong messages about the need to be perfect.

Likewise, if we had parents who frequently compared themselves to others, we learned another tool for developing perfectionistic habits. "My father would get angry and insecure any time one of our neighbors got a new car or a promotion," another contributor related. "Somehow, he felt that this reflected on him—their success was his failure. In retrospect, it doesn't make any sense at all, but it taught me to constantly measure myself against other people."

This model for scarcity thinking, a win-lose characteristic of dysfunctional systems, installs a belief in limited resources, whether referring to food or money, or intangibles like happiness and success, with never enough to go around. It's a part of what makes it so hard for perfectionists to come in second, or to have less of some desired attribute than someone else.

But perhaps the most dangerous role models were the ones who projected an image of flawlessness. "I grew up with a mother who was perfect," writes another contributor. "It was a heavy burden." She tells how her mother "swore that she only ever got one answer wrong on a test," and that it never occurred to the daughter to question her mother's claim until well into adulthood (and with the help of a therapist).

All fantasy aside, "Having a parent who is a superstar in some way . . . leads children to feel that they can never be good enough," writes Basco. These parents hide their mistakes and always seem to make good choices. They look fantastic, keep a perfect house, and continually perform successfully at work, and in doing so, they cast a pretty big shadow. "From a kid's perspective, this looks too hard," she adds. There is no way a child can live up to a model like that![116]

Living in a Toxic System

Healthy organizations create supportive, accepting, and caring environments for us to grow as thriving, authentic individuals. And I believe that the vast majority of parents (and others who affect the quality of children's lives) truly want their influence to have positive outcomes. So why do so many people describe their upbringing with words like *obstacle course* or *land mines*?

I would hardly argue that all perfectionists came from what we might call challenging childhoods—there are simply too many potential factors that can contribute to the development of this disorder. But if our parents and teachers got caught up in some bad habits, they certainly came by them honestly. Even with the best intentions, we seem to be mired in social constructs left over from eras long past, threads in a cultural tapestry that evolved in very different times. These patterns characterize a rather tenacious systemic dysfunction that has come up through generations, continuing to inspire beliefs and behaviors so common and familiar that we rarely bother to question them. When we step back far enough to see the big picture, perfectionism can seem like a very logical response to the ongoing exposure to this context.

For example, it's hard to imagine a perfectionist who hasn't been influenced by the social convention of impression management, the thing that keeps us scrambling to control how others perceive us. "I'd hear this all the time," said one of the survey respondents. "'You can't go out like that.' 'You can't wear that in public.' It was always about what the neighbors might think. Even strangers, people we'd never see again." Even if these admonitions were attempts to protect us from criticism and judgments, the ultimate lesson emphasizes the critical importance of serving up whatever we believe the world demands from us. We base the choices we make on anticipated reactions from others. We absorb the message that mistakes and flaws are bad, even shameful. We assume the responsibility for reflecting well on our families.

Clearly, impression management drives a great deal of perfectionistic striving. A cultural tendency toward negativity and criticism wields similar power, drawing our attention to shortcomings and imperfections, rather than appreciating effort or progress. Scarcity thinking layers on fear and competitiveness, connecting our safety and worth to an image of success that demands someone else's deficiency or defeat. Likewise, valuing product over process leaves many of us impatient for results, unwilling to persist and refine our skills if we don't achieve greatness right off the bat. Further, conformity and the need for belonging and approval keep us looking over our shoulder as we try to get it right.

There's one other pillar holding up this social paradigm, and it's one I encountered in almost every bit of research on perfectionism: all-or-nothing thinking, sometimes called black-and-white thinking or dualism. A form of oversimplification, this term refers to the notion that something is either good or bad, a success or a failure, or a winner or loser, for example—with very little space for anything in between.

This may well be an understandable response to a never-ending avalanche of new information and rapidly evolving cultural imperatives, an attempt to make sense of a complicated and overwhelming world. Unfortunately, this type of thinking also costs us our tolerance for complexity, conflict, and paradox, and for someone with perfectionistic tendencies, the results can be brutal.

Table 6.1. Cultural Traditions That Can Contribute to Perfectionism (and Other Bad Stuff) [117]

HARMFUL (Familiar)	HEALTHIER ALTERNATIVE
Impression management: pressure to look good; people-pleasing; shape-shifting to get others' approval; cover up mistakes (shame)	**Authenticity:** safety to be self; tolerance for disapproval from others; accountability; accepts mistakes as part of the process (separate from value of self)
Oversimplification: black-and-white thinking; one right way to do things; judgment; simplistic; prone to extremes; need for certainty	**Complexity and paradox:** ability to see shades of gray, multiple ways to do or see things; can tolerate differences, dimensionality, ambiguity
Scarcity thinking: competitiveness; win-lose; resistance to change; fear of losing or loss, "not enough"; only one winner; hoarding resources	**Abundance thinking:** cooperative; synergistic; win-win; "plenty for everybody"; creative use of resources; multiple winners (and ways to "win")
Negativity: focus on flaws, lack, what's not done, what's not done right; pessimism; despair; "never good enough"; inner critic: loud and clear; fear	**Positivity:** focus on accomplishments, what's done, what's done right; optimism; "good enough for now"; inner critic: present but not in charge (can override, acknowledge, ignore); gratitude
Product orientation: focus on outcome; learning to know, finish, check something off list; resistance to refining, going back to improve something once it's done; orientation: future, past	**Process orientation:** focus on experience; learning to learn, grow; persistence, willingness to make mistakes, go back and correct errors, and refine our work (product); orientation: present time
Conformity: limited, rigid set of rules and tolerances; fear of rejection; acceptance of restrictions; willing to self-abandon if necessary	**Creativity:** flexibility; open to challenge status quo; resistance to restrictions; loss of self is more threatening than rejection

CHAPTER 7

Building Our Identity

How often do we hear people say things like, "Oh, I'm no good at math" or "I can't draw to save my life"? Where do these statements come from? Most of us, when we are learning something new, are bound to make mistakes. If our messy first efforts are met with encouragement and instruction, we're much more likely to try again (and actually improve) than if we encounter the impatience, annoyance, disappointment, or anger of the person we look to for guidance. It doesn't take too many negative reactions—or even the lack of support when we are struggling with something new—before "I can't" becomes a part of

> It doesn't take too many negative reactions before "I can't" becomes a part of our identity.

our identity. Even in a safer environment later on, the stronger these beliefs, the less likely we are to step into the same arena and try again.

A friend from dance class recently shared, "My gym teacher once told me that I got an F in class because that was the lowest grade she could give me." She's one of several successful, seasoned professionals

who nonetheless carry an "unathletic" self-concept riding on memories "of being the fat kid in class, the slowest one on the track, or
the one whose PE teacher rolled her eyes in utter disgust at some
clumsy attempt at something." Even though those experiences happened decades ago (and even though we have all enjoyed this class
for quite some time), for some of us, simply showing up week after
week is a monumental achievement.[118]

What Labels Tell Us About Who We Are

The human brain has a fascinating tendency to simplify the world
by organizing it into patterns and categories. This process is essential
for the development of reasoning and thought, and although previously thought to develop much later in life, psychologists Denis
Mareschal and Paul C. Quinn contend that even newborns can display "primitive categorization abilities."[119] So this need for order
starts early. It's what helps us understand differences and similarities
in things we encounter throughout our lives.

The outcomes can be great when we apply these skills to, say, our
closets or music collections, making it easier to store and retrieve
what we need. But employing the same organization processes with
people doesn't work quite as well. Even positive labels can be surprisingly dangerous and limiting, dismissing our complexity and potential for continual growth and development.

And yet, how often do families adopt this convenient sort of short-
hand, using simple adjectives to identify their kids? "In families with
more than one child, every sibling seems to get a label in contrast
to every other sibling," writes journalist Robin Marantz Henig. So if
your kid sister is highly social, you might end up labeled "the quiet
one," even if you're only really quiet in comparison. Or you might not
get as much credit for your intelligence if your older brother showed

his brilliance before you. "There's only room for one 'smart one' per family—you'll have to come up with something else," she counsels.[120] Words create beliefs, and even if no one in the family carries a negative designation ("the messy one," "the lazy one"), these labels do more harm than good.

Years ago, I started looking at problems with praise, including issues that come up when adults use positive labels. My main concerns centered on patterns that connected children's worth to their accomplishments or their ability to please adults, compared children or complimented one child to motivate another, or used praise publicly to elevate the adult's status or skill.

I saw too many instances of praise-hungry kids and adults, whether the behavior showed up as people-pleasing, learned helplessness, a need for continual reassurance, or dependence on external approval for a sense of value and worth. I also found a far more effective approach when kids were recognized for their efforts or accomplishments instead of receiving praise for being "good" or making the adults happy. Further, connecting kids' choices to positive outcomes —privileges, for example, instead of the adults' conditional approval— also reinforced positive behavior without encouraging dependence or other negative patterns from developing.[121]

Research by psychologist Carol Dweck confirms yet another dimension of destructive outcomes of praise and positive labels, information that happens to be extremely relevant to the development of perfectionism. In Dweck's studies, students were given fairly simple tasks, which all completed successfully. However, students in one group were praised for their intelligence: "You must be smart." When kids in the other group achieved the same results, they were recognized for their efforts: "You must have tried really hard." The results of these studies consistently showed that the difference in the feedback the children received not only affected their self-concept, but also their confidence and willingness to challenge themselves with more difficult tasks.[122]

Children who were identified as "smart" tended to get quite attached to that label. When offered a choice between staying at the level at which they had been praised or going on to a more challenging task, most chose the easier activity. This way, they could continue to succeed and maintain the appearance of being competent and intelligent. They were also likely to give up when they ran into trouble and inclined to lie or exaggerate their performance if they didn't do well.

In the results of Dweck's studies, we see evidence of impression management in the children's concern for how smart they look. And we certainly see all-or-nothing thinking in their fear "that failing at some task—even a relatively unimportant one—meant they were dumb." These children were "obsessed with their intelligence, and with proving it to others," she writes. They were also concerned that having to work hard at something showed a lack of brain power. "Intelligence seemed to be a label to these kids, a feather in their caps, rather than a tool that, with effort, they could become more skillful in using."[123]

Interestingly, in Dweck's experiments, the children whose *efforts* were praised (rather than their intelligence) were far more willing to attempt more challenging tasks, and when they encountered difficulty, they proceeded as if the obstacles simply required more

> The children whose *efforts* were praised (rather than their intelligence) were far more willing to attempt more challenging tasks, and when they encountered difficulty, they proceeded as if the obstacles simply required more work or a different approach.

work or a different approach. "Children praised for effort generally want those hard [tasks] that they can learn from," Dweck observes. These students were willing to persist despite initial failure, perhaps because they had little attachment to a particular label and no superficial image to protect.[124] Her findings have important implications for parents and educators, whose feedback plays a big role in the development of children's beliefs—what Dweck calls mindsets—about their potential and ability, as well as their commitment to learning and their willingness to make mistakes.

Kids praised for being smart come to "believe that their intellectual ability is a fixed trait," she says. "They have a certain amount of intelligence, and that's that." Their primary goal involves "seeking tasks that will prove their intelligence and avoiding ones that might not. The desire to learn takes a backseat." Alternatively, the effort-praised children developed what she calls a growth mindset, believing "that they can develop their intelligence, [and] they focus on doing just that. Not worrying about how smart they will appear, they take on challenges and stick to them."[125]

Internalizing Negative Messages

It's pretty clear that the labels and feedback we get from others can increase the appeal of the deception, shifting our attention from learning and risk-taking to protecting our image. Ann Smith writes, "In painful families, children must create a pseudo-self to maintain attachment for both physical and emotional survival."[126] Well, sure. What's scarier for a child than the possibility of physical or emotional abandonment?

The more real this threat feels—regardless of the actual intentions or behavior of the adults—the stronger the drive to secure the attachment by any means possible, even if the strategies are ultimately harmful or self-destructive. This is the fear that lies at the center of our dependence on other people for approval and our sense of worth. And it would certainly explain why, among beliefs often held by perfectionists, the idea that "regard from others is conditional to personal performance" often pops up at the top of the list.[127]

Writer Jennifer Santos Madriaga admits, "For years my life was defined by deep feelings of inadequacy as well as concurrent actions of striving to keep those feelings at bay. Even as a young child, I felt nothing I did was good enough." Like many other self-professed perfectionists, she was raised (by well-meaning parents, she acknowledges) to believe that being loved required "having to prove your worth each and every day . . . I could not be of value unless I achieved something."[128]

These sentiments were echoed in many interviews, correspondences, and blogs about perfectionism. "I don't think I'm worthy of rewards or gifts or grace unless I've surmounted a series of challenges," shares attention deficit hyperactivity disorder (ADHD) advocate and family coach Margit Crane Luria. "I don't get to be Margit and live happy. I have to be super-Margit and then my reward is still conditional on passing other tests that present themselves."

Price-Mitchell writes, "I grew up in a household where no matter what I achieved, it was never enough. Believing my parents would love me more if I achieved more, I set my goals higher and higher. It wasn't until I became a parent myself that I realized my perfectionism wasn't healthy."[129] And artist Susan Klebanoff described the "double whammy" she experienced in receiving criticism of her imperfections combined with proclamations that nobody was good enough for her. How does a child process information like this?

Burns observes that in a relationship with perfectionistic parents, "a child is regularly rewarded with love and approval for outstanding performance . . . When the parents react to the child's mistakes and failures with anxiety and disappointment, the child is likely to interpret that as punishment or rejection."[130] This is a fair assessment of the process in some families. However, based on feedback from a number of contributors, the presumption of "praise for good" does not apply universally. In fact, many contributors came from homes in which they rarely received any positive feedback, or even a hint that they could ever get it right. "My parents were hypercritical about everything," business manager Jerry Tereszkiewicz reflected. "If something was done as expected, there was no comment. If there was something slightly wrong with it, we were told it was terrible."

Young children need confidence in their parents' judgment and wisdom. Whatever our parents' feedback or reactions, we naturally assume these messages must say something true about us.[131] "As little children, we acquire certain beliefs about ourselves," writes Liesel Teversham. "We give the experience certain meaning, like, 'My dad shouted at me. That means he doesn't love me.' Later that becomes 'I'm

> Whatever our parents' feedback or reactions, we naturally assume these messages must say something true about us.

unlovable, I can never get it quite right.' And those are the glasses we continue to look through our entire lives." Her way of coping with her father's criticism was to believe that she would have to be perfect to be lovable. 'There's a deep driving that makes me petrified to do anything halfway, or not perfectly. I know that I can get my 'love' by getting it right."

And if disapproval and disparagement weren't enough, many children are also held directly responsible for their parents' feelings and behavior psychotherapist Karyl McBride states, "Many times parents in dysfunctional families will blame their children or project onto

their children the bad feelings the parent is feeling at the moment."
Since kids don't know any different, these messages create an internal landscape in which the child comes to believe "'It must be me.'
'It must be my fault if my parent is mean to me, or can't love me.' 'I
must be unlovable.'" So what's a child to do? McBride suggests that
given the need "to be loved and cared for, [children begin] to try to
'fix' the adult problems so they can achieve their goal. They don't do
this consciously, of course, but many start this at a very early age."[132]

Custodians of the Family's Well-Being

Owning our reactions to other people's words or behavior can be a
challenge on a good day. In dealing with our kids, it can be even more
difficult—especially if our identity and sense of adequacy depends
on them looking or acting a certain way. Common remarks like "You
make me angry" or "I feel sad when you don't get good grades" throw
a whole lot of responsibility for our emotional well-being on a child's
shoulders. (Messages like "I'm so happy when you do well in school"
convey a similar accountability.)[133]

Projecting responsibility and blame is easy and convenient, and it
happens frequently in troubled families. As a result, "the child ends
up carrying the emotional baggage of the family," says McBride. "Kids
want peace, love, and harmony in their lives and need it to thrive
emotionally. So, if it is not there, guess what they do? Try to fix it by
trying to be a better and better kid, or they may also try the opposite
and act out to get their parents to focus on them. But they are learning and internalizing that no matter what they do, they cannot fix
their parent's problems."[134]

Even if adults don't come right out and say, "Hey, things are kind
of crappy right now so we're counting on you to pull us out of this
hole," subtle cues can trigger a rescue reflex, especially in a sensitive,

hypervigilant, or overly responsible child.[135] Plenty of people become perfectionists without direct negative projection and, in fact, many children assume the role of custodian for the family's status and well-being without ever being specifically asked to do so.

"I never thought about where the desire to succeed came from," writes contributor Michelle Tillman, who does not remember ever being pressured by her parents to do well in school or be involved in numerous school activities. "They never said anything, but I always felt that if I didn't, I would fail my parents—not myself, but my parents. I don't know what would have happened otherwise, but I have a feeling that I might even have felt worse than my parents did."

Others talked about their fear of hurting or disappointing others. Adderholdt and Goldberg relate a story of a woman who would cry when her son didn't win an essay contest. The son, not surprisingly, came to believe that if he didn't win, "my mother will cry and it will be all my fault."[136] Another resource cited a woman with similar sentiments, stating "I'm scared of failure . . . If I failed, I'd be letting myself and other people down. I've always lived my life for others."[137] And Teversham cites the frightening prospect of being responsible for hurting anyone, along with the responsibility "for 'fixing' their feelings again."[138]

Children who take on the responsibility for managing the emotional lives of their parents clearly, if understandably, have a distorted sense of their own power. Nowhere is this more evident than in the examples shared by people whose early lives included episodes or ongoing stretches of stress, violence, addiction, or other mental health issues in their parents' lives.

Silke Powers recalls the impact of her mother's alcoholism on her perception that "good was never good enough." Despite Powers's efforts to control her mother's drinking and make her happy, her mom "would still find fault and criticize [and drink]. Now I understand that it was a losing battle. But it deeply ingrained the thought in me that no matter what I do, I should be doing it better. No matter how many things I tick off my long list, I should have gotten twice as many done."

Another contributor offered her experience as the family caretaker. "My parents fought a lot," she shared. "Even as a young child, I remember this chronic urgency to *do something* to make it better. I worked hard and got good grades. I even hung out with kids they approved of, whether I liked them or not." Her comments included a willingness to withhold any opinions that were not consistent with her parents' beliefs, and to even surrender her wants and preferences to avoid upsetting them. "I thought if I could be good enough, maybe they would stop arguing all the time. At the very least, I didn't want to add to their unhappiness."

These efforts were no more successful than those of the contributors who tried to keep their parents clean and sober, but as children, we really have no way of understanding that these are not our problems to fix, nor are they our burdens to carry. We rarely realize that we are up against a hopeless enterprise until much later in life (and often with a good bit of support and therapy), if at all. Even then, it's hard to resist the temptation to keep trying, spinning faster and faster, taking on more and more, until at some point, sometimes, we just throw in the towel and quit trying. Because even that—not bothering anymore—can be a type of perfectionism, one of many ways this disorder can manifest.

PART III

The Problem with Perfect

CHAPTER 8

Through the Looking Glass: Living in a Distorted Reality

Trying to define a term as elusive as *perfectionism* presents a bit of a challenge. Because there are so many ways for this disorder to show up, any definition is going to leave loopholes, a way for us to not see ourselves in any list of characteristics we encounter —kind of like the guy who insists he's not an alcoholic because he doesn't beat his wife.

Of course, it's easy to find examples of perfectionists in the media, perhaps most interesting in the variety of ways in which these individuals express their perfectionism. Authors Martin Antony and Richard Swinson see some examples associated with anger, while others are identified with depression, anxiety, inflexibility, or a lack of spontaneity. The commonality among all of these individuals, they claim, "appears to be strict standards or expectations for oneself or others that either cannot be met or can only be met at a great cost."[139]

In the time I've been researching this topic, I have found material on perfectionism that focused on fitness and body image, fashion, housekeeping, studying and achievement, parenting, creativity, car maintenance, job performance, relationship issues, and various addictions, to name a few. Other resources slid into related areas like obsessive-compulsive disorder, hyperactivity and attention deficit, narcissism, dissociation, projection, personality disorder, and even Munchausen syndrome by proxy. The literature also offers a range of categories, including self-oriented, other-oriented, socially prescribed, overt, covert, neurotic, narcissistic, principled, hyperattentive, maladaptive, frustrated, and defeated perfectionists.[140]

I have no objection to any efforts to focus or clarify this topic—with the exception of attempts to identify perfectionism as a healthy way to go through life (often labeled as "normal" or "adaptive"). Based on this data, I could probably come up with some complex, multidimensional matrix with overlapping flow charts and lots of circles and arrows, but rather than chasing my sanity down that particular rabbit hole, I thought I'd simply share some examples of what perfectionism can look like from one person to another.

Please note that this is not a test. Some of the topics in this part of the book may look familiar, but you do not need to relate to a specific number of ways perfectionists think, act, or interact with others to qualify. You don't need to give yourself points for the degree to which each example applies. If you see yourself here, just know you're in good company. If not, well, good for you. (However, do try to notice if this material starts sounding like everybody *but* you.) Read on for some ideas for healing in the next section. In the meantime, let's start with some of the beliefs and mental constructs that many perfectionists share.

Stinkin' Thinkin'

The most obvious demonstrations of perfectionism show up in our behaviors, our relationships, and its impact on our physical and mental health. But all of this evidence has its beginnings in unhealthy thought patterns, including distorted beliefs about who we are and how the world around us operates. There's even a name for it: "stinkin' thinkin'." A familiar concept in recovery circles, the term is defined by the online Cambridge dictionary (using the more proper "stinking thinking") as "a bad way of thinking," one that "makes you believe you will fail, that bad things will happen to you, or that you are not a very good person."[141]

If we are constantly bombarded with negative messages and pressure to perform, it's easy to see how our thinking can get pretty twisted. (And as we have seen, empty praise can have the same effect.) The result is a set of beliefs that fall under this broad umbrella, what David Burns refers to as cognitive distortions or irrational thoughts that "have little or no basis in reality."[142] While several resources offer slightly different examples of this type of thinking, all present a version that is ultimately harmful. "What people think will have an impact on how they behave," contends an article on an alcohol rehab website. "Experiencing negative thoughts all the time is bad for people. Such thinking can cripple the human spirit. It can lead to depression and stops people from getting the most out of life."[143]

This road is paved with contradictions, generalizations, and rigidity in thinking, with behavioral outcomes that can include overcommitting and overdoing, underachieving and paralysis, physical and mental disorders, and failed relationships. The ingredients and proportions can vary from one perfectionist to another, but certain patterns pop up fairly consistently throughout the literature, and were evident in many of the exchanges with contributors to this book.

Zero Shades of Gray

Even by its most basic definition, perfectionism is a pretty simple, black-and-white concept. Merriam-Webster calls it "a disposition to regard anything short of perfection as unacceptable," and the dictionary app on my laptop describes it as a "refusal to accept any standard short of perfection."[144] Beyond these stripped-down definitions, most research explains perfectionism in terms of personality traits or beliefs. One of the most common of these is all-or-nothing thinking. This is actually a good place to start because so many of the behaviors perfectionists exhibit and so many of the outcomes they experience can trace their roots back to this very basic thinking disorder.

"Perfectionists frequently believe that they are worthless if their accomplishments are not perfect," advises the counseling center website for the University of Illinois. They give the example of the straight-A student who receives a B and feels like a "total failure."[145] Burns uses similar language, noting, "If a situation falls short of perfect, [perfectionists] see it as a total failure." He uses an all-too-familiar example in which eating a spoonful of ice cream translates to the perception that "I've blown my diet completely" and to the behavior of subsequently polishing off the entire carton.[146]

Stress-management expert Elizabeth Scott contrasts perfectionists with high achievers, people who strive for excellence but who don't cross the line into perfectionism. While both "tend to set high goals and work hard toward them . . . a high achiever can be satisfied with doing a great job and achieving excellence (or something close), even if their very high goals aren't completely met." On the other hand, "perfectionists will accept nothing less than, well, perfection. 'Almost perfect' is seen as failure."[147]

Even a cursory glance at the research will offer plenty of examples. "You're not satisfied unless you have it all," write Adderholdt and Goldberg. "All the track trophies, all the academic awards your school can give, all the leadership positions in your clubs. One B or one second place is enough to tip you over into the feeling that you've failed, that you're not good enough."[148] Psychology professor Les Parrott observes, "Perfectionism leaves no room for error. It pushes us to be number one, and if we aren't at the top, we feel like losers. No matter that you've done your best, says the perfectionist; what matters is not making mistakes."[149]

All-or-nothing thinking is sometimes referred to as the saint-or-sinner syndrome, contributing "to the failure of the perfectionist's efforts at self-control in activities like eating, smoking, and drinking."[150] (We're either on the wagon or way, way off.) It makes ambiguity hard to tolerate and provides the temptation to simply give up when absolute perfection seems out of reach. It's why we walk away from new tasks and activities before we've had a chance to improve the skills we need, much less master them. And it's what makes it so hard to try again when we slip or fail.

All-or-nothing thinking is also behind the rigid insistence that there is only one right way to do something, making it hard for perfectionists to compromise. It's the "off switch" that precludes opportunities for second chances, commitment, or change. It can wreak havoc on relationships because it makes win-win solutions hard to reach. (Winning can only happen if someone else loses; being right requires making someone wrong.) It's what makes parents and teachers worry that kids won't grow unless we criticize their mistakes and point out the flaws in their judgment, and what makes us think that focusing on the positive means accepting or condoning the negative. And it's what makes self-compassion so difficult for people who see the only alternative as self-indulgence or lower standards, with no balance or gray area for growth in between.[151]

Assumptions and Generalizations

Looking over my notes for this section, I flashed on a memory from my childhood. Whenever my father would run into a negative situation—and this would include little things like traffic delays or a baseball game being rained out—his typical reaction was to throw up his hands and say, "It figures." What I learned from this particular model (and have worked very hard to un-learn), was a generic anticipation of negativity and defeat, with disappointments and obstacles being the norm. A logical outgrowth of all-or-nothing thinking, this example combines scarcity beliefs with overgeneralization, both of which are common among (if not necessarily limited to) perfectionists.

Burns describes overgeneralization as a type of mental distortion in which perfectionists "jump to the dogmatic conclusion that a negative event will be repeated endlessly." He describes a patient who had convinced himself that if one person looked down on him, then naturally everyone else would feel the same.[152] This cognitive distortion can includes a wide range of assumptions and reactive behaviors. It's a special type of all-or-nothing thinking we see in people who often use words like "always" or "never" in negative ways to describe their reality. "Perfectionists fall into certain traps," observes author Lata Jagtiani. "When they err, they conclude, 'I always make mistakes.'"[153]

Professor John Tagg has observed problems with overgeneralization in his students, especially in the assumptions they make about their performance and capabilities. He cites students who have done poorly on essay exams in the past, for example, who automatically believe that they can't be successful when facing a similar test in the present, "generalizing from one or two experiences of a certain kind to all experiences of a certain kind."[154] We hear evidence of this inclination in all sorts of "I can't . . ." statements. A bad grade on an art project becomes "I can't draw." A missed step demonstrates "I'm clumsy (or accident prone)." Being overlooked for a promotion translates to "I'll never get ahead."

Frequent companions to overgeneralizing include worrying, catastrophizing, jumping to conclusions, and mind reading (assuming what others are thinking). Antony and Swinson remark, "Perfectionism is often associated with a tendency to predict that negative events are more likely to occur than they really are. We call these predictions probability overestimations." Listen for catastrophic thinking at the extreme end of this continuum, indicated by a fearful anticipation of a negative outcome as well as "incorrectly assuming that one could not cope with a negative outcome if it were to occur."[155]

These fallacies can trigger anxiety and depression. They keep us from saying yes because we figure we'll probably fail anyway. And they also prevent us from saying no because we're afraid of alienating someone important, or looking like a bad parent or an incompetent employee. These are the thoughts that make every request look like a last chance, the ones that assure us that we'll never, ever get another opportunity if we turn down an invitation we just can't squeeze into our life right this minute.

But how many of us adopt this habit of disaster orientation as a talisman, believing that it can somehow prevent bad things from happening, or show us as caring and concerned people? It's hard to dispute the rational pointlessness of worrying, or the mental and emotional stress it can produce. Yet these habits persist, promoting a glass-half-empty (or worse) perspective about who we are and what we have to offer this world.

CHAPTER 9

Living on the Dark Side: A Tendency Toward Negativity

You don't have to be a perfectionist to notice that there's a whole lot of negativity going around these days. Even a brief scan of the news, social media, or hateful consumer reviews can ruin a good day and leave us reeling. Whether or not this cultural orientation encourages the negativity we see in perfectionists, it's hard to ignore the propensity for negative distortions warping perfectionists' thought patterns and beliefs.

"Perfectionism is not a quest for the best," writes artist and creativity expert, Julia Cameron. "It is a pursuit of the worst in ourselves, the part that tells us that nothing we do will ever be good enough."[156] If this observation seems kind of harsh, consider the number of mind tricks we have up our sleeves to feed our sense of inadequacy. Whether blowing off a compliment, dismissing our achievements,

> We continually set ourselves up to perpetuate our not-good-enough beliefs.

comparing ourselves unfavorably to someone else, obsessing about a complaint, or feeling unworthy of our successes, we continually set ourselves up to perpetuate our not-good-enough beliefs.

Only Letting the Bad Stuff Come Through

Comedian Steve Bluestein (no relation) has had a good year. His book generated sixty-six five-star reviews and his play received five rave reviews. However, two other book reviews came in with one star and one additional play review was lukewarm. Despite the overwhelming accolades in the positive reviews, Bluestein posted, "In my head, those three people are the only ones who know the truth."[157]

Burns refers to this process as mental filtering. "You pick out a single negative detail and dwell on it exclusively."[158] Author Jon Acuff calls negative feedback the squeaky wheel that gets the oil, a model that

> "Critic's Math": by which one insult plus one thousand compliments equals one insult. No matter how much good feedback we get, we have the ability, he says, to ignore it all in the face of one negative comment.

has "caused many of us to ignore the people who liked our dream in order to focus our energy on the people who hated it." He refers our tendency to use what he calls "Critic's Math," by which one insult plus one thousand compliments equals one insult. No matter how much good feedback we get, we have the ability, he says, to ignore it all in the face of one negative comment.[159]

Antony and Swinson see filtering as "a tendency to selectively focus on and magnify negative details at the expense of positive information, which is dismissed as less important."[160] Jagtiani notes that this filtering can be so effective that "when complimented for work done well, [perfectionists] pay no attention."[161] In fact, if we're really good at this, we will even twist actual accomplishments into failures! Consider the university student who studied hard and aced a class he believed he needed to pass with an A-plus. Despite achieving his goal, he was depressed because, according to perfectionism researcher Paul Hewitt, "the A+ was just a demonstration of how much of a failure he was . . . If he were perfect, the student argued, he wouldn't have had to work so hard."[162]

What a setup! "The need to be perfect places a person in a self-destructive double bind," authors Hendrie Weisinger and Norman Lobsenz explain. "If one fails to meet the unrealistic expectation, one has failed; but if one does meet it, one feels no glow of achievement for one has only done what was expected. There is no objective way to measure effort or improvement, no chance to relish success, no reason to build up one's self-image."[163] We end up minimizing our accomplishments, and if we manage to hear a compliment, we tend to dismiss it by pointing out some flaw that our supporter has missed. "I could have done better" becomes our mantra, suffocating any sense of joy and fulfillment we have earned.

This type of negativity is sometimes referred to as *telescopic thinking*. "Perfectionists use both ends of the telescope when viewing their achievements," writes Adderholdt. "When looking at unmet goals, they use the magnifying end, and these goals appear larger than they really are." Turn the telescope around and achievements are minimized and insignificant.[164] Telescopic thinking makes it possible to disregard positive recognition, obsessing instead about the point we forgot to make, the notes we played wrong, or the typo we failed to notice. (Or we ignore accolades because as soon as we accomplish something, we immediately start thinking about the next unfinished item on our list.)

This telescope metaphor comes in especially handy when we start talking about our imperfections and slip-ups. I was recently watching a short clip in which I was being interviewed. I understand that we can all be a bit self-conscious watching ourselves on video, but I was disturbed by the fact—especially in light of the work I'm doing on this book—that despite being articulate and passionate in offering some very worthwhile tips to the audience, there was this weird running commentary in my head that obliterated my ability to appreciate the value of what I was saying. *Why in the world did I wear that? It sounds like I have a cold. Could my hair look more stupid?* And so on.

And yes, like my friend, Steve Bluestein (still no relation), I can recall wading through a stack of rave reviews after one of my presentations, my attention to comments like "life-altering," "uplifting," and "career-saving" dashed by two evaluations that filled the page with complaints about the sponsor's failure to provide bagels at the beginning of the seminar. (As one superintendent once told me in what may be some of the best advice I ever got, "Some people would bitch if they was hung with a new rope." Her words exactly.) If you're looking for perfect, there really is no way to win.

Regrets and Rumination

I'll admit that things like the bagel-related evaluations are more of an annoyance and distraction than an actual blow to my self-worth, and they've mostly stayed with me because of their absurd irrelevance to the question about what those participants gained from the presentation. But what about the comments and interactions that cut closer to the core of who we are, especially when they reveal things we hope people don't notice, or involve times we really messed up because we weren't adequately prepared or said something careless or hurtful, for example?

That kind of feedback is far more difficult to shake off. Even when we can eventually appreciate the learning and growth we gained from these experiences, when that sense of shame gets triggered, the associated release of neurochemicals can lock in the memories of that event for a long, long time.

Perfectionists seem to be especially vulnerable to this phenomenon, possibly because so much of our identity can get tangled up with our performance. "Perfectionists have a hard time forgetting past mistakes," claims Adderholdt. "Many can remember specific test questions they missed many years earlier."[165] Shift the attention to achievements,

> "Perfectionists have a hard time forgetting past mistakes."

and it's the future that becomes so important, she adds. "What must be done for tomorrow far outweighs the accomplishments of yesterday."[166] Staying grounded in present time can be a significant challenge for perfectionists.

In an article highlighting the habits of miserable people, psychotherapist Chloe Madanes includes a tendency to glorify the past (imagining how good things *used* to be) or vilifying it (blaming what's not right today on bygone mistakes and traumatic events). Either way, she assures, "no matter what's happening in the present, you won't be happy." And if that's not enough, there's always rumination, another skill familiar in perfectionistic circles. Her tongue-in-cheek advice to "worry constantly about the causes of your behavior, analyze your defects, and chew on your problems" will guarantee a pessimistic (and very self-absorbed) view of life.[167]

Although not specifically geared to perfectionists, these distorted thought patterns are worth noting because they are so common among this population. Adderholdt and Goldberg cite the frequency with which they have heard "If only . . . " and "Why didn't I . . . "

among the individuals with whom they worked. "You don't let things go. You chew on them relentlessly, like a dog gnawing on a bone."[168]

This is hardly the road to peace of mind and may be part of why Scott claims that "perfectionists are much less happy and easygoing than [non-perfectionistic] high achievers." Further, she claims that "high achievers are able to bounce back fairly easily from disappointment," while "perfectionists tend to beat themselves up much more and wallow in negative feelings when their high expectations go unmet."[169] Author Carolyn Gregoire agrees. Perfection seekers "tend to obsess over every little mistake," she says. "This can add up to a whole lot of meltdowns, existential crises, and grown-up temper tantrums."[170]

Sadly, these patterns can undermine the very goals perfectionists seek. One study of male gymnasts attempting to qualify for Olympic competition found that the more successful athletes "tended to underemphasize the importance of past performance failures, while the athletes who failed to qualify were more likely to rouse themselves into near-panic states during competition through mental images of self-doubt and impending tragedy."[171]

Twenty-twenty hindsight gives us all great wisdom and understanding after the fact. We've all said and done things we regret, whether mindfully and deliberately because they seemed like a good idea at the time, or automatically and unaware of the potential impact. Learning from these events and becoming more conscious and responsible can lead to productivity and peace of mind. This is a far more righteous outcome than we can expect from using our regrets as tools to perpetuate self-loathing and shame.

Losing an Imaginary Competition

Blogger Luminita Sauvic admits, "I never felt good enough, so I never celebrated my successes. . . . None of [my] accomplishments mattered because all I could hear was the negative chatter of not having done as much as everybody else."[172]

Like many people, Sauvic used other people as her metric and mirror. Margie Warrell, a blogger and expert on courage in the workplace, observes, "Too often we fall into the trap of comparing our insides with others' outsides." Assumptions are enticing and often unconscious, amplifying existing insecurities when we hold our weaknesses up against the light of another person's strengths.[173]

This is one of the most dangerous aspects of perfectionism, making it far too easy to build our judgments on superficial, external factors, assuming that someone's got it easy, got it soft, got it made. "Every time I look at a hot girl, I think about how happy she must be," admits lifestyle writer Lauren Martin. "It's sick and disgusting, but I figure if she's pretty, she must be happy." Martin wonders how this person could "possibly be sad or worried about anything?"[174] But sadness and worry don't always show. "People who need help sometimes look a lot like people who don't need help," advises author and blogger Glennon Doyle Melton.[175]

Of course the problem is that the comparisons and competition never, ever end. "When a woman looks in the mirror, she doesn't see everything you see," advises Martin. "She sees everything she's not."[176] The most beautiful women have the most to lose. How could this not create anxiety and insecurity? But perfectionists can put a pretty distorted spin on priorities. We see the beautiful, the rich, the accomplished, and the privileged, and we immediately slip into less-than mode. These special folks get treated differently than "the ordinary," and we assume we want what they have. Of course we can't begin to imagine

> We see the beautiful, the rich, the accomplished, and the privileged, and we immediately slip into less-than mode.

their actual lives, much less consider that the objects of our envy may well be struggling with their own insecurities and personal issues.

Antony and Swinson notice that perfectionists tend to get caught in this trap of comparing themselves to others more frequently than non-perfectionists, and may also be "more likely to experience negative emotions" as a result. They also note that "perfectionistic individuals may also compare themselves to others in a manner that serves to maintain their perfectionistic attitudes."[177] Whether focused on appearance, achievements, talent, popularity, financial status, or some other asset or quality, the habit of measuring ourselves against others rarely ends well—and this includes the temporary fix we may get from fixating on someone we consider inferior.

> "Comparison is an act of violence against the self."

"Comparison is an act of violence against the self," warns author Iyanla Vanzant.[178] Warrell reasons, "Comparisons are always subjective, often biased, and rarely helpful." She notes that as we struggle "to keep our head above water and fulfill expectations, we often mistakenly assume others are getting by more effortlessly."[179] And yet, the tendency to believe that others are more easily successful is common enough to show up in several lists of negative feelings, thoughts, and beliefs associated with perfectionism. "Perfectionists tend to perceive others as achieving success with a minimum of effort, few errors, emotional stress, and maximum self-confidence," explains a post on one university counseling website. "At the same time, perfectionists view their own efforts as unending and forever inadequate."[180]

Business executive Neeta Patel notes concerns about the media glitz and glamour attached to celebrity and wealth, coverage "often omitting the struggles and failures the individuals likely encountered along the way. While these images may inspire ambition, the approach often makes success look a little too easy." She believes that the "relentless press coverage" may be giving young people the message "that all you have to do is have an idea, set up a company, and you're on your way to fame and fortune." Patel addresses the importance of learning to cope with failure, citing the risk of depression and suicide if their efforts fail to deliver.[181] Clearly there are dangers in setting goals based on what we see as others' successful outcomes.

Waiting to Be Found Out

Perfectionists are "excellent when it comes to contemplating disaster and failure," writes psychologist Kevin Leman. "They're also great at seeing rejection and criticism everywhere."[182] But what happens when we actually succeed at reaching our goal? We get the promotion, the book deal, the acceptance letter from our first-choice college. Now what? Just as the fears and risks associated with failure are fairly well recognized, there are similar concerns related to our responses to achievement and success.

"There was this boy I liked back in high school," wrote one contributor. "When he asked me to prom, I assumed he was either kidding or planning to get me to say yes and then not show up on prom night. Either way, I turned him down." The possibility that she would have been worth inviting had never occurred to her as a legitimate option at the time. Even when we say yes, we are haunted by the sense that being chosen was just some weird mistake. "Often successful people have such a deep sense of shame that they put on masks to hide their hurt," writes Parrott. "Instead of shielding them, the masks only serve to make them feel like phonies."[183]

This inclination is known as the "impostor syndrome." The Caltech University counseling center describes this condition as "a collection of feelings of inadequacy that persist even in face of information that indicates that the opposite is true," noting that "it is experienced internally as chronic self-doubt, and feelings of intellectual fraudulence." Although not specifically attributed to perfectionists, there's no doubt a good bit of overlap among the high-achieving individuals who attribute their success to luck, timing, being good at fooling people, or the insignificance of their accomplishment.[184] At its core, says Parrott, is "the belief that you do not deserve your success and that someday you will be exposed as a fraud."[185]

Ann Smith describes a high-performing salesman who frequently outperformed his coworkers. Nonetheless, "he was in constant fear of getting fired or going broke . . . Despite appearances, he was waiting to be revealed as the impostor that he believed himself to be."[186] Warrell sees this syndrome to be remarkably widespread. "The list of people who sometimes worry about being uncovered as an impostor is as impressive as it is long. Having to live with a nagging fear of being 'found out' as not being as smart or talented or deserving or experienced . . . as people think is a common phenomenon."[187]

She quotes Nobel Laureate Maya Angelou, who once said, "I have written eleven books, but each time I think, 'uh oh, they're going to find out now. I've run a game on everybody, and they're going to find me out.'"[188] Political journalist Rachel Maddow has likewise expressed her fear that her success "is going to go away at any moment. People are going to realize that I'm a great fraud and it'll end, so I better make sure this is a good show because it'll be my last. Part of me feels that way every day."[189] Considering the number of well-known, highly successful individuals who have admitted to laboring under this syndrome, you'd think it would be easy to dismiss our habit of relentlessly comparing ourselves to other people unfavorably, and instead, recognize the common humanity and frailty we can easily share.

CHAPTER 10

Establishing
Our Value

I n a meme making the rounds on Facebook, personal growth activist Jessica Ortner cautions, "You can't hate yourself happy. You can't criticize yourself thin. You can't shame yourself wealthy. Real change begins with self-love and self-care."[190] It's hard to argue with these sentiments. We know. Wrangling with a harsh inner critic and years of self-loathing can leave a well-meaning perfectionist exhausted and cranky. Any achievements these voices may have compelled probably came at a very steep cost.

If you really want to see the connection between perfectionism and self-worth, check out the way we respond to mistakes, flaws, or criticism. Do we get angry and defensive, or defeated and depressed? Does making a mistake translate to *being* one? How quickly do we quit or drop out when we don't get something right the first time? When our sense of safety and worth depend on doing things exceptionally well, even the slightest slip can compromise both.

> But even in the absence of errors, for many perfectionists, there is a certain emptiness we keep trying to fill.

But even in the absence of errors, for many perfectionists, there is a certain emptiness we keep trying to fill. This "hole in the soul" drives a fear of not being good enough, if not a generic fear of imperfection itself. Some refer to this state of anxiety as *atelophobia*, a disorder that can leave sufferers with the feeling that everything they do is wrong.[191] If that sounds extreme, it's also a good place to bring up a word that is a lot more common: shame.

The Corrosive Voice of "The Committee"

Yesterday evening, after an hour or so of fairly mindless nibbling—a habit I tend to indulge while writing since I quit smoking years ago—I got a bad stomachache. *Really* bad. As I was curled up in bed, doubled over in pain, I had this flash that "normal" people in this situation would probably be thinking, "Well *that* certainly wasn't a good idea." Having previously introduced the voice of my Inner Critics, what I often refer to as "The Committee," it may come as no surprise that the conversation in *my* head was more of a screaming match about what a stupid, out-of-control, self-destructive idiot I was.

Please note that I would never in a million years *ever* talk to another human being this way. But for many of us, this voice is the default setting for the broadcast running round the clock in our head. (I have since learned to turn down the volume, but boy, when I'm hurting, embarrassed, or otherwise vulnerable, it can sneak back in with a loud and nasty vengeance.) This, my friends, is the voice of shame, the internalized critic that confuses our actions with our essence, our choices with our worth. The Committee is not restricted to perfectionists but there's just no getting around the topic of perfectionism without talking about shame.

"Where perfectionism exists, shame is always lurking," claims Brené Brown. "In fact, shame is the birthplace of perfectionism." She defines shame as "the intensely painful feeling or experience of believing that we are flawed and therefore unworthy of love and belonging."[192] Psychologist Kristalyn Salters-Pedneault uses similar terms. "Shame is an emotion in which the self is perceived as defective, unacceptable, or fundamentally damaged."[193] The connection is clear in Michael Lewis's definition, which views shame as the negative, painful result of a presumably unfavorable comparison of "the self's action with the self's standards."[194]

> "Shame is the birthplace of perfectionism." Brown defines shame as "the intensely painful feeling or experience of believing that we are flawed and therefore unworthy of love and belonging."

It's important to include shame in our discussion because so many types of distorted thinking and compensating perfectionistic behaviors emerge out of shame-based reasoning. Shame is how the tribe keeps us in line, cautions Gilbert. "Shame makes people sick," she adds. "Shame can literally take years off your life. At best, it just makes you terribly, lingeringly sad."[195] Salters-Pedneault warns that shame "is associated with a desire to hide, disappear, or even die."[196] This is different from guilt. "Guilt says I've done something wrong; shame says there is something wrong with me," explains counselor John Bradshaw.[197] Or as Brown puts it, guilt is about our behaviors while shame is about who we are.[198]

Shame forces authenticity into hiding. It bullies us into believing that we are not only inadequate but also helpless to change. It kills creativity and shuts down our ability to hear sincere guidance and feedback that would help us grow. It keeps us looking over our shoulder, seeking approval and worrying about what others are thinking. It inclines us to self-destructive behaviors and legitimizes the belief that it's necessary to attack and shame others in order to get them to change. We can also thank shame for turning human beings into "human doings," evidence of another core belief that hinges our sense of adequacy and worth on our ability to produce and achieve.[199]

Twisted Reasoning

Here's another bit of perfectionists' math: self-worth equals achievement equals self-worth. "If you are a perfectionist, it is likely that you learned early in life that other people valued you because of how much you accomplished or achieved. As a result you may have learned to value yourself only on the basis of other people's approval."[200] In other words, according to this thinking, the more I do and the better I do it, the more likely I am to be accepted and valued. (Oh, and that will *only* happen if I can meet certain standards and expectations I have created or accepted.) This formula applies to many areas of perfectionism, including anything that can be measured, counted, or weighed.

Luria shares her version of this kind of reasoning—"Here's how my head goes: There's a point system in life. The idea is to accumulate as many points as possible but, unlike many systems, I have to figure out the rules myself. No one will tell them to me because that would be cheating. My job is to avoid getting 'zinged' because that means losing points and losing points equates to misery and poverty. Sometimes I just don't want to even start because I know I'll get it wrong and I'll get zinged anyway. Aside from the anxiety, depression, fibromyalgia, and assorted intestinal issues, I've become very good at surmounting obstacles. I wonder if I can just stop my obstacle-surmounting and just *live*."

Look at the equation from another angle—fear of failure—and the math works out the same. "Perfectionists often equate failure to achieve their goals with a lack of personal worth or value."[201] Kimbriel Dean notes, "When our minds are twisted with the fear of falling short, we fall into the trap of believing we will not be loved if we don't measure up." This is not a great plan because "the perfectionists' burden is we never believe we're good enough."[202]

Greenspon explains the connection with shame. "Perfectionists believe themselves to be what psychologists call conditionally acceptable. Their sense of themselves is that there may be some inherent flaw within them that makes them unacceptable people and that perhaps, *if* they can be perfect, acceptance will follow."[203] In other words, if I make a mistake, I'm a failure. And if I weren't flawed, I wouldn't be screwing up and making mistakes.

This thinking factors into several different types of cognitive distortions, including a strange logic common among perfectionists called *emotional reasoning*. This is what happens when our sense of reality is defined by negative feelings, regardless of any evidence to the contrary. Tagg offers an example of a student who was very nervous about taking a test on some material she actually knew fairly well. "When she said she didn't understand the material, what she meant was that she didn't feel secure about the material. To her, that amounted to the same thing. But she was wrong. Her feelings lied and misled her. We can't reason well on the basis of emotions, and if we try we almost always make our problems worse."[204]

Emotional reasoning breeds ideas like "Life will begin when I get skinny," "I can't get into college unless I get perfect grades," or "If I were good at my job, I wouldn't be nervous about this evaluation." So we put on our masks and we try to look good because the alternative is unbearable. We learn to stuff feelings and we learn to keep up the deception because we don't want anyone to know that we're frightened or sad or not as strong as we seem. We develop a type of disclosure phobia because perfectionists can have a very hard time "letting themselves be exposed or vulnerable,"[205] even with the people with whom they are closest. And sometimes we just shut down or run away.

"The core of the problem," says Richard Winter, "is that when . . . self-worth depends on reaching those high standards, it is an inevitable script for self defeat and [our] own personal hell of repeated failure and eternal regret."[206] Adderholdt concurs, warning that tying self-esteem to achievement leads to what she calls a "roller coaster" existence.[207] This belief—and the pressure it exerts on anyone who credits certain standards and requirements as a prerequisite to being worthy of love and acceptance—is hardly conducive to mental health or social well-being.

The Tyranny of "Musts" and "Shoulds"

Relationship coach Sherie Venner recalls feeling a bit of panic as she stood outside the church the first time she got married. She was a "very young and naive" nineteen-year-old and despite the impulse to leave, she went through with the wedding because she was worried about what other people would think. She felt obligated by the promise she had made to her fiancé and dismissed her doubts and fears as simply having cold feet.[208]

How many of our decisions are compelled by ideas we have about what we're expected or supposed to do, rather than by what we truly *want* to do, choices we could make in our best interests? Commitment is great when the things to which we're committed are appropriate and fulfilling—for us, and at that moment. "Think of all of the things you've started, lost interest in, but kept doing long after it's lost its appeal," challenges fitness enthusiast Steve Kamb."If I had ever started something in the past, I was damn sure I was going to finish it. And if there was a way to get to 100 percent on something, I would do everything in my power to get there, even at the sake of shirking other responsibilities and no longer enjoying myself . . ."[209]

Perfectionists have a lot of rules. Sometimes referred to as *shoulds,* they represent the distorted logic that leads to extreme standards and self-demands, many of them based on fallacies and limiting biases. "Sure, chubby girls get boyfriends too, but they are way lower quality," wrote a young blogger, including this point among her reasons for wanting to be perfect (and thin).[210] Overloading our schedules with honors classes because we are convinced that we won't get into college without them comes from similar thinking, as does fixating on the need for a certain brand of clothing or a certain type of car to fit in with a desirable social niche.

"Shoulds" are automatic thought patterns, projected values based on personal beliefs or preferences, generally without much thought given to costs or benefits. In relationships, they can be especially destructive and toxic. Shoulds shift priorities, allowing us to forego sleep or exercise or time with loved ones in favor of studying, cleaning, or finishing an important project.

Consider some of the common mandates guiding perfectionistic beliefs. Among these, Adderholdt includes the ideas that "regard from others is conditional to personal performance; being ordinary is shameful; anything undertaken cannot end in failure, particularly in perceived fields of competency; emotions should not be expressed; tasks must be done over and over again until they meet exact standards; there is no room for desires, only for self-demands; or . . . there can be no 'I want,' only 'I must.'"[211]

"'Have to,' 'got to,' 'should,' 'should have,' and similar verbal expressions create the discomfort of time urgency and anxiety while reducing our effectiveness and sense of personal power," claim authors Chick Moorman and Thomas Haller.[212] Our shoulds become the basis for a core belief system by which we navigate our lives. Believing that perfection and achievement will win us approval and acceptance, we become what poet Theodore Roethke calls "time-harried prisoners of Shall and Will."[213]

We scramble for brownie points—if not actual badges—looking for evidence that we really are good enough. We get strokes for keeping our rooms clean, looking nice, getting good grades, scoring the goal, and doing what we're told, connecting our social and emotional safety to pleasing others. And, says Brené Brown, "somewhere along the way, we adopt this dangerous and debilitating belief system: I am what I accomplish and how well I accomplish it."[214]

In the process, we can lose touch with our inner striving and our creative voice, if not our confidence outright. This is more than just a fear of making mistakes. It is a very legitimate fear of rejection, exclusion, and abandonment—experiences that, by the way, light up the same parts of the brain that respond to physical pain. So the perfectionist performs with one eye on the audience: "Instead of enjoying the process," says Cameron, "the perfectionist is constantly grading the results."[215]

And, I might add, constantly second-guessing ourselves along the way. "In the real estate business, I learned that whenever I buy a property, I always wonder if I could have bought it for less," notes entrepreneur Beth Bauer. "Or if I am selling, could I have sold it for more?" While Bauer has learned to make peace with the outcomes of her efforts, her example illustrates a lack of certainty that often accompanies perfectionistic decision making.

Besides, how many of us follow the shoulds all our lives just to end up feeling empty and discouraged? Despite continually achieving and collecting accolades, writer Jennifer Santos Madriaga started wondering what the point was "to all this 'doing.'" She was deeply ashamed of the secret voice "always asking, 'Is this all there is?' After all," she comments, "society was reinforcing that I was doing things the 'right way.'" As she dutifully checked off the items on her checklist of success, rather than closing in on happiness with each accomplishment, she found herself further and further away from where she wanted to be. "I had become an adult and done everything that was expected of me. And I was completely miserable."[216]

Evidence of Our Value

Thomas Greenspon claims that perfectionism is not a struggle to achieve excellence. "Although many times it will seem as though the motivation comes entirely from within, the developing perfectionist most often wishes to be perfect to fulfill the desires of someone he or she seems to have disappointed."[217] So it makes sense that some of us would look for ways to inflate our value by taking on lots of important tasks, doing more than is necessary or required, and when-ever possible, becoming a most-important-person—sometimes for everyone in our lives!

Teversham thought it was rather selfish to admit how good it felt when someone needed her, so instead, she preferred to think her involvement was for *their* good, not hers. "Those poor people," she writes, "they really need my help . . . And no one else will be able to help them as well as I can."[218] Let's face it—most of us enjoy being needed, feeling useful, valuable, and significant. But those of us who aspire to being indispensable, whose "niceness" and worth depend upon it, have too often purchased this balm for our ego with the loss of self and denial of personal needs, seething resentment, and the alienation and abandonment that self-righteousness can inspire. For Teversham, any rescue plan simply had to involve her. Others couldn't possibly cope or manage, "and that leaves me to do it all."[219]

This exaggerated sense of responsibility also pushes us to finish uninteresting books, complete irrelevant projects, and hang in long after we've outgrown certain relationships or jobs. (How many hours do we invest getting to the next level of some video game that's become frankly tedious to play?) This call to duty can show up in some interesting displays of overdoing and overcommitting, com-mon traits among perfectionists, and many of the contributors to this project had their own special spin on getting it right.

Engineer Piero Mattarelli relates his version of perfectionism as a manic pursuit of formal neatness—especially in writing. Back in the days before computers offered him "a providential interven-tion," he notes that when writing out his assignments in high school and college, "if I happened to write a wrong word, I would tear off the whole page rather than draw a line through the mistake." In addition to contributing to "an environmental disaster in terms of paper waste," this habit also required an extra year or so in order to complete his course.

Author Linda Sorenson recalls a "reading contest in the early grades where we got caterpillar segments for each book we read," noting that her "caterpillar was three-quarters of the way around the room before the rest of the class had barely shot out a head." She'd turn in ten-page papers instead of the required five—typed up, hunt-and-peck style, back in the days before any of the other kids typed up their work. And Michelle Tillman is hardly alone in feeling like she's "juggling too many balls at once."

Feeling overwhelmed has become a bit of a cultural cliché, and for many of us we simply don't know how or when to say no. Business coach Christine Kane jokes about the potential payoff of being able to complain about how much there is to do, describing the satisfaction of seeking sympathy from friends and coworkers "for how hard it is to accomplish your goals and dreams." (This, she notes, is especially valuable if you can get them to agree, "citing how special you are because you have been given so much talent, and how it must be quite a burden.")[220]

In all seriousness, though, how many of our activities truly deserve our time? What is overcommitting and overdoing costing us? Do we *really* need to find one more piece of information or check our work dozens of times? And why do so many perfectionists labor so hard on projects they never finish or bother to submit?

Blogger Marc Chernoff cautions, "Being busy does not mean being productive. Busyness isn't a virtue, nor is it something to respect." We're running nonstop but don't have time for the things that matter most. We wrap

> We're running nonstop but don't have time for the things that matter most. We wrap ourselves in the illusion that busy equals importance.

ourselves in the illusion that busy equals importance, but in the end, we're just "hamsters running on a wheel."[221] It's hard to delegate things we enjoy doing, even when we can, because when we depend on our accomplishments to prove our worth, it's like giving up pieces of ourselves.

CHAPTER 11

The Perfect Sabotage

"For some reason, I really liked drawing horses," said one of my contributors in a personal interview. Recalling an experience from when he was about seven years old, he continued, "I don't know what turned me on to them—probably cowboy shows. I drew them for months and I thought I drew them very well. They looked very much like horses to me." Unfortunately, his mother had a different opinion and did not hesitate to share it. "That's ugly," she remarked, looking over his shoulder as he drew. "That's not what a horse looks like."

"I just balled up the paper and threw it out. I never drew another horse after that, and in fact, stopped drawing altogether," he said. "There was no opportunity for learning. If we didn't know how to do something or if we did something wrong, we just got yelled at." Growing up in this environment continually reinforced the idea that "if it isn't perfect, don't bother." A number of contributors weighed in with similarly heartbreaking stories. Powers decided early on that if she couldn't be perfect ("and who can be?" she asked), going "the route of the mediocre underachiever" was a much safer choice.

"By the time I was in middle school, it seemed like my mom was angry and stressed all the time," wrote another survey respondent. "I decided to clean the entire house while she was at work, hoping that would cheer her up. This was far beyond the usual chores I was expected to do and I did a really good job." But when Mom came home, instead of being happily surprised, "she simply noticed one of the rags I had left on one of the steps. 'What's *that* doing here?' she asked. Now as an adult, I like to keep my own house neat and clean, but I always have this nagging feeling that I've forgotten something, that something's still not right."

Childhood housekeeping issues came up frequently, with a surprising number of contributors apparently unable to make their bed correctly. "Being raised by a mother who is very particular about cleanliness and keeping the home tidy, I had to manage the frustration of having to do chores over again," shares relationship coach Hamidah Bahashwan. "Over the years both of us gave up on the hope that I would be able to reach her standards, so she ended up doing it over, and that was okay to me." Another contributor said that no matter how hard she tried, her mom would always find something to straighten or fix. "I change my sheets every week, but I just shut the bedroom door rather than bother trying to make the bed," she wrote.

"Perfectionistic behaviors can be divided into two main types," claim Antony and Swinson. "Behaviors designed to help an individual meet his or her unreasonably high standards and behaviors that involve avoidance of situations that trigger the need to be perfect."[222] We don't typically associate perfectionism with underachievement, but this outcome is not at all uncommon.

Avoidance behaviors all share a common fear of failure and a desire to self-protect from anticipated consequences of not doing as well as we (or others) feel we should.

Avoidance behaviors all share a common fear of failure and a desire to self-protect from anticipated consequences of not doing as well as we (or others) feel we should.

How Not to Reach Goals

Actually, the process is fairly simple. First, let's set unreasonable, impossible goals, which we then fail to meet. The pressure and failure reduce productivity and effectiveness, which leads to self-criticism and self-blame. This process prevents us from ever really grasping what realistic, reachable goals look like. So we end up in this strange contradiction in which we are pulled in one direction by a desire to achieve and in another by the impulse to self-protect.[223]

This polarity can result in a great deal of stress and dysfunction, which may result in our not starting a project, neglecting to submit work we've finished, or starting so many projects that we leave ourselves no time or resources to complete any one of them.[224] By "zooming too far out when setting goals," says lifestyle coach, Kris Ward, we reach for step twenty when we are only on step two. This turns out to be a great way to self-sabotage with feelings of pressure, doubt, and overwhelm that keep us from starting a task, much less generating any momentum.[225]

"I know that perfectionism stood in the way of developing any talents I had," Powers relates. "I had a hard time starting out 'not perfect.' I wanted to arrive to the first lesson already knowing how to do it, and then gave up quickly if I wasn't perfect from the start." She is not alone. Kane meets "countless would-be entrepreneurs, artists, and world-changers who hold themselves back because they need to 'do it perfect.'" She advises them of an unfortunate truth that many perfectionists know all too well. "When you wait to be perfect, you never get it done. It's a painful loop, and it often leads to depression, disease, and a nagging feeling that you're not quite stepping into your life's purpose."[226]

Of course, there is a certain comfort in playing it safe. "I know there is a lesson to be learned from failure," shared one contributor, "but throughout my life, I only went after challenges where I figured I had a good chance to succeed." Braverman saw a similar tendency toward underachievement in many of her gifted students. "They will not attempt to do something unless they can feel 100 percent successful." She mentions young people who look to celebrities in, say, sports or music, and don't realize the amount of time and practice most of these individuals have invested in their careers. These are the kids who aren't practicing or putting in the time they need to be good at something but who quit because they're not perfect at the first try. "They think they should be naturals, like you're born a winner. No," she adds, "winners work at it."

The Challenge of Completion

The word "done" has many definitions in perfection-speak. The research and media offer numerous accounts of perfectionists who take forever to get projects "right," if they ever complete them at all. I'm not talking about the times we get distracted by more pressing matters or the times we drop an undertaking because it's somehow lost its relevance or value. This is more about ongoing feelings of inadequacy about our efforts, a lack of satisfaction with what we've done, and an unwillingness to see our work as "finished enough" to let it go and move on to something else.

Blogger Jeff Goins compares his perfectionism to a ritual his dog practices: walking in circles before lying down. Often when Goins is writing, he can't finish a project "unless it is 'just right.' I can't start something new until what I'm working on looks like what I have in my head." While he agrees that "there's a lot to be said for excellence," he also notes that sometimes, he's simply not satisfied that the writing is good enough. "I keep going around and around in circles . . . being a perfectionist. And I'm making myself miserable."[227]

Light show artist and visual pioneer Marc Rubenstein admits, "It is so very hard for any artist—especially a Virgo perfectionist—to let go and deliver any product, creative or otherwise." At some point, he says, we simply have to be done. However, he notes that by "done" he is not saying "finished or complete." There will always be one more tweak, one more layer, one more bit of information to add. "I've known grad students who have been working on their dissertation for ten or fifteen years," remarked one former university professor. "A lot of them have actually finished the bulk of the writing, but are constantly looking for another piece of data or update, or just feel too uncertain to share what they've done."

Perfectionistic goals can get hung up when we hyperfocus on details. Joseph Ferrari, a psychology professor and expert on procrastination, observes, "Some people put way too much time on one aspect of a project while allowing little or no time for the rest. They can then blame any failure or incompleteness on lack of sufficient time" which also allows them to "rationalize that any failure was not due to lack of effort, since they spent so much time trying."[228]

Cameron sees perfectionism as "a loop—an obsessive, debilitating, closed system that causes you to get stuck in the details of what you are writing or painting or making and to lose sight of the whole." She argues that it's not about getting it right or fixing things, and even discounts the relationship to standards. "Perfectionism is a refusal to let yourself move ahead."[229]

> "Perfectionism is a refusal to let yourself move ahead."

It's not just the people we think of as creative types who have a hard time determining when enough is enough. One technician shared a work experience in which he "asked an engineer for a rough order-of-magnitude answer to a question. The engineer asked if I wanted the answer to the second or third digit right of the decimal point. My expectation was within ten." Clearly there was a different set of expectations for which each considered to be an acceptable level of quality. In fact, citing perfection can also give us a handy excuse for a *poorly* executed job. Safety consultant Wale Balogun K. reports hearing people use the expression "nobody is perfect" as a way to shrug off their laziness or incompetence.

But there's another side to "done" that I've also noticed in my work on this topic, one that has more to do with the emphasis on product over process. Once perfectionists finish something, that thing is completed, done, checked off the list. Braverman acknowledges a resistance in her students to revise, rewrite, or redo something they already handed in. "They assume that their first try is a good try, or a good-enough try, or the best they're going to get because this is what they turned in." They've moved on to the next task, leaving previous efforts in the dust. In the reverse version of the perfectionist who never stops modifying a project, for these individuals, once they submit their work, they see no reason to go back and try to make it better.

Scott notes that "high achievers can enjoy the process of chasing a goal as much or more than the actual reaching of the goal itself. Conversely, perfectionists see the goal and nothing else. They're so concerned about meeting the goal and avoiding the dreaded failure that they can't enjoy the process of

> "High achievers can enjoy the process of chasing a goal as much or more than the actual reaching of the goal itself. Conversely, perfectionists see the goal and nothing else.

growing and striving."[230] As a result, once perfectionists are done, they expect that to be the end of it.

Life in the Land of Diminishing Returns

A few weeks ago, I decided to take advantage of an invitation to a professional conference to add on a bit of time for what I'm calling a writer's retreat or working vacation. I was starting to bog down at home with a few too many distractions and interruptions, so getting a little distance from my usual work environment has proved to be a very good move. I've written the last three chapters at a little apartment we rented for our stay, a place in which I've been holed up for almost the entire time I've been in the area.

I've restricted the usual sightseeing, visits with friends in the area, and, for the most part, even going out for meals during this intense work period. I'm here to write, right? But I've noticed that even on my most productive days, at a certain point, I end up spinning my wheels. The words start running together, my mind wanders, and I end up with maybe a single, messy paragraph to show for hours of work.

"Over time, quantity versus quality are often the inversely proportional factors when striving for perfection," notes my technician friend. "At what point do we find ourselves operating in a region of diminishing returns?" When I'm focused, alert, and in the flow, clarity and coherence are far more accessible than when I'm mentally fried and trying to force these connections to happen.

Besides, how often do our efforts go beyond anything anyone would notice or appreciate? "Perfection assumes that you are smarter than your audience because you know the rules and this leaves no room for your audience to be involved," claims artist James Victore. "So good job, smarty-pants. You spent hours tweaking details that real human beings don't care about."[231]

"In business there is a cost for perfect information," writes Bauer. "One can keep asking for more information or analyzing information repeatedly and in different ways in order to get more perfect information to make a decision. But it takes time and people to get more information and more analysis. The key is understanding how much information you really need to make a rational decision." She applies the same reasoning to our appearance or a piece of art. "We find that the more we search and strive and do to reach perfection, we can never attain it. We keep seeing new things and wanting more. The more we try, the more elusive perfection becomes."

Fear of failure is a harsh task master. In our efforts to self-protect, we make things harder than they need to be, spend longer than we need to spend checking and re-checking our work, make unreasonable demands on our attention and cognition, jeopardize relationships, and compromise our physical and mental health. And of course, if that doesn't work, we can drag our feet or just give up.

Procrastination as a Classic Defense

"Believe it or not, the Internet did not give rise to procrastination," claims writer Eric Jaffe. "People have struggled with habitual hesitation going back to ancient civilizations."[232] We all let ourselves get distracted and put things off that we don't want to do—or at least don't want to do quite as much as what we end up doing instead. But if everyone procrastinates, the practice is especially common as an avoidance tactic among perfectionists.

Adderholdt and Goldberg explain, "For the perfectionist, procrastination acts as an insurance policy . . . To delay the possibility that a performance might not be perfect, the perfectionist puts things off."[233] Scott agrees, noting that "it seems paradoxical that perfectionists would be prone to procrastination, as that trait can be detrimental to productivity, but perfectionism and procrastination do tend to go hand in hand."[234]

"Self-sabotage is when we say we want something and then go about making sure it doesn't happen," explains author Alyce P. Cornyn-Selby.[235] The logic goes something like this. The prospect of failure is so terrifying that we try to prevent failure by failing to do anything at all. (No, that doesn't make sense to me, either, and yet I've done it all the same.) Then we feed the cycle by feeling like crap because we missed the deadline or didn't make it to the gym or had the cable go out because the bill is still sitting on our desk because we've been busy the entire time so hey, get off our back!

It's unusual to find articles on procrastination without finding the term "self-defeating behavior" nearby. Writer Alina Larson shares, "Commonly you'll hear procrastinators say they work better under pressure. But Ferrari says his studies have shown that people are not more efficient when under time constraints. What they perceive as adrenaline is actually anxiety."[236] Procrastination can be tied to worry, lack of goals or planning, low motivation, a distaste for a particular task, overestimating the difficulty of the activity we're avoiding, or a lack of training or skill to handle what we're expected to do. However with perfectionists, it's also likely to be related to the fear of judgment, ridicule, and rejection by others.[237]

Of course, procrastination can give us a short-term break from dealing with stress-producing tasks, but the hours devoted to distracting e-mails, texting, social media, and video games are bound to catch up with us. "Procrastination is the absence of progress," writes Jaffe. He cites studies done in the late nineties with college students in which the procrastinating kids showed lower levels of stress, which initially suggested a beneficial side to pursuing more pleasurable activities. "In the end, however, the costs of procrastination far outweighed the temporary benefits. Procrastinators earned lower grades than other students and reported higher cumulative amounts of stress and illness. True procrastinators didn't just finish their work later—the quality of it suffered, as did their own well-being."[238]

Some sources also mention being overcommitted, overextended, and overscheduled as a cause of procrastination. "When we are trying to do too much, our bodies and minds scream for a rest," says freelance writer Lisa Rivero, "and we often unconsciously put off necessary work precisely when we have the most to do just to give ourselves a break."[239] Educator Barb Clark mentions how hard it can be to sort out priorities when the list is long. She observes that sometimes "it's easier to start new projects to distract yourself when you run into difficulties with your current project." We ignore what's hard, she says, because in order to achieve our own internal perception of "correct," we fail to see that other acceptable ways exist. "Knowing you can do better prevents forward progress. You end up with so many undone project that become obstacles."

Winter calls procrastination a "practical consequence of wanting to do everything right." He proposes the following as a motto for perfectionists: "nothing ventured, nothing lost."[240] But just as "never finishing" can work as an avoidance tool for dealing with the fear of failure, never getting started can be just as effective.

> But just as "never finishing" can work as an avoidance tool for dealing with the fear of failure, never getting started can be just as effective.

Freezing in the Face of Overwhelm

There seems to be a whole group of perfectionists who fall into a category described with adjectives like "frustrated," "defeated," or "discouraged." On the surface, their behavior and attitudes would hardly invoke the image of what most of us would think of as perfectionistic. These individuals represent the ultimate in procrastination. They don't just put things off. They don't even bother to begin.

"I feel like I am the opposite of a perfectionist," says Tammy Fuller, a nurse and fitness coach who was labeled a frustrated perfectionist by a friend. "My natural tendencies lean toward lazy and sloppy." However, from her friend's perspective, Fuller was simply someone who tends to see things as too big to tackle so she just doesn't tackle them at all. "If it can't be perfect then I might as well just let it sit there."[241] Chad Jones, a contributor to comments on a blog on the topic, says that as a frustrated perfectionist, in practical terms, he's done before he begins. "That's right. I don't even start because I know it won't be perfect."[242]

I think that a number of people come to this point in a number of ways. Perhaps the hardest hit are those to whom success has always come easily and who suddenly find themselves in much more challenging circumstances. Carol Dweck offers an example in the reaction of a "fixed-mindset" student confronted with algebra for the first time. "Up until then, he has breezed through math. Even when he barely paid attention in class and skimped on his homework, he always got A's. But this is different. It's hard. The student feels anxious and thinks, 'What if I'm not as good at math as I thought? What if other kids understand it and I don't?' At some level, he realizes that he has two choices: try hard, or turn off. His interest begins to wane, and his attention wanders. He tells himself, 'Who cares about this stuff?'"[243]

David Burns has seen a similar trend. "As perfectionistic children grow up . . . they find it increasingly difficult to live up to the unrealistic standards they have learned to set. As they enter high school and move on to college and graduate school, the competition stiffens, and the level of work becomes increasingly sophisticated." This is especially rough as training gets more specialized and entrance requirements get more competitive. After living so much of their lives at the top of the class, students are now surrounded by others with similar standing. When their best performance places them in the middle of the pack, these students, who are "psychologically unprepared for an 'average' role," often react "with frustration, anger, depression, and panic," seeing themselves as second-rate losers.[244]

If we haven't had much experience bouncing back from failure, this experience can hit especially hard. After years of "that old effortless perfection," Linda Sorenson found herself "collecting rejections" for her picture books and anthology anecdotes. "I was crushed," she writes. Her confidence shaken, "I hemmed and hawed, second-guessed myself, rewrote and rewrote, and then finally just put them all aside. I was so hurt and stuck. What was up? Where was that perfect creative flow? I boldly decided if I couldn't write perfectly to be accepted, I wouldn't do it at all."

Everyone goes through setbacks and slumps, but it's easy to fall into what Kane calls "a case of the 'used-to-be's.'"[245] We stop moving forward, focused instead about how talented or fit or thin we used to be, how consistently we would practice or write or exercise, how much easier success used to be, thinking that our moment in the sun has passed us by.[246]

Even the mere possibility of failure is enough to break a successful person's stride. "I was the best Ping-Pong player in the family," one contributor shared. "I beat all my friends. I was told I should definitely play against the top players in town. I was overwhelmed with such negativity, I thought, 'Why go to that level where I was certain I would lose?'" Unwilling to overchallenge himself and feeling like he was cheating when the people he knew couldn't compete against his shots, he simply quit playing altogether.

"Perfectionism paralyzes," warns educator Virginia Zeuli. "It keeps us from moving forward and affects all aspects of our personal and professional lives." As we establish our talents, reaching incremental goals, "the gap between expectation and actual performance widens," says Burns.[247] So even the improvement we desire and achievements we earn can work against us. We push ourselves harder and harder, only to discover that our efforts simply raise expectations and demands to do more. Rechtschaffen describes it as learning to juggle three balls and then driving ourselves to manage four and then five. "What's the reward?" he asks. "A sixth ball."[248]

Workloads increase, assignments get tougher, competition stiffens. When the hurdles get too high to clear easily, it's tempting to wander off the track. If we don't feel confident or prepared, or the climb is too steep, the perceived demand for flawlessness can stop us cold. "The problem, when you expect perfectionism from yourself, is that it often will stop you from trying new things or working toward a goal," claims Nisha Naik, a talent acquisitions manager. "If you don't allow yourself to make errors, you can never learn from your mistakes. And if you require perfection from yourself, you are always courting disappointment." The fear of failure, and the fear of failing to do something just right, "stops you from even making an attempt."[249]

Many of us who have spent time in education can vouch for this behavior, even among very young children. Sherry Bolinger remembers an intelligent and articulate third-grade student who refused to attempt assignments "or write for any purpose. He couldn't allow himself to be inaccurate in his work." Ego and dignity can feed a why-bother approach. My classroom experiences often included kids who started off the year trying to convince me to not expect too much from them. (This is a big part of the reason that so much of my work as a teacher educator has focused on preventing disruptive and oppositional behaviors from defeated, discouraged kids who see no benefit to behaving more cooperatively—preferring to be seen as *bad* instead of *dumb*.)

A piece of this puzzle, I believe, has to do with motivation. Scott suggests that non-perfectionists who strive for excellence and high achievement "tend to be pulled toward their goals by a desire to achieve them." They appreciate progress and can enjoy the process of making steps toward their goal. "Perfectionists, on the other hand, tend to be pushed toward their goals by a fear of *not* reaching them, and see anything less than a perfectly met goal as a failure."[250] These are two very different processes. Fear rarely motivates anything much deeper than surface, survival-type outcomes. Being motivated by positive outcomes involves a very different energy dynamic, one that leaves room for the love of the process and enjoyment of the journey—mistakes and setbacks notwithstanding.

> Fear rarely motivates anything much deeper than surface, survival-type outcomes. Being motivated by positive outcomes involves a very different energy dynamic, one that leaves room for the love of the process and enjoyment of the journey.

Educational administrator Virginia Duran Ginn noted a difference among perfectionistic striving and those students and colleagues who had a sincere and healthy desire for successful results. "The perfectionist was more invested in personal outcomes and recognition while those who were after healthy excellence had a bigger picture in mind. Both types experienced stress, frustrations, and even failures, but the perfectionist might rather call it quits than to move forward in the midst of any messiness or uncertainty. It would be too personal and too much ego at stake."

Among perfectionists, arbitrary standards can become obstacles, and fear of negative feedback can undermine our greatest talents. How many of us have dropped classes or sports or music or art before we had a chance to discover our gifts? How many manuscripts sit, forever unseen, on basement shelves or in boxes in the garage? How often have we declined an invitation or missed seeing friends because we had gained a few pounds since our last encounter? "Perfection stops you from starting projects or even relationships because you are not perfect," says Victore. "And it also stops you from finishing or shipping projects because it's not perfect. The timing will never be perfect. You know what's better than perfect? *Done!* Done is better than perfect."[251]

"There was a time, long ago, when I would have fancied myself to be a bit of an artist," writes Jennifer Bostic blogging about an art project she had completed that day. "But somehow, for some reason, I gave up on creating things." In typical perfectionistic fashion, she had lost faith in her creations, believing that others could "do it better," so why even bother to try? She writes about how perfectionism can leave us stuck, talking ourselves out of doing things we want and need to do. "The problem with perfectionism is that it isn't just about giving up on art or some other passion," she says. "Perfectionism makes you give up on yourself."[252]

> "The problem with perfectionism is that it isn't just about giving up on art or some other passion," she says. "Perfectionism makes you give up on yourself."

CHAPTER 12

The Perfect Relationship: Power and Perfectionism

Perfectionists can be quite effective at creating stress, anxiety, and hardship for themselves. Put them in relationships and we find that many are equally adept at doing the same for others. The literature frequently splits on this topic, separating the perfectionistic behaviors we apply to ourselves from the perfectionism we impose on others. To be fair, the observable behaviors of the people who look in the mirror and say critical, derisive things to themselves may appear slightly different from the behaviors of those who inflict similar abuse on other people. However, looking at the wide range of possible perfectionistic behaviors, you'll find the spectrum stretching from highly self-focused on one end to outwardly hypercritical at the other—with plenty of people likely to be quite capable of *both* extremes.

That said, I'm frankly more concerned with the feelings and needs at the core of these expressions of perfectionism than I am with the direction in which they are projected. Whether our actions represent a lack of self-worth or a disregard for the dignity and emotional safety of someone else, I see similar threads of anger, impatience, frustration, disappointment, and even contempt. So I'd prefer to examine the destructive impact of perfectionism on relationships as an issue of fear and power. Because regardless of where and how this disorder is directed (self or other), I believe that the various compensations emerge from a very similar empty and frightened place.

Perfectionism Is Also About Power

I've shared a good bit about the connection between perfectionism and fear, the need for approval, the need to fit in, and the tendency to measure self-worth against appearance and achievement. These are all components of a basic equation that tells us that *we will never get something we see as important unless we do certain things a certain way, and that we won't feel okay about ourselves unless we make that happen.* To achieve this goal we need another ingredient in the mix—power.

While some accounts of perfectionists include a desire for order and control, I believe that the literature generally underplays the role of power in all forms of perfectionism. In relationships, power can look arrogant, judgmental, aggressive, or bitchy, but it can also show up as compliant, helplessness, passive, submissive, or self-destructive.[253] Any strategy that we believe will secure our social, emotional, academic, financial, or physical safety is fair game. It doesn't really matter if this process involves pushing ourselves or pushing others: power is a critical component of perfectionism. Period.

"Perfection is a myth," says Victore. "It's been called a flaw disguised as control."[254] Look closely and you can see a certain similarity between the preschooler who insists on arranging her toys in a certain order, the teens who starve themselves or take steroids, the parents who push a child to make the team or be first in the class, the people who can't work with one thing out of place on their desk, the artist who never finishes the revisions on the painting or song, the people who find other people's flaws as a way to feed their sense of superiority, or the folks who take their work commitments out on the people at home. The common thread I see in every example of people chasing perfection is a very basic need for power and control.

> The common thread I see in every example of people chasing perfection is a very basic need for power and control.

The Basic Ingredients for Connecting

Early in my career, I noticed something interesting in my work with young people, many of whom came from unstable and unsafe home environments. These kids had few positive role models and, early on, had developed a rather creative repertoire of survival skills to help them navigate a world they could not trust. Anticipating hurt and disappointment, many were fairly adept at managing their attachment to others—some hungry for a connection but too prickly to let anyone close, others putting their safety and well-being on the line for any illusion of affection.

In power plays with adults and one another, there was always this sense that winning was achieved only by someone else's loss. Put-downs and insults were common social currency, and attempts to connect with kindness were met with suspicion and defensiveness. Cooperating, respecting other people's needs, even the most basic giving could be contorted to feel like surrender, giving up, giving in. Considering their models and experiences, what skills and strategies would these kids have to bring to a friendship or romantic relationship?

Sadly, it's not just kids raised in dire dysfunction who struggle to form healthy, caring relationships. Few of us have had many examples of positive, respectful, win-win ways to connect with one another. Healthy relationships require trust, respect, understanding, and vulnerability—attributes that can challenge anyone, including individuals with a far less rocky early start. Add perfectionism into the mix and things can get really wonky because many of our most basic needs involve interactions with other people, needs that can be hard to satisfy if people don't want to be around us.

"If you are a card-carrying human being, chances are that you share the same fear as all other humans: the fear of losing love, respect, and connection to others," comments Vanzant. "And if you are human, in order to avoid or prevent the pain, trauma, and perceived devastation of the loss, you will do anything to avoid your greatest fear from being visited on you."[255]

Despite the fact that perfectionistic behaviors can be incredibly annoying, divisive, and alienating, I see no contradiction here. Because short of an extreme, pathological lack of moral responsibility and social conscience, even the most destructive uses of power can seem to provide access to status, assets, or control, which can either prove that perfectionists are worthy of the connections they desire, or can serve as a cheap substitute.

When Our Priorities Get Twisted

Perfectionists have a hard time when things don't look right, get done right, or get done fast enough. In order to fend off fear, anxiety, and anger, we can go to great lengths to control how others behave, how they treat us, or how we think their actions or appearance will influence other people's opinions of us. But blogger Henrik Edberg urges, "Realize that you hurt yourself and the people around you by buying into myths of perfection." Despite media images that can draw you into believing perfection is wonderful and desirable, he says, "in real life, it clashes with reality and tends to cause much suffering and stress within you and in the people around you."[256]

One contributor who works in a highly technical profession offers, "I have worked in fields of endeavor where we have referred to obsessive-compulsive disorder or anal-retentiveness as a desirable characteristic." While he concedes that these traits work well "for performing repetitive tasks with a high level of meticulous attention to technical details, this level of resolution to focus is not necessarily appreciated when interfacing with other humans."

Nonetheless, it's easy to get caught up in details and goals to the point that we deny ourselves time for relationships, self-care, or other ways of enjoying our lives. "A person who insists on getting every detail perfect, such as the hostess who keeps hungry guests waiting while arranging the dining table down to the last detail, can be difficult for non-perfectionists to relate to or live with," notes health columnist Melinda Beck.[257] Winter offers a similar example in describing a woman so keen to keep her house absolutely perfect that "her children could never have friends to come for a meal, let alone stay the night, because she was so terrified that they would put their dirty hands on the wall on the way up the stairs." If friends did come over, "she would run around after them . . . scrubbing the walls." Winter believes her behavior is driven "by guilt, a deep fear of failure, and underneath that a fear of rejection."[258]

Carrey points out, "The effect you have on others is the most valuable currency there is."[259] Yet how often do we take on so much or spend so much time on a task that we end up stressed and resentful, missing important events, and short-changing the people we care about most because when we do have time to spend with them, we're too tired or wound up to make a meaningful, positive connection? Teversham recalls the resentment that built up at work as she continued to take on more and more, hoping to be rescued by people who never seemed to notice that she needed help (which she never asked for). "They kept expecting more of me and I kept giving and doing more. . . . Sometimes I was so tired it felt like I could not face my life, even though I was busy with people and work I loved and enjoyed."[260]

Boundary issues are common among perfectionists. We lose sight of the line where our responsibility ends and other people's begin. We can feel personally responsible for things over which we have little or no control—not that that stops us from trying. But when we personalize our child's failure as a sign of poor parenting, or see a spouse's infidelity as an indication of our inadequacy as a partner, or assume that the friend who doesn't immediately respond to a text is mad at us, the outcome is likely to be anger and resentment, neither of which do much to enhance any relationship. "Too much hustle and not enough self-care and connection," says Ward, citing one cause of perfectionists' self-sabotage. "When our 'love tank' is empty because we've put ourselves last for too long, we won't make clear decisions and we're likely to sabotage even our most precious relationships."[261]

The Right Stuff

In what has become a bit of a family joke, my husband and I can spend the entire day together in the house, yet the minute I reach for my keys to leave for a meeting, class, or appointment—one he's known about this entire time—my imminent departure seems to remind him of something important he needs to share or ask me about.

His requests have always been reasonable: I would never mind helping him find something or sort out a software problem. The only issue is the timing. On a bad day, my programming triggers a knee-jerk annoyance: I plunk my keys down, listen and respond impatiently, and then run out the door, angry and stressed out about being late. Lately, I am learning to stay calm and keep moving, cheerfully assuring him that I'll be happy to help as soon as I get home. However, even when I can pull this off, I often have to bite back the temptation to ask why he always waits until I'm about to leave.[262]

Even with the best intentions, this is not an easy journey for anyone. When we come to believe that our safety and acceptance depend on never making mistakes, we can develop an intense attachment to being right, and that usually means making someone else wrong. This tendency is reinforced by a cultural belief that every problem needs a culprit, insisting that it's not only okay but *necessary* to inflict some form of emotional, psychological, or physical pain to inspire others to more positive behaviors. The more rigid we are about how things should be, the more stress we'll experience in our encounters with others—especially if their "shoulds" are very different from ours, or if they don't care about certain things to the same degree we do.

"When I had my first child, I basically shut my husband out because he couldn't do things the 'right' way," admits education professor Betina Hsieh. "The clothes had to be folded a certain way, the meals had to be balanced and nutritious, the baby had to be put down in a certain routine, our older adopted children needed specific support that only I could give them." Because her husband's attempts to help didn't meet up to Hsieh's "perfect standards," she wouldn't let him do anything to support her. "This nearly destroyed our marriage and family and I ended up getting really ill before realizing that if I didn't let go of my perfectionism, I wouldn't be around to supervise how things were going."

This is a common theme among perfectionists. Basco describes an individual who "is often disappointed and frustrated by others who always seem to let him down." He sometimes "does the job himself rather than ask for help, just so he doesn't have to deal with their procrastination and excuses."[263] We're all extra fussy about certain things in our lives, and what bugs you might well be something I'd never notice (and vice versa). "I'll do it myself" is fine so long as the "doing" doesn't generate feelings of resentment or victimization. And that gets tricky, especially if we've made our preferences known.

"Any critique is harmful to relationships because it implies there is a right and wrong way to do things. Our egos get ruffled," claims educator Peter Bowman. He recommends expressing personal preferences and explaining your reasons, taking ownership of the problem. "No one likes to be told what to do, even less so when the way they do it is [seen as] not quite right."

Retired librarian Rhea Alper reports, "If I want it done right, I do it because I'll have to redo it anyway." She's adopted this attitude, at least in part, out of a respect for her husband's feelings, anticipating that he would be hurt "when I redid something he thought he did correctly." She admits that earlier in their forty-year marriage, frustration would have been an issue for her. "But now I just do it. Sometimes it's not important enough to care one way or the other."

I agree, and I also understand that it can take a great deal of conscious intention (and time) to get to that point. "I see so many young couples angry about 'I did it last time' or saying things like 'I shouldn't have to tell you that,'" observes one contributor who has counseled many families over the years. "And they don't let up until they get some kind of reaction from the other. I think they're looking for remorse, but more often what they get is push-back and anger. It's like they just have to be right, but I don't think they realize how destructive it is to make their partners wrong."

When We Don't Get What We Want

When I was training to become a teacher, people kept telling me to have high expectations, so when I walked into my first classroom, that's exactly what I did. I told my kids I expected this and I expected that and after exhausting my list of high expectations, my students just looked at me and shrugged. They had absolutely no investment in all those things that were important to me, and all the "expecting" in the world wasn't going to change that.

Over the years, it's become clear that this whole expectation thing can cause a great deal of friction, disappointment, and distress in all sorts of relationships. This issue can be especially problematic for perfectionists because we tend to have a whole lot of expectations and rules about how things are supposed to be.

When we live and work with people who share these same ideals, we generally get along fine. But when they think our standards are unreasonable, if they don't see why those things are such a big deal, or if they tend to be perfectionistic about different stuff, conflict and resistance are likely to ensue. Simply expecting people to behave in a certain way—and this includes feeling entitled to these feelings because, after all, they're just *right*—is not only ineffective as a method of motivating people but can be toxic to the relationship and demeaning, dismissive, and alienating to the others involved. Unexpressed expectations, assuming others know what we want, can create even bigger obstacles.

The way we communicate our standards and expectations, and the degree to which others fulfill them, affects how we feel about one another. "I like partners who are neat, who keep common areas clean daily, and who clean up as they go as they cook," shares writer and editor Deborah Drake. "As much as I claim to say I am good with cleaning up after you to please myself, it impacts how I see you when we turn in at night."

Few of us have had many positive models for getting what we want. So instead we respond to our disappointments with the tools we have at hand, creating a cloud of stress and toxicity through which we try to connect. "My partner and I are both perfectionists," writes a contributor in a relationship for many years. "Together we have accomplished a lot and have the respect of those who know us. Unfortunately, we also squabble regularly because of falling short in one way or another. Both of us are on the defensive and constantly have to fend off the controlling nature of the other. It's tiring and takes the shine off what should be a more fun and loving relationship. We keep working on it and maybe we will perfect grace as we age."

As an educator, my job has always been about encouraging people to grow and change, and I think there are nondestructive ways to do that. However, when we try to turn people into our idea of who they should be (even with their apparent consent) we are sure to create problems. "Hammering someone to fit inside a set of unrealistic expectations that can never be met is a recipe for disaster," advises an article on a dating website, "not to mention cruel and unusual punishment for the unsuspecting parties who are just being themselves."[264]

Psychologist Alan Entin remarks, "Perfectionism is very difficult to live with because you are always striving for some kind of magical fantasy ideal that no one can ever live up to." He encourages couples to work to establish attainable goals in their relationship instead.[265] Or, as author Edith Schaeffer relates, "People throw away what they could have by insisting on perfection, which they cannot have, and looking for it where they will never find it."[266]

But oh, we so want what we want, don't we? Perfectionists "are hard on themselves, and many are even harder on others," writes Ann Smith. They "may appear arrogant and judgmental (they know what is best and everyone should do it that way). They fear failure and try to prevent it by being in control."[267] Lisa Cramer, a field manager for adult-living facilities, says that she almost divorced over wanting her spouse to be "a more perfect husband." She ultimately realized that she was too tired of being frustrated and disappointed and instead "decided to surrender to his being his own person and me being my best self. Since then, we get along with much greater ease. It took about five years to get to that place."

How to Alienate the People
We Need in Our Lives

Being deprived of something we want can provoke anger and frustration in the best of us. Even when these feelings are self-directed, being around this energy isn't easy. Retired teacher Mel Alper explains, "I don't expect anyone to be perfect except me, and when I'm not I get very frustrated and angry, which [my wife] takes personally. It has nothing to do with her."

Intellectually, we might be well aware that another person's feelings are unrelated to us, but maintaining adequate distance to not get sucked into someone else's emotional vortex can be hard to do, especially for people who have their own perfectionism issues. Throw in a bit of personalization—a common trait among perfectionists—and we may end up owning what's not truly ours, taking responsibility for things that have nothing to do with us. (Sometimes people just need a bit of space to work through whatever they're feeling. Insisting on explanations or being critical will likely aggravate the situation, creating an even greater disconnect.)

But it's not just being around negativity that's a problem. Perfectionists don't do well on either end, whether giving or receiving. Although feedback is essential for our success and stability in our relationships and jobs, it can be hard to hear when there's even a hint of criticism involved. "Because the perfectionists fear and anticipate rejection when they are judged as imperfect, they tend to react defensively to criticism," reports Adderholdt. "Their response usually frustrates and alienates others and may bring about the very disapproval perfectionists most fear. This reinforces their irrational belief that they must be perfect to be accepted."[268]

Sure, we could learn from our mistakes if we weren't so busy denying them,[269] but how can we admit to something that could fracture the deception? Especially since perfectionists "take every setback and criticism personally," defensiveness seems to protect against a fragile self-image and low resiliency, claims Gregoire, offering a sense of control against perceived threats, "even when no defense is needed."[270]

Going on the offense makes things even worse. It's hard to restrict the pressure we put on ourselves *to* ourselves, and often these attitudes spill over in the form of irritation, micromanaging, criticizing, and nagging. Management expert Sheri Staak notes that expecting perfection from others causes "a tense, stressful work environment, second-guessing and immobility due to fear, stifled creativity and innovation, decreased performance output, missed opportunities for growth and change, [and] negative, defeatist attitudes."[271] (Clearly this comment applies to personal relationships, as do most of the work-related remarks in this section.)

Scott mentions the "Critical Eye" tendency "to spot tiny mistakes and imperfections," after which it becomes hard for perfectionists to see anything else.[272] With so much attention focused on errors and flaws, many perfectionists are simply not wired to notice and acknowledge what others are doing well. "A perfectionist cannot appreciate others and cannot appreciate their efforts," writes computer scientist and consultant Don Tillman. While perfectionistic leaders want respect, "they are incapable of giving praise or being respectful to others since no one can meet their expectations."

Even efforts to deliver positive feedback can be loaded, a backhanded compliment with a put-down or agenda: "That was a great report. I didn't think you could pull it off." "Your speed is really improving. I'll bet you could do much better." (Or at home: "You played that beautifully. Why can't you keep your room neat?") These cruel power plays inspire mistrust and fear, and keep people off-balance and insecure—hardly ideal for building healthy relationships, commitment, or cooperation.

Working for a perfectionist can be a nightmare—and a big factor in why people leave their jobs. Government worker Victor Allan C. Ilagan admits that he learned a lot from a perfectionistic boss, although she also inspired sleepless nights and anxiety attacks. "My heart would throb on the way to the office." Ilagan was about to resign when that boss was replaced. "She still gives me the creeps when I think of her." Another contributor talked about working for a "gotcha" type of boss. "No matter what I did, he would find something wrong with it. If I changed it to what he wanted, he suddenly wanted something different." Not surprisingly, that individual was very happy to leave that no-win situation.

Employers who are hung up on perfection often end up with the exact opposite, according to clinical psychologist Marc Schoen. "Pressuring employees to be perfect leads them to take desperate measures and cut corners."[273] And although you might think that perfectionism would increase someone's chances of advancement at work, the truth is quite the opposite. "Portraying yourself as a 'perfect' leader, or expecting perfection from yourself, is actually detrimental to your leadership or career success," writes Staak. "Striving to meet goals and attain best practices will keep you moving forward, but striving for perfection can actually backfire and impede growth and performance."[274]

Confusing quality work with hyperfocused efforts to be perfect "could be doing more harm than good," writes business reporter Emmie Martin. Among the qualities that can ruin a career, she includes poor use of time, lack of flexibility and authenticity, and a resistance to admitting to needing help (or not knowing something).[275] Adderholdt seldom sees perfectionists reach the top of the totem pole. They often remain "just a painstaking worker," working alone because their demands bring them into conflict with others.[276] Further, Ginn sees perfectionists having difficulty collaborating, being unwilling to assume responsibility for errors, and requiring recognition for any contributions they make.

Certainly, perfectionists struggle in personal relationships as well, their expectations creating unhappiness for both partners. In one study, when asked if their partner was a perfectionist, "those who said yes were more likely to use nagging and sarcasm to deal with their relationship troubles. These strategies, the researchers found, led both sides to have less satisfaction within the relationship."[277] Few relationships are immune. Jagtiani describes parents who deny their children "proper sleep or playtime just so that they can top the class," for example, and partners who "sulk for days because something was not kept back in its usual place."[278]

Leman describes a client whose insecurities and lack of self-worth led to an inability to connect, finding petty reasons to reject "anyone who really began to care about him."[279] An article on a dating website warns, "The scariest time in any romantic relationship is when it starts to look like it's actually going to work out." Criticism and doubts begin to surface and "the validity of the entire relationship comes into question. It seems that chronic dissatisfaction and criticism of a mate may speak more to fears of disappointment than any real incompatibilities in a relationship."[280]

Clearly, perfectionism doesn't work well as a relationship enhancer. Whether we're dealing with family, friends, coworkers, employees, bosses, or other important people in our lives, getting along will serve everyone involved. Unfortunately, perfectionists can be more than unpleasant people to avoid. At our worst, we can be appallingly destructive.

Beyond Alienation

If you really want to assure your alienation from others, throw in a little arrogance, indifference, contempt, and shame to finish the job. A perfectionist out to win at all costs can be ruthless in using these hateful weapons. Truly vicious perfectionists can go to great lengths to undermine another person's confidence, self-assurance, and even competence. "There are two ways to dehumanize someone," writes Wong, "by dismissing them and by idolizing them."[281] Either can give the perfectionist with a need for superiority some power and leverage.

Treating people as though they don't matter also shatters the possibility for connection and understanding, leaving others doubting that they have a shred of worth to offer the world. Consider the man whose romantic advances included putting his wife on the scale and agreeing to make love to her only if her weight was under a certain number. As extreme and bizarre as this story sounds, it was only one of several accounts from both men and women who were rejected because they did not live up to someone's random fantasy.

Author Robin Korth, a fifty-nine-year-old woman in "great health and good physical shape," was getting along great with a man she met online. After several seemingly successful dates, he explained his lack of desire for intimacy. "'Your body is too wrinkly,' he said without a pause. 'I have spoiled myself over the years with young women. I just can't get excited with you. I love your energy and your laughter. I like your head and your heart. But, I just can't deal with your body.'" Although this encounter may have inspired Korth's "brutal scrutiny" of herself, it also allowed her to reclaim a body that she refused to hide—especially for the benefit of a self-absorbed, entitled guy who, to the end, remained clueless to the "hurt and horror he had inflicted."[282]

While deliberately shaming did not seem to be a factor in Korth's encounter (as her needs and feelings were apparently not even considered), shame is clearly another powerful relationship wrecker. Inflicting shame requires others to feel diminished. Not just remorseful or embarrassed, but diminished. Even for someone with good intentions, trying to inspire positive behavior with shame is terribly misguided.

"If you want to motivate friends or family members . . . or simply are seeking motivation yourself," registered dietitian Lauren Slayton recommends checking negativity and shame at the door.[283] Brené Brown offers powerful support, claiming that "shame corrodes the very part of us that believes we are capable of change," insisting that it is more likely to inspire a negative, numbing, resistant response instead. "Shame never works as a catalyst for healthy, lasting change," she adds.[284]

Another poisonous ingredient for relationships: contempt. We can recognize contempt in eye-rolling, sarcasm, or a deprecating tone of voice that says "I matter, you don't." A power play that disregards, dismisses, and denigrates others, contempt is also one of the top indicators that a relationship will fail. "Contempt signifies rejection," remarks author Susan Heitler. It suggests that whatever flawed quality being targeted is "hopelessly unfixable."[285] Contempt is one of the nastiest ways to communicate that someone isn't living up to our expectations. (Expressing disappointment isn't much different, although it usually lacks the element of disgust and disrespect that contempt often carries.)

As we can see, perfectionism can do serious damage to relationships. None of us can avoid running into jerky, disrespectful people from time to time. My concern keeps coming back to the factors that make us vulnerable to attempts to control or belittle us, the beliefs that allow us to justify staying with unkind or abusive people. I want to dig underneath the anxiety that make us feel responsible for keeping everyone else on the planet happy, and gives the not-good-enough voice of the Inner Critic its credibility. Because these are the messages and images that have such a strong influence on our sense of adequacy and worth, information for which we would willingly compromise our mental and physical health as a way to cope.

Stress-Producing Obstacles in Relationships [286]

+ Needing to be in charge or in control, especially when doing so depends on disempowering or controlling others, or when it disregards other people's desire for autonomy.

+ Needing to be right, when it depends on others being wrong, when it requires making others wrong, or when it insists that others agree or support our views and actions.

+ Needing to be needed or feel important, when it requires others to feel dependent or insecure.

+ Needing others to exhibit certain behaviors, appearance, values, preferences, or abilities in order to feel worthy or adequate (or successful as a parent, spouse, or leader, for example).

+ Expectations, especially when our preferences or desires are not communicated or agreed to beforehand. Having an agenda for how another person should be or behave: "I expected you to be home by now," "If you really loved me, you would have called," "I can't believe you didn't get me a card."

+ Being arrogant, self-righteous, or disappointed because of unfulfilled (and often unexpressed) expectations.

+ Assuming that others operate with our priorities and values (and judging them negatively when they don't): "How can you spend so much time watching football?" "I can't believe you haven't read that book." "How can you find anything in this mess?"

+ Assuming that someone will think, feel, act, or react in a certain way: "I didn't tell you because you'd get mad," "I didn't want to bother you," "I was afraid you'd be hurt." Thinking for another person.

+ Tunnel vision. An inability to see the "big picture."

+ All-or-nothing thinking. A tendency to think in terms of opposite extremes. An inability to see multiple options or other points of view.

+ Fear of conflict, rejection, or abandonment. Compromising personal values or standards, making decisions based on someone else's reaction or possible reaction.

+ Denying that a problem exists or making excuses for someone else's unacceptable behavior, rather than confronting that person or asking for more reasonable behavior.

+ Reactivity. Overreacting.

+ Victim thinking. The perception of having no power to change situations (or thinking) for the better or to do things differently.

+ Abdicating personal responsibility. Being afraid or unwilling to let people know what we want.

+ Blaming: "If you would shape up, there wouldn't be a problem."

+ Double standards. Expecting or demanding behaviors from others that we do not model or demonstrate.

+ Criticizing, shaming, ridiculing, judging, or attacking. Focusing on the negative (especially in someone else's behavior, choices, preferences, or values).

+ Asking others to defend or explain their behavior rather than asking for what we want: "Why did you borrow my sweater without asking me first?" instead of "I want you to ask before you borrow my things."

+ Assuming that others are committed to an agreement simply because we have expressed what we want. Not asking for agreement.

+ Lack of consideration for others. Focusing on our own needs to exclusion of others' needs. Failing to respect another person's boundaries, privacy, or time.

+ Focusing on another person's needs to exclusion of our own. Discounting or dismissing our needs in favor of someone else's (when doing so will have a negative or harmful outcome). Self-sacrifice.

+ Resistance to being conscious and present in the relationship.

+ Resistance to personal change: "I've always felt that way," "This is just the way I am (or do things)."

CHAPTER 13

The Perfect Stress for Body and Mind

Early in this book, I mentioned that perfectionism—not the pursuit of excellence, but a quest for flawlessness—could put us on the fast track to crazy. Regardless of how our perfectionism manifests, the disorder *will* take its toll on our body and mind.

We need to look at both cause and effect here. We know that the seeds of perfectionism are sown early in our lives as we run through various attempts to engage or maintain attachment, attention, and care from the people we depend on for our safety and survival. During this time, says Susannah Grover, "we receive bushels of conditioning to help us survive in various life situations." But this conditioning also disconnects us from our true selves, what she calls our deeper Nature, and ends up creating "what can be subjectively experienced as 'psychic holes,' each one bringing with it the sense of being internally deficient."

As these feelings accumulate, "we start looking for fulfillment out-side of ourselves, learning to manipulate the people around us and our environment, so as to maximize pleasure (by way of popularity, posi-tive feedback, or acquisition of things, for example) and attempt to minimize pain," she says. We do our best to avoid direct contact with these psychic gaps, places where we have, through necessity, discon-nected from ourselves. In the process, we end up developing "a phobic nervousness about contacting anything deeper than our 'surface self.'"

We reach for positive reflections from the world around us, Grover observes, directing our life force "towards fabricating a positive image, expressing personality cleverness, or becoming an enticing object for others or an invaluable expert so people will hold us in high esteem (when we, ourselves, don't)." Underneath these efforts exists a "grow-ing secret sense of a fraudulence, which keeps the whole mechanism going ad nauseam, until we are ready to get off this wheel of misfor-tune and take the risk of moving in the direction of becoming Real."[287]

These efforts create a good bit of anxiety because keeping up the deception—not to mention ignoring the parts of ourselves from which we have disconnected along the way—is incredibly stressful and exhausting. Many of the perfectionistic behaviors we see have emerged as a means of coping with these feelings of emptiness and fear, or as an attempt to cover them up.

Stress and Anxiety

Everyone experiences stress and anxiety from time to time, but per-fectionists seem to have their own special reserve tanks for these feel-ings. According to the U.S. Library of Medicine, "Stress is a feeling of emotional or physical tension. It can come from any event or thought that makes you feel frustrated, angry, or nervous." On the other hand, "anxiety is a feeling of fear, unease, and worry."[288] Anxiety can linger after the stressful event or it can be tied to feelings of vulnerability about something awful that we believe will happen in the future.

Information about anxiety will often be accompanied by information about anxiety disorders, depression, addiction, identity issues, and suicide, among other psychological problems—similar conditions to those often associated with perfectionism. Not only that, but "perfectionists are very rarely obsessive about only one aspect of their lives," says freelance writer Jennifer Drapkin.[289] Clearly there is a great deal of overlap in the numerous ways perfectionism can affect mental health.

Playwright Victoria Maxwell describes her perfectionism, anxiety, and depression as a "vicious triangle," one that often prevents her from starting or accomplishing tasks. "My generalized anxiety disorder, and bipolar disorder (especially the depression side) co-mingled nicely, if not destructively with my need for everything to be beyond excellent," she shares. "The result for me was horribly cruel self-talk, piercing feelings of inadequacy, constant free-floating worry, and ongoing depression that wouldn't lift even if I did complete something well. My mantra was 'it's never good enough . . . it's never good enough . . . it's never good enough.'"[290]

The dread of falling short keeps pushing us to write one more version of our best verse, top off our weight loss by losing one more pound, shave one more second off our best time. But here's where it gets circular: "Many people with anxiety have difficulty gauging when tasks are completed to their satisfaction," reports clinical psychologist Kathariya Mokrue. Regardless of how much time and effort they've invested, it's hard for these folks to know when to stop. Fatigue and exhaustion kick in and loved ones beg them to come up for air. But the "risks associated with being wrong or imperfect" can generate anxiety, which signals even more frantic work. "It is only when this signal is drowned out by physical or mental exhaustion that people stop."

Mokrue also notes that this may be what makes it so hard for perfectionists to celebrate accomplishments, and why so many "still harbor feelings of insecurity and anxiety" despite all their good works.[291] And no matter how hard and fast and furious our schedules, somehow the to-do lists never seem to get shorter. "We convince ourselves that if we stay busy enough and keep moving, reality won't be able to keep up," writes Brené Brown. "Of course, the irony is that the thing that's wearing us down is trying to stay out in front of feeling worn down."[292] Gregoire reiterates the corrosive impact on resiliency. "Rather than bouncing back from challenges and mistakes, the perfectionist is beaten down by them, taking every misstep as evidence for the truth of their deepest, continually plaguing fear: 'I'm not good enough.'"[293]

Shape-Shifting for Inclusion and Approval

I remember the messages that accompanied any recognition I got when I was a kid. The warnings went beyond the fear that my success might go to my head, and instead cautioned me to not let too much talent or intelligence show. Tone it down a bit. Don't shine too brightly. Although this was a generic caution apparently intended to protect me from social rejection, the caution was particularly emphatic with regard to relating to boys. My desirability, I was informed, depended on this deception, fitting into a mold that would ultimately deny a great deal of who I actually was for a very long time.

Sadly, some fifty years later, this suffocating model still very much exists. Despite any gains by women in past decades, girls are still getting the message that "female empowerment simply comes from being sexy."[294] According to author and counselor Lisa Hinkelman, "girls continue to say that they 'dumb themselves down' around boys." Her research also shows that "girls as young as six equate being sexy to being popular."[295] Much of the literature backs up her findings. "It can be a tough, desolate world out there for girls who put more emphasis on what's inside their brains than what's outside of them," writes editorial advocate Jamie Varon. "It's not like you can't be both smart and pretty (of course you can), but it's frustrating when—no matter how smart you are—there's more emphasis put on how you look."[296]

Senior lifestyle writer Lauren Martin compares "the dating landscape with the same risks many face going into the arctic tundra." Learning the tricks and tips for the journey, "we've changed our clothes, hair, and grooming styles to fit the destination." Yet the women who refuse to check their intelligence along the way are more likely to find themselves single and alone. With some exceptions, of course, these cultural stereotypes and gender biases, create a no-win outcome for a whole lot of people. "There are plenty of women who will give up their lives for men, who will refuse to challenge them, fight them, and refuse to see them as their equals, but their saviors," she says.[297] That's a pretty steep price to pay for meeting cultural standards of desirability.

And once ingrained, these beliefs can last a lifetime. "I am a teacher who is passionate about her students, her subject, her family and friends," asserts educator Mollie Rosenfield, "but I am still, sickly perhaps, proudest of my sexual abilities. Recently divorced, in my sixties, I have already begun to go back to the old patterns of getting male approval through sex. I am terrified." Some of the most talented, brilliant women I've met discount their creative and intellectual assets, favoring appearance and sexual competence as what really matters.

But it's not just about intelligence and looks, and it's not only women who bear this burden. Although young girls are still chided for displays of anger, for example, so are boys who dare to exhibit sadness. (Notice how often adult women express angry feelings by crying and how frequently men demonstrate grief with rage.) We learn the social consequences of our emotional authenticity, although the impact on our mental and physical health of stuffing our feelings can be far worse.

Following the rules and doing what's expected can buy us belonging and safety, but this can come at a high price. We pick on the new kid to be accepted by the popular crowd or laugh at a derogatory joke to fit in with office associates, even though at some level we are squirming in discomfort at our internal hypocrisy. Denying the best parts of ourselves to please others creates a perfect breeding ground for resentment, depression, and self-doubt. And sacrificing our integrity and the essence of who we are to accommodate someone else's ideas about what is acceptable, desirable, or cool is perfectionism at its most soul-killing.

> Following the rules and doing what's expected can buy us belonging and safety, but this can come at a high price. We pick on the new kid to be accepted by the popular crowd or laugh at a derogatory joke to fit in with office associates, even though at some level we are squirming in discomfort at our internal hypocrisy. Denying the best parts of ourselves to please others creates a perfect breeding ground for resentment, depression, and self-doubt.

The Walls Come Tumbling Down

Ann Smith tells of a client whose children were always clean and well-dressed, whose purse was filled with anything anyone might need, and whose house was always ready for guests to drop by. Every aspect of her life was extraordinarily well-organized, but by the time this woman finally sought help, she was angry, depressed, and hated her life.[298]

Middle-school teacher John Spencer explains the set-up, "Perfectionism is the belief that things can be perfect and *will* be perfect with the right amount of effort." As long as we hold this belief, it means that the inevitable errors and failures will keep telling us we're not good enough or working hard enough. We rationalize our attachment to this belief in all kinds of ways. In Spencer's case, he insisted it was just the high expectations he held for himself and his students. "It wasn't about high expectations," he writes. "It was about insecurity. I felt a need to prove to others that I was a great teacher. I was arrogant but that arrogance was fueled by insecurity."[299]

Perfectionism can eventually precipitate a mental health crisis. "Someday, sometime, you will be sitting somewhere . . ., and something bad will have happened," writes Quindlen. "You will have lost someone you loved, or failed at something at which you badly wanted to succeed. And sitting there, you will fall into the center of yourself. You will look for some core to sustain you. And if you have been perfect all your life and have managed to meet all the expectations of your family, your friends, your community, your society, chances are excellent that there will be a black hole where that core ought to be."[300]

> Perfectionism can eventually precipitate a mental health crisis.

Somehow, that core gets lost in our search for external definition and validation, and in the messages we receive that helped construct our belief system. "When you were growing up, were you taught that others' needs were more important than yours? Were you even allowed to have needs?" asks Teversham. She also comments on the fact that many of us were held responsible for how we made others feel or act.[301] Whether being praised for making others happy or being warned to behave so Daddy wouldn't get mad or so Mommy

> Whether being praised for making others happy or being warned to behave so Daddy wouldn't get mad or so Mommy wouldn't start drinking again, children grow up with a distorted sense of their obligations and abilities to manage other people's emotional lives.

wouldn't start drinking again, children grow up with a distorted sense of their obligations and abilities to manage other people's emotional lives.

So we keep trying to get it right, choosing our outfits or houses or cars hoping others will respond to them in positive ways. We are told what will make us marketable—economically, socially, or romantically—with the implication that these choices will make us happy. Klebanoff recalled growing up with the pressure to marry "the right guy" and how that affected her judgment. Pushed to focus on status and money "rather than how they made you feel," she is currently divorced from all three prestigious, high-achieving, husbands. "It didn't work out," she shared, sadly.

A number of contributors mentioned the impact of never being able to live up to others' expectations and how continually trying just wore them down. "The patterns were always the same," writes therapist Shelly Bullard. "I'd give a lot in a relationship, and feel like I didn't get that much in return. A man would pursue me strongly in the beginning, only to distance himself once I fell for him. I'd fall for unavailable men who were unable to show up for me in a strong, consistent way . . . I'd sacrifice my own needs for a man. I'd feel like I had to prove myself to a man; I'd do the right things to keep his love."[302]

A number of similar stories came out in correspondences and conversations with contributors. "Throughout my childhood, my father never missed an opportunity to criticize my social behavior," wrote one contributor. "He would watch me with my pals and later dissect every mistake he thought I had made, often saying, 'It's no wonder you don't have any friends.' Although I actually had many close peers and playmates, I grew up more inclined to believe my father's words, mistrusting anyone who was especially nice to me or interested in me romantically." This outcome was neither surprising nor especially unusual. "After a while," one woman explained, "if you get ground down enough, you start to believe that you're lucky you have anyone in your life. Period. Abuse starts looking like attention and you get twisted around enough to accept it as love."

Lack of confidence seeps into relationships, often creating friction and distance, which further damages whatever sense of worth or connection remains. "I had a friend who used to call after every get-together to apologize for some perceived offense he had committed," shared another individual. "This was after a really nice night of hanging out together. Nothing had been weird until that call. One time he even sent a card," he recalled. "This guy was so sure he had done something wrong when nothing bad had actually occurred that he ultimately destroyed any desire I had to spend any time with him."

Ruminating, beating ourselves up, second-guessing our behavior, and tearing ourselves down puts our mental health in a tenuous position, vulnerable to a variety of illnesses and disorders. Psychologist Katherine Muller often sees professional clients to help them break through their belief "that if they didn't flog themselves, they wouldn't be as successful." Her work includes helping them understand that "people usually succeed in *spite* of their Inner Critics, not because of them."[303] Beck connects "unrelenting self-criticism" with depression and anxiety, as well as "eating disorders, self-mutilation, and body dysmorphic disorder—[the] preoccupation with one's perceived physical flaws."[304]

Most of us can only maintain the delusion for so long before the cracks start to show. Perfectionists and control freaks "are more susceptible to emotional and physical problems than those who are open-minded and flexible, or 'non-absolutist,'" says psychology lecturer Alistair Ostel. He explains the risk of absolutist (all-or-nothing) thinking, including impediments to problem-solving and coping skills, which can show up as anger and higher levels of stress hormones, suppressed immune systems, insomnia, heart palpitations, chronic fatigue, high blood pressure, and lower levels of job enjoyment than people in similar jobs who are more flexible and open-minded.[305]

Body Image and Food Issues

Taryn Brumfitt, the founder of Body Image Movement, asked 100 women to describe their body. Many had a hard time keeping their responses to a single word, but among the responses shared, none of the words was particularly kind or loving. In fact, the most common responses included "imperfect" and "disgusting." Apparently, this was no surprise to Brumfitt, who used to address her image in the mirror in similar terms. "I loathed my body," she reported.[306]

When I first started researching this project, many of the articles and reports I found were built around the impact of perfectionism on how people perceive—and treat—their bodies. And while you're more likely to find body-issue research and articles focused on women, this issue is by no means gender specific. I've known few men who are unaffected by images projecting unrealistic and often unachievable standards. Writer Chris Tognotti confirms, "Sinewy, fit male bodies are held up as an ideal, and it's easy to conclude that falling short makes you undesired, unwanted, and unlikely to become otherwise."[307]

A mock ad posing four "normal" men next to professional ads for men's underwear "show how men are also held to the near-impossible body standards of models and professional sports players, and inundated with images of far-from-average male bodies on a daily basis," writes poet and freelancer Nina Bahadur. "Studies have shown that idealized images affect men and boys, and may be linked to male eating disorders."[308]

Perhaps the body-image dimension of perfectionism comes to mind so quickly because some version of it is in our face everywhere we look. From magazines to billboards, commercials to e-mail offers, we are constantly confronted with examples of "the look" we all should somehow emulate, as well as the products and programs that can help us achieve that goal. We get the message. Even before adolescence, the conditioning is well in place.

"By the age of ten, around a third of all girls, and 22 percent of boys, say how their bodies look is their number one worry," says educational consultant Nicky Hutchinson. "And ten is also the average age when children start dieting." Colleague Chris Calland adds, "The current population of young people have lower body confidence than ever before—and that's borne out by the rising numbers of youngsters with eating disorders and serious anxieties about their appearance."[309]

Calland also sees an increase in concerns expressed by boys. "Boys worry about it far more than in the past," she says. "Traditionally girls have always shown greater concern about their weight and appearance, but the research shows boys are also worrying. They want to be tall and, when they're a bit older, to be muscular—and they worry about weight too."[310] In a study of 1,500 kids aged seven to eighteen, "40 percent of under tens worry about their weight and almost a quarter have been on a diet in the past year." Thirty-eight percent of kids under ten "say they are influenced by a 'diet obsessed society,'" with 61 percent slightly older youngsters (aged eleven to thirteen) "saying they worry about their weight and 45 percent admitting they have been on a diet."[311]

A video project in which fifty people were asked to describe how they would change their bodies yielded some interesting results. While adults of both genders "struggle to decide on just a single area they would want to change," young children seemed far more comfortable in their bodies and were frankly baffled by the question. (They were, instead, more likely to suggest a super power, or enhancing their body with wings or a shark's mouth, for example.)

These responses suggest that our appreciation for our bodies decreases as we get older, illustrating how ingrained insecurities about our bodies become as we transition into adulthood. Only one of the adults in this small sample, an older woman, spoke about how comfortable she was with getting older. She mentions her white hair in particular, noting her decision to "stay this way because it wouldn't be me if I totally changed the way I looked."[312]

Jennifer Smith reports, "While working as a residential counselor, I can recall countless conversations about perfectionism. Many residents took strides to have the perfect body, leading them to do whatever it took to achieve this unrealistic goal. Interestingly, they were never satisfied and thus continued treating their bodies in harmful ways. The desire for perfection spilled over into other areas of life causing anxiety, insecurities, and disappointment." Tandy, a recovering bulimic who "exercises like a maniac every day," has struggled with food, weight, and body issues her entire life. Despite having achieved her weight goals several times, when I asked, "At what point did you finally feel good enough?" she responded dismissively, "Oh, never."

This awareness and hyperfocus on flaws is stressful and depressing. In addition to the mental health strains, the willingness to do "whatever it takes" can seriously impact our physical health, and not in a good way. It's easy to throw around glib advice about the health benefits of being skinny, but there's nothing healthy about thinness that comes at the expense of starvation, fad diets, laxative abuse, or forced vomiting. Although Calland suggests that messages about healthy eating and obesity may be necessary, these campaigns can have a negative effect. "Some children have absorbed the anti-obesity message to such an extent that they dread gaining weight."[313]

And let's not forget the control factor. "When my daughter was in middle school, she developed a very serious case of anorexia," wrote one contributor. "At some point in therapy, she revealed that she was frustrated with things going on that she had no control over, that eating (or not) was something she felt she could control. She was at a new school, competing with students who were also perfectionists. Somehow, in her middle-school brain, she figured she could be the skinniest—the most perfect skinny. I would think she might have been an aberration, but as a middle school teacher, I have witnessed this multiple times."

Food and body issues take us into some dangerous waters. "For perfectionists, eating disorders are another side of the 'all-or-nothing' mindset," offer Adderholdt and Goldberg. "The more you focus on being perfect, the more aware you become of your faults."[314] Words like "cleanse," "never," and "perfect" only add to the stress and distorted thinking when applied to food, says nutritionist Ellie Krieger, who would like to see these words eliminated from our vocabulary.[315] Antony and Swinson observe, "In general, dieters are more perfectionistic than non-dieters . . . Dieters also set up unrealistic standards for eating, often restricting their intake to dangerously low levels."[316] In fact, statistics compiled by the National Association of Anorexia Nervosa and Associated disorders note that "eating disorders have the highest mortality rate of any mental illness."[317]

Nonetheless, look into some of the darker corners of the Internet and you can find support, encouragement, and even instructions for self-starvation on "thinsporation" and "pro-ana" websites. (Although some sites provide nonjudgmental forums to help people seeking recovery, this term frequently refers to the "movement, largely Internet-based, that portrays anorexia and sometimes bulimia . . . as a lifestyle choice rather than a disease or disorder.")[318] Nor is there any shortage of I-hate-my-body sites or those that "rate" women, ridiculing and maligning the 95 percent of us whose natural body type doesn't fit the ideal portrayed in advertising.[319]

> Depending on self-destructive strategies and hypercritical mindsets—ours or anyone else's—is unlikely to yield healthy choices.

Depending on self-destructive strategies and hypercritical mindsets—ours or anyone else's—is unlikely to yield healthy choices. Besides, most perfectionists who reach one goal will simply find another flaw to detract from any satisfaction they may find in whatever success they achieve. "I've had the perfect body and it's not all it's cracked up to be," says Brumfitt, who spent fifteen weeks of very hard training and 100 percent discipline with her diet to lose weight and tone up.

"And of course people just focused on how good I looked, and how inspirational I was and completely glossed over the fact that there was a heap of blood, sweat, and tears (and not just my own tears) to get to that position." Reaching that short-term goal for her meant sacrificing most of the things she loved.[320] But how easily our priorities can get scrambled when we are seeking achievements, a sense of control in our lives, and some relief from the pressure and pain.

> How easily our priorities can get scrambled when we are seeking achievements, a sense of control in our lives, and some relief from the pressure and pain.

Addictions and Abuse

I've been off diet pills and amphetamines for more than 35 years, yet there is still a part of my brain that is convinced that every problem I have (including meeting the deadline for this book) will disappear with a few good hits of speed. For many years, that was the preferred path to achieving my goals, not just in terms of how much I could accomplish in a day, but also for controlling my food intake and weight. In the old pictures, I look frighteningly thin— although I certainly didn't think so back then. The external rewards and approval only encouraged me, allowing me to believe that I was doing a good thing and, for a long time, making it easier to ignore my body's attempts to convince me otherwise.

It's no surprise that stimulants are quite popular among perfectionists, especially when eating disorders *and* workaholism are present, as they commonly are. However even without the food component, work is often the drug of choice for many people with this disorder. Gregoire comments, "Although perfectionists aren't necessarily high achievers, perfectionism is frequently tied to workaholism." She quotes Burns stating that the perfectionist "acknowledges that his relentless standards are stressful and somewhat unreasonable, but he believes they drive him to levels of excellence and productivity he could never attain otherwise."[321]

To that end, certain substances appear to offer a similar boost, plus a hint of creativity and cleverness, as well. "I was a stand-up comic in the eighties and coke was the drug of choice for many of my buddies," says addiction counselor Willy Drinkwater. "They believed that they were much funnier on coke than without. They felt their energy captured the audience. Many times they just ended up frenetic and disorganized." Drinkwater claims that the writers and musicians with whom he currently works "often feel that coke and other stimulants fuel the creative process. After coming down, when they look at the work they created, [they often say] 'hmm, it was really great when I wrote it last night. I don't get it.'"

Being busy can create its own buzz, making us "feel more alive than anything else for a moment," says Chernoff, noting, however, that "the sensation is not sustainable long-term."[322] However, it's another arena in which we can create a sense of control, as well as tangible evidence of accomplishment that is not always discernible in social interactions. It satisfies our desire for exhaustion and overwhelm as a symbol of our status and worth. But as Cameron notes, "There is a difference between zestful work toward a cherished goal and workaholism. That difference lies less in the hours than it does in the emotional quality of the hours spent. There is a treadmill quality to workaholism. We depend on our addiction and we resent it. For a workaholic, work is synonymous with worth, and so we are hesitant to jettison any part of it."[323]

> Being busy can create its own buzz, making us "feel more alive than anything else for a moment."

> It satisfies our desire for exhaustion and overwhelm as a symbol of our status and worth.

Using work or food (and often both) may be extremely popular among the perfectionist crowd, but these are certainly not the only distractions available. Other drugs, alcohol, relationships, sex, shopping, cleaning, social media, video games, even perfectionism itself can take on an enticing and potentially addictive quality. Not all will contribute to our productivity, and in fact, may be most valuable as a vehicle for procrastination and avoidance.

Part of the attraction is that each of these substances or behaviors can satisfy a need for power in some way. They may help us establish a sense of control over chaos and unpredictability, or help us carve out a space in our lives where others can't make us do something (or make us stop). I've rarely met anyone struggling with a substance abuse or behavioral addiction problem that did not also have unresolved power issues. I believe that in addition to any chemical or neurological factors in the development of all addictions, power and control are significant components.

> I've rarely met anyone struggling with a substance abuse or behavioral addiction problem that did not also have unresolved power issues.

However, I suspect that for perfectionists, the most treacherous aspects of addictive substances and behaviors lie in their potential to quiet the voice of our Inner Critic and any feelings it may arouse. "Emotions are precious gifts," writes author and communications coach Lynn Collins. "They are all important parts of getting to know who we are." The problem starts when our early feelings trigger deep-seated, unresolved issues in [the adults in our lives,] who don't always handle our emotions in positive, supportive, or understanding ways.[324]

> I suspect that for perfectionists, the most treacherous aspects of addictive substances and behaviors lie in their potential to quiet the voice of our Inner Critic and any feelings it may arouse.

"We got sent to our rooms for having huge feelings," writes Anne Lamott.[325] Being dismissed, ridiculed, criticized, or shamed for our feelings compounds whatever problem we were having in the first place. If our emotions provoke responses that threaten our emotional and physical safety, we get the message that it's not okay to have feelings—and when we do, we need to keep our feelings to ourselves because our emotions "cause even more upset," says Collins. It doesn't take long before we figure out that "whatever we can do to eliminate feeling sad, bad, guilty, or shameful is a positive thing to do."[326]

If we believe we can distract ourselves from feelings of inadequacy, doubt, fear, or despair by getting busy, getting high, getting laid, or getting numb, those options start looking pretty good. "People like to not have to think," says musician Grace Slick. "It feels good to just relax. It feels good to not worry about whether your thighs are too fat, and drugs do that for you for a period of time." She cautions against talking about how terrible drugs are. "They're not terrible," she claims. "What they are is real dangerous."[327] And if we're trying to disconnect from emotional discomfort and the demands we place on ourselves, that makes us *real* vulnerable.

Numbing and Self-Harm

The emotional landscape can be a dark and scary place for perfectionists, and many of us spend a great deal of effort to avoid contact, especially with sad, angry, frightened feelings we've managed to keep hidden for a long time. We look to the "distractions" to keep the feelings at bay. The problem, says Chernoff, is that when we desensitize ourselves to vulnerability or hurt, we also numb ourselves "to love, belonging, empathy, creativity, adventure, and all of life's goodness."[328] Nonetheless, many of us are willing to sacrifice access to the good stuff if it means we can avoid the bad.

In addition to the behaviors and substances previously mentioned, there is another coping strategy that can work toward these ends, one that may be difficult to understand. "Some perfectionists purposefully take their frustration, anxiety, and sense of worthlessness out on their bodies" by cutting or injuring themselves.[329] The intention is not suicidal, but instead to provide a release from pain and tension, distract from overwhelming emotions or difficult life circumstances, express feelings that are difficult to put into words, or help the individual feel in control.[330]

The behavior usually starts in early teen years, although experts more recently report seeing it in children as young as eleven or twelve. It is often associated with eating disorders and may accompany "a history of sexual, physical, or verbal abuse." Wendy Lader, an expert in deliberate self-harm behavior, describes many of the people who engage in this practice as sensitive, perfectionists, or overachievers. "The self-injury begins as a defense against what's going on in their family, in their lives. It is definitely a coping strategy for unhappy kids."[331]

"Self-harm is a way of expressing and dealing with deep distress and emotional pain," write Melinda Smith and Jeanne Segal. "As counterintuitive as it may sound to those on the outside, hurting yourself makes you feel better. Injuring yourself is the only way you know how to cope with feelings like sadness, self-loathing, emptiness, guilt, and rage." Smith and Segal warn that "self-harm can become addictive. It may start off as an impulse or something you do to feel more in control, but soon it feels like the cutting or self-harming is controlling you. It often turns into a compulsive behavior that seems impossible to stop." Further, they add, "the relief is short lived, and is quickly followed by other feelings like shame and guilt. Meanwhile, it keeps you from learning more effective strategies for feeling better."[332] In this way, self-harm is much like any other addiction.

Glennon Doyle Melton claims to have spent twenty years "lost to food and booze and bad love and drugs." She attests to the fact that no matter how fast we run, our efforts to numb ourselves fail when our feelings eventually catch up with us. "That's how you can tell you're filling yourself with the wrong things. You use a lot of energy, and in the end, you feel emptier and less comfortable than ever." There really isn't much point in chasing what's not good for us. "You can never get enough of what you don't need," Melton states.[333]

When the Pain Exceeds the Resources for Coping

The statistics are pretty grim: more than 1 million people worldwide commit suicide each year, with more than 40,000 in North America.[334] Are all suicides perfectionists? Of course not. However, a combination of factors can throw perfectionists to the higher end of the at-risk scale, with all-or-nothing thinking possibly being the most critical.

Drapkin cites what expert and researcher Gordon Flett calls the "just right" phenomenon, saying "if something isn't 'just right' to a perfectionist, then it might as well be thrown away."[335] This thinking might apply to a stain on a shirt or a chip in a dinner plate, but it could likewise pertain to a setback or perceived failure in that person's life. Clinical science researcher Kelly Ann Haker observes, "If their lives are not perfect, and they do not perceive a way of changing it, then they irrationally conclude that it is not worth living."[336]

"When perfectionists fail to achieve their unreasonable goals, they turn inward and become excessively self-critical and demoralized," writes Haker, who also attributes the higher risk for suicide to the tendency to dismiss accomplishments and exaggerate mistakes, along with the accompanying frustration, anger, guilt, hopelessness, and lack of contentment regardless of achievements. "As the stresses and pressures pile up and their coping abilities are depleted, suicide might seem like the only way out," Haker reports. "Their negative self-evaluations and incredibly high expectations lead to distress and dysfunction, which puts them at an increased risk for suicidal ideation."[337]

In general, the combination of being more inclined to depression and anxiety than non-perfectionists, with a greater need for approval, higher sensitivity to rejection and failure, lower resiliency, and weaker self-compassion skills can increase perfectionists' risks for suicide, especially in an environment in which we feel we don't have much support. Specific incidents in which we believe we have disappointed someone significant in our lives, experience acute embarrassment about a mistake or bad review, or anticipate some future event with tremendous fear or anxiety can take us closer to the edge.

Our adeptness at managing the deception only increases the risk. "The dangers of perfectionism, and particularly the link to suicide, have been overlooked at least partially because perfectionists are very skilled at hiding their pain," says writer Melissa Dahl. "Admitting to suicidal thoughts or depression wouldn't exactly fit in with the image they're trying to project. Perfectionism might not only be driving suicidal impulses, it could also be simultaneously masking them."[338]

Public health author Eric Metcalf agrees. Perfectionists "may keep their doubts and worries to themselves, secretly stewing on flaws they think they have. In the meantime, they give off the impression that nothing bothers them. As a result, perfectionists might not ask for help or look for sources of support. Their death may then come as a complete surprise to their loved ones."[339] Maintaining this pretense can drain crucial resources on which we might otherwise rely. "Eventually," warns Dahl, "that façade may collapse."[340]

David Conroy, a professor of preventative medicine, cautions that suicide "happens when pain exceeds one's resources for coping with pain."[341] Once perfectionists cross that line, Dahl claims they "act deliberately, not impulsively, and this means their plans for taking their own lives tend to be very well thought-out and researched. In a sad twist of irony, once a perfectionist has made up his mind to end his own life, his conscientious nature may make him more likely to succeed. "[342] True, says Metcalf. "Perfectionists also expect to reach their goals—which can be deadly when the goal is suicide."[343]

Table 13.1. How Perfectionism Feels and Looks

FEELINGS OR BELIEFS	POSSIBLE BEHAVIORAL AND EMOTIONAL OUTCOMES
Sense of adequacy, identity, or worth tied to (or dependent on) appearance, performance, or achievements as perceived by self or others, or as anticipated as these would be seen by others (what others would think or how others would judge)	Self-criticism, comparisons to others; fear of failure; reliance on external approval; measuring self against images or information in media and popular culture; making choices primarily based on anticipated responses of others
Feelings of dissatisfaction regardless of actual accomplishments; sense of not measuring up regardless of effort	Sense of inadequacy, self-loathing, despair; self-harm; continual attempts to gain approval to create a superficial sense of worth; basic feeling: *not good enough*
Feelings of dissatisfaction regardless of recognition, acclaim, or appreciation by others	Inability to take a compliment without turning focus to a flaw or imperfection; tendency to dismiss, disregard, or not hear others' positive comments or regard (not just modesty)
Fear of inability to perform a task successfully; frustration with inability to perform a task successfully the first time	Paralysis; failure to start a project (or diet, for example); procrastination; delaying, or derailing possible completion; over-compensating: repeating, correcting, or redoing but never actually finishing; resistance to trying again or doing over (should get it right the first time); under-achieving; real or feigned indifference to task; avoiding something that can't be done well the first time

Unrealistic sense of what is expected by others or self-imposed pressure to live up to expectations and standards that are far beyond or excessive to actual requirements for the task	Overcommitment; overdoing (beyond satisfying curiosity or passion for topic or project); need to prove self, gain approval, or self-protect; setting excessively high goals (example: trying to lose 50 pounds when 20 pounds overweight, or writing a 50-page paper when 15 was assigned)
Constant or consistent focus on performance failures, mistakes; sense of never being able to get it right; equating imperfection with failure and lack of worth (or lovability)	Discounting the positive aspects of performance; not being able to see or value effort or progress; difficulty using internal feedback to course-correct, improve, or revise goals; sense of defeat, discouragement; underachieving; dropping out, giving up (project, diet, career, relationship, for example); fear of trying again; ruminating on flaws or errors; addiction, self-harm; suicide
Having standards and expectations for others (communicated, though often not); expecting or demanding adherence to personal values and priorities; belief that there is one right way to do things	Impatience, disappointment; criticism (focus on other person's failures, flaws, mistakes, shortcomings, omissions, or inadequacy); nagging, anger, or contempt; lack of appreciation for effort or intentions (or too distracted by negative perceptions) to provide adequate or effective feedback, guidance, or request; self-righteousness, arrogance, judgment; stress in relationships; alienation of others, or giving up on relationships
Fear of criticism; defining self and worth according to reaction and feedback of others	People-pleasing, approval seeking; internalizing criticism and negative feedback or perceptions (including teasing, meanness, bullying, ridicule, or hostility) as shame; fear of even reasonable negative feedback; difficulty applying or taking value from external feedback; defensiveness; disclaimers or excuses; counterattack; avoidance; quitting

Belief in the necessity of holding the marriage, family, workplace, or world together through personal power, skill, or effort; inflated sense of power and responsibility for another person's happiness or an institution's survival: "If I don't make the team, it'll kill my mother." "If I don't fix the errors in this report, no one else will (and the results will be catastrophic)."	Overexertion, overcommitment, overcompensation; pressure to perform in order to not let someone down; tendency to withhold request or feedback for fear of another person's reaction or hurting someone's feelings; impression management, disclosure phobia; assuming others' responsibilities; feeling victimized, resentment toward people or organizations; difficulty setting boundaries or saying no; making decisions based on perceived or assumed external realities rather than internal needs; self-abandonment

PART IV

Getting Real,
Getting Well

CHAPTER 14

Living with Imperfection

W riting has always been a bit of an all-consuming undertaking for me, and on the best of days I'm challenged to
maintain a degree of balance and perspective. Working
on a book on the topic of perfectionism has been like swimming in
the deep end of the pool holding a bowling ball in each hand. Having been immersed in these particular demons for the past two years,
I'm noticing a degree of obsessiveness that has surpassed those of all
previous writing experiences.

Clearly, this project has brought up a number of perfectionistic behaviors and feelings that I thought I had long since worked
through. Despite having far more material than I can use, I can't
seem to stop digging for studies and quotes to add to my notes. I'm
nibbling nearly nonstop as I work, procrastinating with social-media
distractions between paragraphs, and spending way too much time

making sure that the hundreds of resources in the draft of the bibliography are all formatted *exactly* the same way.

Perhaps this is why some of the most fascinating (if bewildering)
comments I've come across in the research are those made by people
claiming to be "recovered perfectionists." I guess I'm a little suspicious
about the idea that a perfectionist can just stop being one. I applaud
anyone who's managed to pull that off, but for me, the process is
ongoing, and on behalf of anyone in a similar position, shooting for
imperfect progress might be a more reasonable goal.

I can attest to certain patterns I've managed to break (often after
some deep personal work and a bit of time), while admitting to others that still sneak up on me when I'm not paying attention. I appear
to be in good company. "I think it'll be a lifelong adventure for me
to become my imperfect self and to see nothing wrong with that,"
writes Powers. "I constantly have to talk to myself to go against what
I learned in my childhood. I don't think I'll ever feel totally relaxed
about just being me without pleasing anyone else."

Victoria Maxwell expressed similar feelings after dealing with perfectionism in therapy for many years. "Deep-seated issues tend to be,
well, deep-seated. They come back to haunt and hunt us in many
forms over the course of our lives. Think of it like the universe's video
games levels, except we have to be a game player whether we logged
on or not." According to Maxwell, once we get the easy levels of
perfectionism licked, "Universe says, 'Okay . . . Let's see what you've
really got. Here you go: try advanced.'"[344]

I offer this section of the book to examine some of the solutions different people have discovered and used successfully at various points
in their personal journeys. I do believe that change and growth are
possible, that our past does not need to define our future. Rather than
looking for a cure—which, frankly, feels like a rather all-or-nothing

approach to healing perfectionism—I think it might make more sense to look at ways we can recognize our inclinations and perhaps get to a point where they aren't running our lives.

Creativity in a World of Human Imperfection

When I first moved to the Southwest, one of my students told me about a Navajo weaving custom that includes creating a deliberate flaw in the work. Weaver Ron Garnanez explains, "The traditional teaching of the Navajo weaving is that you have to put a mistake in there. It must be done because only the Creator is perfect. We're not perfect, so we don't make a perfect rug."[345] Sculptor Harry Benally and Navajo historian Harold Carey add, "Each rug is woven to include one small flaw in the final product in order that any evil spirits residing in the rug may have a way of escape."[346]

Turns out, cautions against perfectionism have global and historical roots. "Cultures around the world have embraced the concept of the perfect imperfect, often introducing deliberate flaws in works of art, either for religious or aesthetic reasons," says artist and designer Krishna Kumari Challa. She mentions Amish quilts, Turkish carpets, Islamic art, Persian rugs, and Zen pottery along with Navajo weaving as examples. "Great sculptors in India always left a flaw in the statues they carved," she adds, noting that a sculptor might break a statue's toe or add a mark "that spoilt the perfection a bit" as an example of "controlled imperfection."[347]

Thomas Backhouse, an artist and self-proclaimed "pattern junkie," describes the intentional errors in Islamic geometric art as a show of humility. As in many other cultural traditions, the deliberate errors are a testament to the idea that "only God is perfect" and "only God can produce perfection."[348] Elicia Brown relates that quilt makers in past centuries "contemplated the dangers of striving for perfection." She quotes author Alina Tugend, who described "how makers of 'humility quilts' in the nineteenth century deliberately included mistakes in their work so as not to tempt the devil."[349]

For another perspective, consider the Japanese principle of *wabi-sabi*, which "emphasizes finding beauty in imperfection, and accepting the natural cycle of growth and decay."[350] This aesthetic appreciates "beauty that is 'imperfect, impermanent, and incomplete'" in works that may be asymmetrical, rough, or irregular.[351] In another Japanese tradition, broken pottery is repaired with gold-imbued resin, transforming a damaged piece "from something to be discarded into a work of art," reports religious historian Zo Newell. The process, known as *Kintsugi*, "makes no attempt to hide the crack, but incorporates it as a design element into something simultaneously broken and strengthened by the break."[352] Clearly, resistance to perfectionism is not a new idea, nor is it restricted to one geographic area or cultural tradition.

Perfectionism can become a particular hindrance when it comes to creative enterprises. "Every idea or project is perfect, as long as it's still just an idea in my head," writes artist, musician, and computer programmer Laura Gutman. "As soon as I put pen to paper and write that first word down—as soon as the idea starts manifesting itself in the real world—it's not perfect anymore. I have to embrace imperfection or I won't ever create anything."

A number of contributors shared a similar conviction. Silke Powers has posted her works-in-progress on social media, along with comments about "happy accidents" or remarking that she has no idea where a painting in its first stages is heading. "I find that I have to totally give up perfectionism if I want to create art that speaks to me," she writes. "I also find that the imperfections in my art are often the parts I love most."

And from a practical standpoint, do we really want perfect art? Benally and Carey observe that a perfect rug "would look as though it were machine made and lose the charm of a handmade piece."[353] Cameron describes "perfect" art as "airless, arid, and dead."[354] And Challa reminds us that "Zen potters deliberately leave glaze drips on pots as 'controlled' imperfections to reinforce that 'perfect is boring.'"[355]

Marc Schoen mentions flaws in the Beatles' early recordings, "like Paul's voice cracking or John singing the wrong word." But this, he claims, is what "made the end result magical. When today's Auto-Tuned artists aim to be perfect, their songs lack the same richness."[356] Marc Rubenstein understands that creative people can "always see that one thing" that's not quite right. "But," he shares, "I have also seen writers continue to improve their work until it was garbage, and musicians refine a work until there was nothing special about it, no spark to inspire and uplift, no edge nor ring of truth to make people think or feel."

"Art is not perfect. Art is *human*," writes Goins. "I want to create beautiful art. Not stale perfection. I don't want to 'get it right.' I want to make it beautiful."[357]

Who Do You Think You Are?

After working as a composer, lyricist, author, and musical theater writer, Hannah Kohl has recently added "papercutting artist" to her résumé. Her work, which she does freehand from an image she holds in her mind, is highly intricate, delicate, and personalized, and it has met with tremendous acclaim.[358] Yet a recent post on her social media page went like this: "Sometimes, when I'm partway through a project, I look at it and think, 'What the hell am I doing? This is ridiculous. What am I doing with these tiny scissors?'"

Creativity—including nonartistic endeavors like creating a business or a new career, for example—takes tremendous courage. How could stepping into the unknown not bring a side portion of self-doubt to whatever excitement we might be feeling? Whether making that first cut in the paper, composing the first line of a song, writing the first word of a book or blog, or declaring ourselves available for training or entertainment events, we're vulnerable. What if nobody calls? What if they don't like our work? What if we mess up a commission, or miss a deadline, or turn in crap? What if this doesn't work out?

Two weeks before the launch of a 2013 writing project, successful software designer Nathan Barry was wondering, "'Would people even buy this book?' I've had this same self-doubt before every product launch I've done, even after a string of successful launches lately. Each time I find something different to worry about." Concerned that this book was about "an entirely new topic," he admits that "at this point I should have had confidence that another book would do well—and I did to a point—but the doubt was still there."[359]

So how do we move forward? Kohl shares, "I remind myself that my job is not to judge what I create. My job is to create. I don't know how my art or writing or music will affect the world, but I think there's a long game when it comes to how our work impacts civilization. My work may inspire someone right now, or it might not find its true target until a hundred years go by. Somehow, that idea takes a lot of pressure off. And instead of putting down the scissors or the pen or walking away from the piano, I just create what I can create. I don't judge it. I do it."

Standing up to the Inner Critic is incredibly liberating. Because there is another side of the "Who-are-*you*-to-do-this?" argument for those of us who have the courage to hang in and keep moving forward, persisting against the doubts and the noise. As Kohl notes, "At some point during the process, that fear of not being good enough flips into pride for what I've done. I think about all the humans out there making things, writing things, doing things, building things, and I truly believe that our most valuable resource is the collective weight and wonder of human achievement . . . because we have no idea, really, do we? Even when we're not so sure what we're doing matters, I think we owe it to each other to keep going."

These days, when I start to question my own authority or my right to compose music, create art, or, say, write a book about perfectionism, I turn to a quote I recently found by author Jean Rhys. Although applied to the idea of writing, I believe her words are relevant to any human endeavor: "All of writing is a huge lake," she says. "There are great rivers like Tolstoy and Dostoevsky. And there are mere trickles like Jean Rhys. All that matters is feeding the lake. I don't matter. The lake matters. You must keep feeding the lake."[360] And that usually keeps The Committee quiet for a while.

Perfectionism or Striving for Excellence?

Even before I started working on this book, I could have identified specific ways perfectionism has affected my life. Although many aspects of perfectionism that appeared in my research really didn't resonate with my own experience, others were so spot-on that it was almost physically painful to add them to the manuscript.

Identifying perfectionism can be especially tricky because in so many ways it resembles a positive, healthy pursuit of excellence. It may be easy to tell that I have crossed the line when I notice that I'm searching a fourth or fifth version of material I already have, or when I'm standing in a closet filled with clothing and can't choose an outfit because The Committee says that everything I own looks terrible on me. But we can slip into perfectionistic patterns without even realizing it. (Sure, I know *now* that agreeing to write that blog in the middle of a hectic travel week when I'm on book deadline was not a brilliant choice, even though it sounded fun and interesting and professionally worthwhile at the time.)

"There is a fine line between striving to reach high standards of excellence and feeling self-defeated through the inability to reach unrealistic expectations of perfectionism," writes Michael Pyryt, a professor specializing in gifted education.[361] For me, the acid test requires mindful, honest answers to some tough questions, most of them having to do with our authenticity, sense of worth, or inclination to make choices that could hurt ourselves or others. "Ambitions are healthy until they become the obsessions by which we define ourselves," cautions Kimbriel Dean.[362]

While author Betty Hatch sees "nothing wrong with striving for perfection," her explanation actually sounds like an argument in favor of the healthy pursuit of excellence. "The problem comes from believing one can and should reach perfection," she notes. "At 75, I'm still striving for it, but I know I have never reached it and that I never will. That fact does not bother me at all." Acknowledging that perfection is an impossible goal doesn't diminish the joy Hatch experiences from doing her best. Instead, shooting for perfection pushes her toward continued improvement and pride in her achievements. "For me, the issue is not about being perfect, but using [perfection] as an incentive to do and be the best I can."

This distinction is an important one. "Healthy strivers tend to set goals based on their own wants and desires rather than primarily in response to external expectations," says a resource offered by a university counseling center. This

> "Healthy strivers tend to set goals based on their own wants and desires rather than primarily in response to external expectations."

post further describes the goals of these individuals as "realistic, internal, and potentially attainable," generally being "just one step beyond what they have already accomplished." It further notes that "healthy strivers continue and they take pleasure in the process of pursuing the task at hand rather than focusing only on the end result," and that their reactions to disapproval or failure "are generally limited to specific situations rather than generalized to their entire self-worth."[363]

Contributor David Maxwell maintains, "Perfectionism is often a cover-up of inner sloppiness, a way to gloss over a failing or weakness we are aware of, and of which we cannot abide others becoming cognizant." On the other hand, he says, "Striving for excellence and achievement will take into account those failings and weaknesses, and figure out a way to grow alongside them." He believes that this approach offers a way to use flaws and errors as a way "to build a stronger base upon which to construct a larger achievement than perhaps originally envisioned."

Regardless of how we mark this separation, I think that the key is paying attention to the impact our behaviors and beliefs have on our physical and mental health, as well as their effects on the quality of our relationships. Art restorer Will Shank claims, "I could not have had a career restoring zillion-dollar paintings if I had not been a perfectionist. It was tiring, and I found that I had little patience left for my personal life, especially after I became Papa to a baby at age fifty-two." Shank has managed to achieve greater balance in his life, and "over the years, learned to stop sweating the small stuff. I still manage to pursue excellence and to go for quality instead of quantity."

Sometimes, just knowing we have options is a good place to start. There is a point, after hours of going through my website looking for spelling errors, bad links, or non-curly quotation marks, and my back is sore and my hands are aching and I haven't seen my husband all day, where I finally snap to the reality of how I've been spending my time and forcibly extract myself from my work. "Whenever I get lost in a perfectionist headspace, I remind myself that it will cause me and my world harm," writes Edberg. "And so it becomes easier to switch my focus and thought patterns because I want to avoid making stupid choices and avoid causing myself and other people unnecessary pain."[364]

So let's start teasing out the destructive patterns from the times we're simply working hard, lost in the flow doing something we love, living and learning and growing in positive, healthy ways. Let's pay attention to times we have trouble saying no even when we know it's the best choice we can make. Let's become aware of any inclination to sacrifice our authenticity or integrity for other people's approval, or be disingenuous to avoid rejection or criticism. Let's watch out for the tendency to overcommit and overcompensate, equate our worth with achievements or awards, or check our work over and over again, as well as instances of chasing reassurance, comparing ourselves to others, avoiding a task, not knowing when to quit, or being tempted to give up easily.

Likewise, let's keep an eye out for the urge to reject positive feedback, notice only flaws in ourselves or others, mistrust our inner guidance in favor of other people's opinions, or be miserable when we don't come in first or get it right. Notice when we're having difficulty making decisions, worrying about how others might react, defining our worth by other people's standards or expectations, or attempting to control others in order to feel adequate or worthy.[365] Because these are among the markers that tell us that we've slipped into destructive, disordered patterns that will indeed sabotage our relationships, make us sick, and hold our happiness hostage.

CHAPTER 15

Being Your Biggest, Baddest Self

There's this story making the rounds online that tells of a man offering a twenty-dollar bill to the participants in his audience, all of whom were keen to accept this gift. He then crumpled the bill and ground it into the floor with his shoe. Nonetheless, the participants were still willing to accept the money. Acknowledging the point of this demonstration, he said, "Many times in our lives, we are dropped, crumpled, and ground into the dirt by the decisions we make and the circumstances that come our way. But no matter what happened or what will happen, you will never lose your value. Dirty or clean, crumpled or finely creased, you are still priceless to those who love you. The worth of our lives comes not in what we do or who we know, but by who we are."[366]

We don't have to look far to see dozens of encouraging, inspiring messages, images, and posters to reassure us of our value, potential, and inherent worth. As delighted as I am to see—and share—these quotes, I have some concern about the gap between our actual experiences and the beautiful memos we might see on a classroom, boardroom, or social media wall. Because if the feedback from people in our most important relationships has been consistently focused on our flaws, shortcomings, or the number of times we've let them down, we are unlikely to imagine that these positive messages apply to us.

Letting Go of the Need for Approval

It's really hard to be our biggest, baddest selves when we're conditioned to hide behind our pretenses. Getting real can be rather terrifying because it exposes us to the very things we've spent our lives defending against. "We sometimes hold back being fully ourselves, or stepping out and living our purpose in a big way because of the fear of what people will think or say," claims speaker and life coach Kute Blackson."When you put yourself out there in the world, and dare to follow your dreams, it is a risk. It is a vulnerable and courageous act. People will judge you. People will talk about you. People will project their stuff on to you. In fact, some people won't like you. Make peace with this up front."[367]

Well, fine. Perhaps we can all agree intellectually with social media strategist Ted Rubin when he insists, "Your value does not decrease based on someone's inability to see your worth."[368] And it's probably true that "Sometimes people try to expose what's wrong with you, because they can't handle what's right about you," as model Maria Rivera observes.[369] But if we've spent our lives cowering behind fears of what others might think, stepping into the bright sunlight of our authentic selves can be blinding. We need to be able to embrace the fact that we're worthy of love, happiness, and success, despite the part of our belief system that tells us we're only okay if other people think we're okay.

Psychologist Michael Kraus connects people's sense of power to feelings of authenticity, "that is, the extent to which one is able to express one's true attitudes and feelings around others." This brings up a bit of a chicken-and-egg dilemma for me because while power may allow people "to feel and behave more authentically in all different situations,"[370] I also contend that authenticity *creates* power—power over our own destiny and our ability to face ourselves in the mirror every day, not to mention the power to avoid having to strategically shape-shift to try to get anyone's approval.

I also contend that authenticity *creates* power—power over our own destiny and our ability to face ourselves in the mirror every day, not to mention the power to avoid having to strategically shape-shift to try to get anyone's approval.

"When you no longer care about what other people think of you, you start being yourself," Sauvic contends. "You start behaving the way you always wanted but . . . couldn't because of all the restrictions and limits you imposed on yourself." In her list of things to give up to be happy, Sauvic includes giving up the need to impress people and giving up our attempts to live life according to other people's expectations. "You have no idea how much freedom comes with letting go of your need to control what other people think of you."[371]

Steve Jobs warned, "Your time is limited, so don't waste it living someone else's life."[372] Isn't it time to commit to ignoring other people's agendas for who they think we're supposed to be? Not just intellectually, but at a core belief level, one that can withstand disapproval and yes, even abandonment. (We are already paying the price of *self*-abandonment.) Finding our own inner voice and trusting its guidance becomes our true mission, then. "To be yourself in a world that is constantly trying to make you something else is the greatest accomplishment," Ralph Waldo Emerson advised.[373] And great cause for celebration.

Real Versus Perfect:
Finding Our Authentic Selves

One of the contributors to this book described an incident during a difficult period in her life. She was sharing her struggle with bouts of panic and depression with a friend who expressed his concern for how fragile she sounded. "That was when everything fell apart," she said. "Of course, at that moment, I *was* fragile, but I had invested so much energy in being strong, protecting my vulnerabilities, that, when they were exposed, I heard my friend's comment as an out-and-out attack."

The deception crumbled under the strain and this comment shattered any illusions she still held about being perfect and in control. "I remember the moment as being one of the most painful in my life. But in retrospect, my friend's observation helped me reclaim parts of myself I had suppressed or denied. I had to come out of hiding. I had to get real."

To a certain extent, I believe that we are all broken—survivors of disappointment, betrayal, and, well, life itself. Very few of us feel completely secure in who we are. "The world breaks everyone," Hemingway once wrote, "and afterward many are strong at the broken places."[374] Sometimes falling apart gets people on the path of becoming whole and many believe that true recovery actually *requires* some sort of breakdown. Ashkay Dubey notes, "Healing doesn't mean the damage never existed. It means the damage no longer controls our lives."[375]

> To a certain extent, I believe that we are all broken—survivors of disappointment, betrayal, and, well, life itself.

Somewhere along the way, we learn to claim who we are, defining ourselves *by* ourselves.

It's difficult to get comfortable in our own skin when the world insists on measuring us against standards that have

> "Healing doesn't mean the damage never existed. It means the damage no longer controls our lives."

nothing to do with who we are or why we're here. We're stripped down to a two-dimensional version of ourselves, and it's easy to buy in to this identity. "Accept no one's definition of your life," cautions Robert Frost, urging us instead to make those distinctions ourselves.[376] And as complex and fascinating as we are, we can certainly do better than accepting an easily digestible version of who we think we're supposed to be. We owe it to the world to show up in our full, Technicolor glory.

Tradition would likewise deny us the right to celebrate our efforts and accomplishments, condemning pride in our hard-won achievements as a selfish and unwarranted response.[377] Even reasonable pursuits can come up against discouragement or dismissiveness. "It's hard being awesome," says author Cindy Ray. "People don't want someone who is awesome. They want someone as screwed up as they are so they don't feel so alone." But what's more awesome than authenticity and the ability to take comfort in our own uniqueness? Consider cartoonist Ashleigh Brilliant's perspective. "I may not be perfect," he claims, "but parts of me are very, very excellent."[378]

Perhaps it's time to redefine our idea of *perfect*, and I appreciate the people who are leading us in this direction. "You know what's really, powerfully sexy?" asks culture critic Courtney E. Martin. "A sense of humor. A taste for adventure. A healthy glow. Hips to grab on to. Openness. Confidence. Humility. Appetite. Intuition. Smart-ass comebacks. Presence. A quick wit."[379] When Christina Huffington shared a pre-summer post with advice on how to get a bikini body, it read, simply: "Put a bikini on your body."[380] A refreshing change from the usual fashion advice! Even for those of us disinclined toward bikini-wearing, a message encouraging self-acceptance is always welcome.

I'd like to close out this section on getting real with a quote from a blog by Courtney Walsh that pretty much sums it up for me. "Dear Human: You've got it all wrong. You didn't come here to master unconditional love. That is where you came from and where you'll return. You came here to learn personal love. Universal love. Messy love. Sweaty love. Crazy love. Broken love. Whole love. Infused with divinity. Lived through the grace of stumbling. Demonstrated through the beauty of . . . messing up. Often. You didn't come here to be perfect. You already are. You came here to be gorgeously human. Flawed and fabulous. And then to rise again into remembering. But unconditional love? Stop telling that story. Love, in truth, doesn't need *any* other adjectives. It doesn't require modifiers. It doesn't require the condition of perfection. It only asks that you show up. And do your best. That you stay present and feel fully. That you shine and fly and laugh and cry and hurt and heal and fall and get back up and play and work and live and die as *you*. It's enough. It's plenty."[381]

Self-Care and Compassion

Think of the first time you heard the airline safety routine telling you to secure your own oxygen mask before trying to assist anyone else. Tell me that didn't sound a little strange. Of course there is logic and common sense behind this plan. "What might look like an act of self-regard is actually the condition for being able to care for the other," writes philosopher James K. A. Smith.[382] I doubt many people would argue with Smith's observation. But how many of us have a hard time considering, much less applying the point of this message beyond airplane emergencies?

When it comes to setting priorities, perfectionists have a tendency to put *self-care* at the end of the list, devoting our energy and attention to other people, work, studying, cleaning, or exercise, for example. It doesn't help that most of us have grown up with a good bit of validation for self-sacrifice. Our culture continues to confuse self-care with selfishness, but there is a difference. Self-caring people know how to respect and honor other people's needs in ways that might never occur to someone who is truly selfish, and they can be very caring and generous without compromising or ignoring their own needs.

Self-care requires a belief in our own deservingness, our right to happiness and peace of mind. It allows us to set reasonable, achievable standards, and leaves space for us to fall short or make mistakes without rousing the Inner Critic to rip us to shreds. Self-care can also improve the quality of our relationships, if only in narrowing the chances that we will feel resentful, self-righteous, disempowered, depleted, or other potential byproducts of self-sacrifice.[383]

We can start by reducing some of the stress in our lives, perhaps taking writer Larry Eisenberg's advice to "resign as general manager of the universe."[384] Peace of mind notwithstanding, this is not an easy task for anyone who has attempted to take on this role. Let's shed the presumption that if it weren't for us, everything that matters would just fall apart. "In the past, things were left up to fate or God," comments author Alina Tugend. "Now we think we can control everything so we get angry at ourselves if things go wrong."[385]

Nor is comparing ourselves with others a self-caring habit. "Accept yourself as you are and as you are not," advises Blackson. "As you unhook yourself from other people's validation you become truly powerful."[386] Freelance writer Chiara Fucarino addresses another danger inherent in making comparisons. "If you think you're better than someone else, you gain an unhealthy sense of superiority. If you think someone else is better than you, you end up feeling bad about yourself. You'll be happier if you focus on your own progress and praise others on theirs."[387]

Let's also get better at carving a little time for ourselves out of the day. "We prioritize all our responsibilities with very little time left over for us," says Rechtschaffen. He recommends a daily routine involving "something you enjoy with no productivity attached to it. Simply find something that 'lights you up' and makes you feel good. And if nothing comes to mind, practice slowing down until you find it."[388]

Wellness coach Melissa McCreery includes an unfed hunger for self-care and me-time as one of several stresses (or hungers) that connect feelings of overwhelm and overload to a tendency toward emotional overeating.[389] Sometimes just a few minutes of not being available to anyone, not checking things off our list—in fact, not doing anything on our list—will speak to whatever part of us needs to know we're worthy of this time.

And for heaven's sake, could we please add *self-compassion* to our priority list? "With self-compassion, we give ourselves the same kindness and care we'd give to a good friend," writes Kristin Neff, a researcher and expert in this field.[390] Her work suggests "that giving ourselves a break and accepting our imperfections may be the first step toward better health," noting that high scores on tests of self-compassion correlate with lower depression and anxiety, and greater happiness and optimism.

Neff points to a fear of self-indulgence as the main reason people aren't more self-compassionate. "They believe self-criticism is what keeps them in line." But when we address our backsliding and errors with self-criticism and negativity, we usually end up feeling even less motivated to change."[391] Nutrition counselor Susan W. Berry similarly urges, "Don't be so hard on yourself. I've never seen anybody truly heal or grow or evolve by being mean to themselves, by bashing or hating themselves, relentlessly driving themselves, or being merciless."[392] Self-acceptance—making peace with our quirks and imperfections—would be a huge step for many of us.

"Does everything really need healing?" asks educator Mercedes Stewart. "Thinking that we need healing all the time suggests a belief that we are perpetually broken." Beck suggests shifting from condemnation to conviction, focusing on positive goals and improvement rather than self-criticism.[393] When Teversham noticed that she was beating herself up for feeling flattered by the demands people were making on her, she realized that "it would be far more helpful to treat that flattered part of me with great compassion and kindness, like I would treat a small child who needs a lot of care and nurturing. Healing is only possible in a loving, caring, compassionate environment."[394]

Owning Our Mistakes

Perfectionists can put a lot of energy into protecting the deception. This practice becomes especially evident when we mess up. If we believe that our worth and safety depend on flawlessness, it's extremely difficult to admit to our failures and mistakes. However, it's important that we eventually surrender to our humanness, which flat-out means that we're not going to get it right every time.

Unfortunately, we don't have many models for positive, healthy, responsible problem ownership, and the alternatives can be quite destructive. "A few years ago, I witnessed a hurtful exchange at a get-together among several friends," one contributor shared. "To be fair, the individual responsible for the unpleasant remarks took the time to write what she felt was a note of apology. However, the note expressed regret only for the fact the recipient had taken offense, which actually felt more like an attack on the woman for having gotten upset." Understandably, this exchange and its unfortunate follow-up terminated the friendship.

On the other hand, I once knew someone who was great at sincere apologies but who never actually changed his behavior. His ostensible remorse became meaningless, creating distance and caution among those closest to him. And it's not just personal relationships that are at stake here. We've probably all had dealings with the occasional coworker, customer-service representative, or tech-support person who ended up passing the buck or making us wrong for a problem we were having.

Chick Moorman and Thomas Haller explore how different teachers respond to making mistakes in front of the class. While some are thankful when students catch a mistake (and feel safe enough to point it out), others choose to give a more negative message, claiming they "did it on purpose" to see if the students were paying attention, casually dismissing the mistake, responding with self-ridicule, or even denying they had made an error. Either way, "our students are watching and learning . . ."[395] Anyone in a leadership capacity who honestly admits to not knowing something—and then takes the time to find out—offers a far better lesson than people more committed to looking good, being right, or knowing all.

"The greatest of all faults is to be conscious of none," says philosopher and essayist Thomas Carlyle.[396] But if the prospect of something as simple as having put something in the wrong place or entering a figure in the wrong column can throw us into survival mode, it's understandable that even an innocent question can provoke defensiveness, blame, excuses, or denial. Healing invites us to examine our attachment to being right at all costs. And it requires that we develop the psychological strength we need to come clean when we aren't exactly on target, remembering that our worth does not equate with flawlessness, even if there is a price to pay.

Apologies can be hard for perfectionists. Withholding an admission of accountability can be based in "the fear of being shamed, being seen as weak, being rejected, or the like," claims Psychiatrist Aaron Lazare. He recognizes that learning to apologize requires overcoming these fears, which "requires honesty, commitment, humility, and courage."[397] And if we've betrayed a trust or said or done something hurtful, the recipient may need time to process and accept our apology.

Likewise, it may take a while for someone we've hurt to gain confidence in our commitment to not repeating the offending behavior. (Pressuring people to apologize or accept an apology does more harm than good, often forcing resentment underground and delaying the openness to trust and connectedness.) Saying "sorry" doesn't get us off the hook; reparations and behavioral changes might.

"It is the highest form of self-respect to admit our errors and mistakes and make amends for them," says Turner. "To make a mistake is only an error in judgment, but to adhere to it when it is discovered shows infirmity of character."[398] Stop making excuses or trying to justify what happened. ("I'm sorry, but you . . ." is an attack, not an apology.)

Let's recognize mistakes and fix what's broken. When we can leave our contact information on the windshield of the car we just dinged or admit to a mistake that might compromise our work or social status, we are definitely making huge strides. Because from a human (and karmic) standpoint, an honest mistake is way better than a perfect coverup.

And Owning Our Progress, Too

When I was in graduate school, one of my courses required something they called a "competency contract." The final project was to include a list of competencies—things we had accomplished or could do well, along with documentation to provide evidence of the variety of skills we had developed during our career. It was one of the most daunting tasks I'd encountered as a student, perhaps because it forced me to focus on the very things I'd tend to forget the instant I checked them off the list.

This class turned out to be one of the most valuable of the entire program for the same reason. It was probably the first time I came face-to-face with my habit of immediately finishing one project and rushing off to the next, barely even noticing all that I'd created, planned, or pulled off along the way. From a day-to-day standpoint, I had just been awfully busy. Stepping back to identify the skills I had learned and applied to the tasks I had performed gave me a monumental sense of perspective—something we rarely take time to appreciate.

If being able to own our flaws and mistakes is a challenge for perfectionists, learning to revel in our growth and successes may be even more difficult. We go over the top in setting goals and, for the most part, reaching them, but our attention always seems drawn to what's left to do. "Do you make lists?" asks author Jinny Ditzler. "What happens when you have ten things and get only seven of them done that day? Feel great? Sense of accomplishment? If you're like most of us, you beat yourself up for the ones you *didn't* do."[399]

I can relate. I wish I could say that I fall into bed at the end of an exhausting, crazy-busy day, drifting off in the sweet satisfaction of all

I've accomplished. But the fact is, no matter how much I get done, I'm more likely to toss and turn, obsessing about whatever is still on my list, waking up to add things to make the list even longer, or worrying about how far I'm falling behind. Common as this pattern may be, there is nothing healthy, happy, or productive about it.

While I am working on de-emphasizing the not-done stuff in favor of recognizing actual accomplishments, this is not my natural inclination. "Just as we must take responsibility for our failures in life, we must also take responsibility for our successes," writes columnist Margie Warrell. "Minimizing them serves no one."[400] Sauvic suggests listing thirty of your assets and then thirty of your major successes. "Keep this list close to you," she writes, especially for when the Inner Critic starts in.[401] (I've started keeping a "done" list, a separate entity from the endless "to do" roster, actually writing down the stuff I managed to finish or work on at the end of the day. Even when I really have to stretch, this exercise helps me keep the volume down on the negative messages, and minimize the panic I feel over what's not finished.)

Because that voice will always be nearby, waiting to tell us that we're not doing enough, working hard enough, going fast enough. It will drag up cultural messages that confuse honest satisfaction and pride with arrogance and conceit. It will inject doubt and look for ways to undermine our confidence in our adequacy. It will draw our smile to the typo, the missing image, the one dish we forgot to wash. So this is the place in the story where we get to fight back. Consider this section a permission slip, a multiuse coupon to tell the Inner Critic to pipe down so we can savor whatever progress we've made—imperfections, incompleteness, and deficiencies notwithstanding.

This is the balance that each of us deserves. "You don't have to attain perfection or mastery to be worthy of the success you've achieved and any accolades you earn along the way," says Warrell. "It's not about lowering the bar, it's about resetting it to a realistic level that doesn't leave you forever striving and feeling inadequate. You don't have to be Einstein to be a valuable asset to your organization and to those around you. Nor do you have to attain perfection to share something with the world that enriches people's lives in some way."[402]

Adderholdt and Goldberg likewise suggest making make time to savor successes. "Perfectionists have a habit of doing one thing after another without ever pausing to feel good about what they accomplished. Put your feet up, relax, and go over the details in your mind. Focus on your triumphs and ignore your mistakes."[403] We each come here with gifts to develop and share with the world. It's absolutely cruel to focus only on the stuff we haven't done or haven't done perfectly. "Flaws are often our gifts misused or overused," notes Ann Smith, who urges us to slow down and spend some unhurried time concentrating on our talents and aptitudes.[404] (And yes, it counts even if these skills come easily to us.)

Let's reflect on the journey as well as the destination, acknowledging the end result of our efforts as well as what we enjoyed and learned from them. And while I don't recommend depending on recognition and accolades as evidence of our worth, I do think it's essential to notice—and accept—positive feedback when it's offered. Practice saying *thank you* to compliments, without qualifying or dismissing them.

> Let's reflect on the journey as well as the destination, acknowledging the end result of our efforts as well as what we enjoyed and learned from them.

"Appreciating your success enables you to take responsibility for your greatness so that your life isn't just about becoming good enough," Ditzler assures. "It's about finding ways to use your special gifts to make a difference. Appreciating yourself is the first step toward giving yourself permission to be who you are and make the contribution you're here to make."[405]

Setting Achievable Goals

Notice how often the words "unreasonable goals" or "impossible standards" pop up in descriptions of perfectionists. Whether over-committing to too many goals, aspiring to goals that don't really match what's manageable or healthy for us, or limiting our commitments and aspirations to avoid failure, this issue can challenge anyone with perfectionistic tendencies.

For some people, having problems with goal setting can just be from a lack of practice. If we've spent our lives following someone else's agendas and mandates, we probably haven't had many opportunities to explore and evaluate our options. We've been told what to do and what to think, so we've been conditioned to look to others —our parents, teachers, peers, or the media—for direction. We make impulsive decisions and grab at things that appear to offer us happiness, coolness, and belonging. How could we possibly know what a reasonable deadline, dress size, or neat house looks like?

When faced with big decisions that could affect our lives in significant ways, it's understandable that we sometimes freeze in the face of possibilities, not having a clue which way to go. When school counselor Eric Katz would question his students about what they wanted to do or be after high school, he claims that many tried to "read" him and come up with an answer they thought he wanted to hear. "The normal anxiety of the transition from high school to this world of new options was terrifying to them." Many had limited experience making decisions on their own. Added to "an age-appropriate lack of certainty as to what they want to pursue," many students froze, choosing to do nothing "for fear of doing the 'wrong things.'"

Katz developed a "softer" approach to "help students self-reflect and assess their interests, values, and goals," assuring them "that what they are feeling is natural and appropriate," and reminding them "that we only need to plan the next step, not the rest of their life! You can see and palpably feel them exhale once this emotional turmoil is both surfaced and validated." How fortunate for young people to have someone to nurture their dreams while helping them learn how to make decisions, and to midwife them through transitions that demand those skills.

Even with practice, it can be hard to anticipate what our commitments can entail. In addition to the usual suspects—wanting to prove our worth, gain approval, or acquire status markers we see as portals to acceptance and safety—many of us end up with unrealistic goals because at the time we agreed to them, they maybe didn't look all that unrealistic. Sometimes simple logistics can become as troublesome as a core belief in our inadequacy.

"Part of being successful is constantly juggling and deciding what's the most important thing you have to do today," shares attorney Kathy Manning.[406] A recent conversation with colleagues in high-level administrative positions exposed our mutual frustration with the fact that we can spend so much time on things and never feel like we're getting anything done. Each of us is a veteran decision-maker, expert juggler and multitasker, yet we can still underestimate the amount of time tasks might take or how much energy we'll have to devote to them.

Despite years of experience and success in our field, we still get caught up on details and minutia. The best planning has little space for unexpected distractions and interruptions. We hate being so overcommitted and resent our failure to maintain better boundaries when we get in over our heads. Our lack of progress weighs on us as a failure, eroding our confidence in our ability to meet our commitments. And we take scant consolation in similar conversations with others in the same boat, and in the fact that we are *so* not alone.

So let's look at some of the things we can do when we're in too deep. To be fair, many of the people I interviewed are in school, work, or home situations that leave little time for enjoyment or spontaneity, much less me-time or fun. Not all have the option of getting help or saying no, and several believe that opting out of an honors class or committee assignment will cost them in the long run. These circumstances may not qualify as perfectionistic as much as situational survival.

Let's continually evaluate our goals, examining them against one very basic question: Is this good for me? Sure, there are times we just have to keep our head down and get through the project, knowing that most of the work our goals demand won't last forever. Sometimes, just knowing that we can change our mind is enough. And sometimes, we won't know that a goal will take us down a toxic and destructive pathway until we're on it for a while. Long-term negative consequences to our mental or physical health may require us to consider alternatives to our current situation.

I think this is a good place to once again distinguish between perfectionism and doing the best we can do with what we have at the moment. Striving for excellence is always within reach. We push beyond our current level of ability without setting the hurdle at an impossible height. And we hold on to our dreams because those are the things that direct our forward progress.

> Striving for excellence is always within reach. We push beyond our current level of ability without setting the hurdle at an impossible height.

We break goals down into manageable tasks because that makes them more achievable. We hold the big picture of where we ultimately want to go, and we quit trying to just suddenly *be* there. We learn to shoot for the next smaller pant size, the next course to take, or the next drawer to clean out, knowing that achieving each of these ambitions moves us one step closer to a healthier weight, finished degree, or clean house. "Learning to set small goals so as to meet larger ambitions is a skill that improves with practice," says Rivero.[407]

When overwhelm starts creeping in, we take a break. Although this may seem counterintuitive, energy therapist Amy Scher suggests that even a brief distraction allows us to re-center ourselves and handle our tasks better. "Take a breather, get out of your head space, take a walk or stretch, then try again," she advises. "You might be surprised about the positive effect this can have on your ability to focus on the task at hand!"[408]

This is important because perfectionists have a tendency to overcompensate when we get bogged down or fail to meet a goal. Effective goal setting requires ongoing evaluation and regulation, but for some of us, missing a mark today means demanding even more from ourselves tomorrow. Rather than backing up and making the hurdles easier to clear, we punish ourselves with goals that are even more impossible to achieve. As Drapkin notes, perfectionists "adjust their standards, but in the wrong direction."[409]

So let's take a breath and assess our priorities, shortening our lifetime goal list to what we can reasonably achieve *today*. Pick out the top two or three things that really, really need attention. (The big list will still be there when those things are done.)

So let's take a breath and assess our priorities, shortening our lifetime goal list to what we can reasonably achieve *today*. Pick out the top two or three things that really, really need attention.

Let's sort the high-priority stuff from the low-priority stuff, and put our time and energy into getting on top of the more important tasks. And let's commit to enjoying the satisfaction of actually *finishing* something before immediately jumping into the next project. Pick something. Anything. It's easier to stay motivated when we see some progress.

And speaking of the next project, can we learn to back off, ask for some time to think about it, and give ourselves a chance to say *no* (or *not now*, or *not yet*) when new opportunities appear? Let's assess the potential benefits or damage. If we have a tendency to deceive ourselves or distort the parameters of the task we're considering, maybe let's bounce the idea off a trusted friend who can hold a different perspective and be honest with us.

Before we agree to the next enticing offer, let's ask: Do I have time? Will this be fun? Will I learn something I want to learn? Where and how will this fit in my schedule? Am I clear on what this task will require? Will I be able to disengage if this doesn't work out? Just how important is it to do this *now*? Am I hesitating because I'm afraid to say no? Trying to prove myself? Chasing something I don't actually need? Is this goal about my passion, or is it more about something I think I need to do to impress someone, attract someone, or keep someone in my life?

The acid test comes down to how our choices are affecting us—physically, emotionally, and psychologically. If we're having a blast doing what we're doing and it's not interfering with our health, relationships, or self-care, then it's probably a reasonable, achievable goal. Remember, "you are likely to realize that perfectionism is not a helpful or necessary influence in your life. There are alternative ways to think that are more beneficial. Not only are you likely to achieve more without your perfectionism, but you will feel better about yourself in the process."[410]

CHAPTER 16

Developing Psychological Strength

W hen children are learning to walk, it's a pretty wobbly affair. They stand up, unsteady, and fall down *boom*. They try again, totter and sway, maybe taking that first little step, and down again they go. We encourage and cheer. We catch them when they fall, celebrate their progress, and hold them up to try again. We record their adorably clumsy attempts and post them online, imperfect though their performance may be.

This is a great example of a Japanese philosophy called *kaizen*, which educator Glenn Capelli describes as a way of "honoring tiny little improvements, incremental shifts and changes, and getting better in small ways."[411] The practice, which focuses on continuing improvement, has been applied in a wide range of professions, from health care and psychotherapy to banking and other industries. It relies on recognition and encouragement to successfully improve productivity and to humanize the workplace.[412]

I love this concept and its expression in something as simple and basic as a child learning to walk. It not only speaks to my educator's heart, but also offers a beautiful alternative to the all-or-nothing thinking that dismisses imperfect effort as failure. Shifting our emphasis to progress and improvement allows breathing room for creation and growth to unfold in a natural, unhurried way. It also provides a foundation by which we can explore some of the components of the psychological strength we need to crawl out from under perfectionism's harsh jurisdiction.

Learning from Failure

My very first teacher evaluation happened on one of the worst days of my brand-new career. Between barely keeping a large, noisy bunch of kids in their seats, running out of the materials I needed, and having the projector bulb blow when I finally got the students' attention, there was little hint of the teaching talent I'd hope to display. By the time the kids left, I was a wreck. I hadn't just failed. I had failed in front of a professor I badly wanted to impress.

I waited for the hammer to fall. I burst into tears and told him, "I quit," before he had a chance to fire me. I started packing up my things, ready to leave a profession I'd aspired to my entire life, when my supervisor said, simply, "Your flag looks great." I am not making this up. He assured me that teaching was a tough job and that it might take a while to learn to take a bad day in stride. "Let's give it another week," he said.

I've shared this story in practically every presentation and seminar I've ever given, in part because the longer I stay in the field after such an awful experience, the more significant his encouragement and acceptance become. Even after more than four decades, it is still hard to admit to such a rough start. However, I also suspect that my admissions of the failures and struggles I went through as a new teacher may be more effective in opening hearts and minds to new ideas than even the best strategies I've offered to that point.

Perfectionists are terrible at dealing with mistakes. "It takes courage to take on challenges and pursue aspirations that leave you wide open to falling short, losing face, and being 'found out,'" writes Warrell. "But when you refuse to let your doubts dictate your choices, you open new doors of opportunity and discover just how much you can really do."[413]

> When you refuse to let your doubts dictate your choices, you open new doors of opportunity . . .

Educator Marvin Marshall urges, "If failure is used as a guide, not an accuser, success will be swifter."[414] And David Guy Powers is cited as the first source for an often-used quote that defines success as "the ability to go from failure to failure without losing enthusiasm."[415]

Surely on some level we all know this. We can nod in agreement when Neale Donald Walsch assures us that "life begins at the end of your comfort zone."[416] We instinctively know that mistakes are necessary for learning. In fact we may even *encourage* this concept, being far more forgiving when others get off track than we would ever allow for ourselves. We might even stand up to a culture that stigmatizes mistakes, defending the vulnerable from criticism and persecution. But when it comes to our own vulnerability, we can be far less sympathetic.

Perfectionists confuse mistakes with failure, claims Spencer, inspiring us to work twice as hard to prove that we know what we're doing. "This gets exhausting until one day, you define yourself as a failure and simply walk away."[417] Well, where's the fun in that? Warrell confirms, "While playing safe removes the immediate risk of exposure, it opens up the greater risk of never knowing just how capable, deserving, and 'more than' worthy you truly are."[418]

"Few things can short-circuit your effort to live fully alive as much as the fear of failure," cautions motivational speaker Ken Davis.[419] This fear affects everything, casting a shadow over our work, our relationships, and our lives, and can keep us stuck in unhappy situations for a long time. I suspect this is why George Burns believed that "it is better to be a failure at something you love than to be a success at something you hate."[420]

There's plenty of good advice for dealing with failure and mistakes. (You can even get some of these on T-shirts!) "When you stumble, make it part of the dance,"[421] a recent meme advises. Zig Ziglar urges us to "remember that failure is an event, not a person."[422] Henry Ford stated, "Failure is simply the opportunity to begin again, this time more intelligently."[423] And Winston Churchill noted, "Success is not final, failure is not fatal: it is the courage to continue that counts."[424]

If you find yourself feeling a bit cynical, keep in mind that cynicism is a prime ingredient in the deception, a common tool for self-protection. Try Luria's approach instead: "I decide—because Deciding for Myself is the first step to serious rebellion—that everyone should make at least 26 mistakes every day. This leaves me open to bumble around as much as I want. Does it backfire? Of course, but only because it's actually fun to be imperfect once I can relax and laugh at myself."

The impact on creativity and self-expression alone would make this topic worthy of discussion. Clearly, "If you're not prepared to be wrong, you'll never come up with anything original," educator Ken Robinson observes.[425] Sadly, once we nail the ability to walk, a lot of the encouragement and celebration that got us on our feet seems to disappear. And if we grow up with the emotional and psychological equivalent of an electric shock every time we get it wrong, it's hard to risk making mistakes, as original as we may want to be.

Hence this section of the book. I want to rally every bit of enthusiasm for trial and error (with *error* being the operative word), and am hoping that at least one of these quotes will resonate in a way that makes mistake-making much less of a big deal. And since so many people weighed in on this topic, we've got several angles to consider. "Forget about striving for perfection. Perfection is unattainable in an imperfect world," advises program developer Mark Ita. "Instead, strive for excellence. Excellence can be achieved." (Ita has coached exceptional growth from dozens of educators and presenters, myself included, by focusing on small, practical, and achievable improvements over time.)

David Burns similarly urges, "Aim for success, not perfection. Never give up your right to be wrong, because then you will lose the ability to learn new things and move forward with your life."[426] Raichart adds, "There is no perfect without imperfect. There is no success without failure. The effort and aim should count for a lot." And educator Eric Chong shares, "Note to Self: Reframe, re-learn, and rebuild."

> "Aim for success, not perfection. Never give up your right to be wrong, because then you will lose the ability to learn new things and move forward with your life."

Moorman and Haller claim we learn better when we believe that mistakes "are simply data that you can use to improve and grow," things that can be instructive and corrected.[427] This freedom to fail is critical to success in the business world as well. CEO Allen Nance describes a "million-dollar mistake" that led to innovation and "raging successes" in his business. "Companies can't survive without growing, and growth requires making mistakes," he shares. "I will keep taking risks personally and encourage everyone I work with to do the same."[428]

Online learning community developer Adda Birnir describes learning to embrace failure after founding her own startup. "Every last remnant of that type-A, perfectionist student inside me was beaten down by the relentless exposure to failure, large and small, and after months of resisting failure, I grew exhausted," she writes. "After your ego has been thoroughly dismantled, you finally let go of your fear of failure (because in fact, you have been failing for quite some time now), you wrap your arms around failure and say: 'Okay, fine. I'm tired of being wrong. Tell me what is right.'" She adds that "the faster and harder you fail, the more you will learn, the less time you will waste, and the closer and closer you will come to finding the answer."[429]

> Sometimes our imperfections may be the most relatable assets we have. Let's remember that we are neither our achievements nor our failures. We are. Period.

Feeling reassured? I hope so. Because sometimes our imperfections may be the most relatable assets we have. Let's remember that we are neither our achievements nor our failures. We are. Period. We don't have to keep hiding anymore. As Warrell advises, "Even if you never accomplish all you aspire toward, you will accomplish so much more than you otherwise would have. In the process you'll come to realize that the only impostor you ever had to worry about is your fear of people thinking you are one."[430]

Dealing with Disapproval and Discouragement

Not long ago, I received a call from a colleague who was on the road doing presentations for an agency that required maintaining certain numeric evaluations as a condition for employment. I've seen this woman's work and can attest to her preparation, skill, and warmth as a presenter. Unfortunately, sometimes that isn't enough, and that week, my friend wasn't pulling her usual numbers.

Having worked in a similar situation, I can vouch for the strain of trying to contort my programs to solicit ratings that can reflect factors having nothing to do with the quality of the work. But whether in the public eye or quietly living or working far more shut off from much of the world, if we have any contact with other people, negative encounters are inevitable. Their remarks can be thoughtless and insensitive, even if well-intended. And with the numerous digital channels available for expressing opinions these days, feedback can also be downright nasty.

As we've seen, perfectionists are notoriously hypersensitive to criticism from others. However, none of us is immune. In fact, according to counselor Karen Wright, the neural networks that process negative information are separate and more sensitive than the ones that handle positive phenomena. She cites experiments that indicate a stronger neural response to negative stimuli whether weighing financial risks or sizing up other people. We may also interpret a simple question or suggestion as criticism, seeing negative feedback where none is intended.[431]

Nonetheless, it's heartbreaking to put your "all" into efforts that don't get the desired response—the joke that doesn't get a laugh, the proposal that gets rejected, the client who goes to a competitor, the scene on the cutting-room floor. Everyone who's ever put themselves out there has no doubt experienced this disappointment. And as bad as that may be, outright criticism can be far more painful, especially when it attacks our passions, dreams, ability, potential, personality, or worth.

So let's see if we can look at criticism and disapproval with fresh eyes, starting with a grudging acceptance of the fact that not everyone will like us. Somewhere along the line, some of us got the message that everyone is *supposed* to like us, and if they don't, we must be doing something wrong. This isn't true now and it wasn't true then. "You will always be too much of something for someone: too big, too loud, too soft, too edgy. If you round out your edges, you lose your edge," writes inspirational speaker Danielle LaPorte.[432]

Our ambition and talent will almost always attract cynics and haters. In fact, that's probably a good sign, although it's hard to remember that *this has nothing to do with us*. "You have enemies?" queried Winston Churchill. "Good. That means you've stood up for something some time in your life."[433] Even Einstein threw down on this one: "Great spirits have always found violent opposition from mediocre minds," he said.[434] "The truth is, you should never waste your time trying to turn someone who hates you into someone who likes you," writes author Jon Acuff. "Instead focus on turning people who like your dream into people who love your dream."[435]

"Courage doesn't always roar," reminds author Mary Anne Radmacher. "Sometimes courage is the quiet voice at the end of the day saying, 'I will try again tomorrow.'"[436]

Although we may never fully dismantle our Inner Critic, we don't need to feed it by trying to get approval from everyone we meet. We may not be able to avoid criticism and rejection, but we don't have to pay it much attention.

"Stop listening to what other people say about you," writes author and speaker Kimanzi Constable. "There's only one of you! All those things that people criticize about you is what makes you special and unique. When you listen to them and try to change those things, they win and the world loses."

Pulling Pearls of Wisdom
from Piles of Trash

Requesting input is not the same as seeking approval, and the best responses won't ask us to change what makes us special and unique. Feedback can be valuable, even when it's not what we want to hear. Not all ideas are good ones and sometimes another person's experience and perspective can help us focus our goals and improve our game significantly.

Wright mentions the rare individuals "who thrive on feedback of all sorts," people who are "more likely to see feedback as an opportunity for improvement rather than as a damning verdict."[437] Few perfectionists would fit into this category, so let's use this section as an invitation to be hungry for other perspectives—and to listen. In the process, we are going to get a whole lot of information, and we'll have to learn to sort the useful, relevant, and helpful from the rest.

Negative comments tend to be the ones that jump out, so this can get kind of tricky. We can't process reasonable suggestions if we're fixated on the one that rips us to shreds. (One of my seminar participants actually took the time to write "I hate your hair" as her only comment on the evaluation, which, at the time, negated piles of raves and reinforcement for what I had done right.[438]) So we need a few filters to be able to pull what could be helpful data from the irrelevant, the hateful, and the junk.

With new messages coming in all the time, it's easy to lose track of what's meaningful, valuable, and relevant for us. It's important to remove the messages meant only to discourage or distract, for example, and to be very careful we don't mistake someone else's opinions, standards, fears, or dreams for our own. Let's screen out expressions of other people's anxieties and insecurities, as well as anything that projects anger or dismissiveness from someone who isn't ready to meet us on our own terms.

We discard messages that are trying to sell us something, or wish to make us weak and dependent. We watch out for "shoulds" from people perpetuating cultural standards they've never bothered to question. We toss input from the cynics, the disempowered, and the haters—people who take pleasure in bashing others but who really have nothing constructive to say. We reject certain other feedback because the topic is outside our job description, or because we really don't care to change our wardrobe, hair, accent, or weight just to appease someone we may never meet or see again. This information goes straight into the trash.

The remaining input can be helpful, even if it's harsh. Let's try sending our egos out for a break so we can look for ideas that can direct us to positive changes and refinement of skills. We can evaluate this data by asking a few questions: First of all, is it relevant? Useful? Will making these changes improve the quality of the work I do? Make me a better person? Are these suggestions consistent with my values and intentions?

Eliminate the spam and sometimes we find absolute gems—a word of appreciation, a life-changing quote, or a suggestion that can help resolve or eliminate a problem that's been baffling us. We'll know the pearls when we see them. "Feedback's goal is to cause improvements," says Acuff. "Hate's goal is to cause wounds. Let them go."[439] Sure, sometimes people just need to vent and sometimes, just listening and accepting where they're coming from (without personalizing anything they're saying) satisfies them. However, I've rarely found it worth my time or energy to engage people with an axe to grind and no intention of finding a solution or changing their behavior or point of view.

Let's pay attention to our evaluations. It helps when we're interacting with someone we trust, but sometimes a stranger can throw
us a curve that ends up moving us forward in a big, unexpected way.
(Even hostile feedback can give us some clues about how to prevent
future antagonism and misunderstandings.) We can always filter out
the stuff that doesn't feel appropriate, or file it away for further consideration at a later date.

Acknowledge input gracefully: "Thanks for that suggestion."
"What a great idea." "You've given me something to think about."
"I really appreciate your input." Even if the feedback feels more like
an attack, we can disengage without defensiveness, even validating
the possibility that "you could be right" (whether or not we actually
agree) and then moving on.[440]

We need to think of ourselves in growth-mindset terms to take
advantage of the information and suggestions we receive, because
some of the most powerful changes can come as we process and
integrate negative feedback. And no, it's not easy. "No matter how it's
delivered, defensiveness is a natural first response to negative feedback," says Wright. "Don't expect heroics from yourself or anyone
else. If you're the recipient, take a deep breath. It's probably going
to hurt. Try not to talk too much. Instead, lean back and learn."[441]

Letting Go in Present Time

Here's the short list: failure, mistakes, regrets, the past in general,
worries about the future. Letting go is tough for perfectionists, for
any or all of these things. We're haunted by an embarrassing moment
from childhood even as we stress about upcoming deadlines. Simply
being in present time is a challenge.

Sauvic suggests that we yearn for a past we weren't present in while
it was happening. She advises having a clear vision for the future and

preparing ourselves, "but always be present in the now."[442] I'm well aware that despite all the advice to do this, simply reading the words "just let go" may not be enough to change our behavior, since "hanging on" tends to be related to deeper issues of old shame and early fears. We may need to dig a bit deeper to get down to where these habits originated, but in the meantime, let me offer some encouragement and permission to consider that this possibility exists.

"Show up and do what's right in front of you," a friend once advised. He didn't have answers for the big issues I was facing, but by drawing my attention to smaller, concrete, and manageable tasks, he helped bring me back to present time and ease me out of panic mode. He was a big fan of focusing on the things over which we have some control, acting responsibly, doing our best, and leaving the outcomes and impact of our best efforts up to some Power greater than ourselves.

He figured there were reasons for everything and managed to trust that the things that didn't work out (which some of us might call failures) were just happening to leave space for something even better to come along. "Accept what cannot be changed," Fucarino advises. "Instead of obsessing over how unfair life is, just focus on what you can control

> I have found that when I work on the more manageable things, the unmanageable seems to work itself out.

and change it for the better."[443] I have found that when I work on the more manageable things, the unmanageable seems to work itself out. Time smooths out some of the sharper edges, and years or even weeks later, most of what I'd obsessed about turns out to be very insignificant in terms of lasting negative impact.

Columnist Regina Brett advises, "Make peace with your past so it won't screw up the present."[444] When we look back on most

embarrassing moments and our most glaring mistakes, instead of ago-
nizing over them, let's look for ways they might have opened doors
to new ideas, life changes, sensitivity and awareness, or progress—
things that may never have happened otherwise. Maybe everything
really is part of a bigger picture and although it's hard to see at the
time, sometimes the painful events in our lives do have silver linings.

It's difficult for perfectionists to appreciate this. We romanticize
the past while living in the land of "if only." We beat ourselves up for
settling for a lousy offer, trusting the wrong person, or thinking of
a perfect comeback two days after we needed it. We've ignored our
instincts, changed for people who did not deserve it, delayed acting
on good advice. We've run out too early and stayed too long.

All of us have done these things, and the healing starts when we
can see each of these incidents as simply another step along the path,
perhaps something that has, over time, shaped the best of who we
are—or might become. "Do not carry your mistakes with you," writes
Ryan Ferreras. "Instead, place them under your feet and use them as
stepping stones."[445]

Parrott remarks, "Your present is inextricably linked to your past.
If you are weighted down by regret, pain, and guilt over things that
happened two decades ago or two hours ago, you will not be able
to live fully in the present."[446] In some instances, just bringing shame
and regret into the light can strip them of a lot of their power. But
sometimes, stronger feelings require a more concrete ritual to help
us let them go.

I know someone who will write down the text of a verbal attack
or the memory of a painful event on a little piece of paper. She then
seals the paper in a plastic bag half-filled with water, freezes the bag,
and then symbolically throws the memory out. The process literally
waters down the power of the event, freezes it in time, and becomes

garbage for her. (Recycle the plastic bag, if you wish, but I wouldn't recommend using it for anything else.)

I'm also a big fan of writing down feelings and memories I want to disempower, and have also found the freezer trick to be helpful. Sometimes just running the paper through the shredder and turning an insult or resentment into confetti is enough. I also find fire to be a great alternative, especially for feelings that are particularly painful and burdensome. I have a special glass bowl set aside to burn up scraps of paper with notes about anything I want to get out of my head. This can take a lot of the power out of offending messages and painful memories. (I tend to flush the bits of ash down the toilet, which I find quite satisfying, and I understand that the ash can also be composted if written on regular paper.)

"Life is a limited time event," cautions Rechtschaffen.[447] And it's only moving in one direction. Quickly. But time can also give us new perspectives as we get more of it under our belt. "When I was younger, I wish I'd known that what often seemed like 'the end of the world' often turned out to be a positive and transformative experience," shares musician Annie Lennox.[448] Let's stop for a moment and look around, noticing where we are this moment. If our present is cluttered with bitterness and resentment, maybe it's time for a spring cleaning.

As Caliph Umar ibn Al-Khattaab said, "No amount of guilt can change the past and no amount of worrying can change the future."[449] Our baggage keeps us stuck, and the better we get at shrugging off insults and defeat, the faster we can cross back into striving for excellence from a healthy place—in present time.

Persistence and Durability

I've been a crafter and fiber freak my entire life, so when I saw an opportunity to take a spinning class, I signed up. Knowing how much

I loved handling wool, I expected that I'd catch on quickly, as similar endeavors had always come fairly easily to me. Imagine my dismay when that turned out not to be the case.

I wasn't bothered by the fact that everyone else was successfully spinning beautiful, uniform yarns. I was, however, a bit freaked out that I wasn't making the kind of progress I expected of myself and couldn't seem to get the rhythm down. My yarn was thick, lumpy, overtwisted in some places and falling apart in others. Responding to my frustration, the teacher reassured me that she'd never lost anyone yet. "Just keep spinning," she advised. "You can't get worse."

I knew exactly what she meant and understood that her comment was in no way meant as an insult. If I just kept at it, I could *only* improve. And I did! My wool continues to be irregular in width and twist, but I find the product interesting, beautiful, and fun to use in knitting projects. (I can *buy* perfectly spun wool when I need it.) In the meantime, I find the process wonderfully relaxing, almost meditative. I'm really glad I hung in there.

"Achievement often follows on the heels of small (or big) mistakes," writes Elicia Brown. Coping with disappointment and imperfection also requires an understanding "that one can't succeed without opening oneself to the risk of failure."[450] When we expect success—if not perfect results—at the first go-round with something new, most of us are going to be pretty disappointed. We get impatient and dejected when things are harder or take longer than we expect, even though our expectations are likely to be arbitrary and unrealistic. We also expect some tangible outcome for our efforts—a good grade, verbal acknowledgment, some prize or reward, or hard evidence of progress and growth. When these expectations are not met, perfectionists are the first ones to throw in the towel.

This makes persistence one of the most valuable assets a perfectionist can develop. This characteristic will keep us going in the face of
frustration, delays, and failure. Calvin Coolidge noted that the world
was full of unsuccessful people with lots of talent, genius, and education. "Persistence and determination alone are omnipotent," he said.[451]
The ability to stick with it and keep showing up regardless of the
outcomes can help move us toward a healthier approach to achieving.
"Being defeated is often a temporary condition," says columnist Marilyn Vos Savant. "Giving up is what makes it permanent."[452]

It's normal to slip in our commitment, make excuses, and get
out of our routines. But performance coach Jason Selk encourages
maintaining even the smallest of efforts, to build what he calls elite
mental toughness. "Instead of striving to be perfect, commit to getting *something* done. Instead of putting it off until the next day or
some other time, do *something*. Even if it's just 30 seconds. Whether
you're working out your mind or your body in the gym, every workout doesn't
have to be perfect. Keep the momentum going, and don't take a zero. That's how
the truly exceptional do it. One foot in front of the other. Done is better than
perfect."[453]

> Keep the momentum going, and don't take a zero. That's how the truly exceptional do it. One foot in front of the other. Done is better than perfect.

"I've been absolutely terrified every
moment of my life," said artist Georgia O'Keeffe, "and I've never
let it keep me from doing a thing I wanted to do."[454] Whatever fears
may have haunted O'Keeffe, they certainly didn't prevent her from
leaving an extensive legacy of her work.

"How are you showing up each day?" asks personal coach Diana
Reid. "Are you just letting life happen or are you creating life and
taking action on the things that will make your life the way you

want it to be?" She encourages, "Follow your heart. Do what you love to
do and do it often. What feels right
to you *is* right for you."[455] The results
don't have to be perfect. They don't
even have to be good. Let's shoot for
good-enough-for-now.

> "Are you just letting life happen or are you creating life and taking action on the things that will make your life the way you want it to be?"

Author KT Witten assures, "Your dream doesn't have an expiration date. Take a deep breath and try again."[456] If we're exhausted after a ten-minute workout, we aim for being *less* tired next time (and well before we push on to fifteen). No matter how pathetic ten minutes might sound, it might be exactly right for where we are right now. We will improve with practice and do better next time, but we have to show up first with whatever we've got and be satisfied with the best we can do—for *now*.

Edberg recommends setting "human standards for yourself by thinking about personal improvement in percentages" rather than absolutes.[457] This is a good place for a reminder about breaking things down. Fuller recommends taking "a daunting task apart into bite-size pieces."[458] Let's stop setting ourselves up by expecting superhuman achievements and outcomes. (My frequent frustration and impatience with the amount of time and effort a book requires does not make me write any faster or more coherently.)

No matter how important a task or a deadline, or how worthwhile a goal or desire, life will sometimes get in the way. "The path to success is not a simple, linear one," writes Pyryt. "Barriers such as rejection, illness, economic misfortunes, and relationship issues can make it difficult for an individual to achieve success and maintain it. One of the key factors is being able to persevere in the face of obstacles."[459] Striving for excellence (instead of perfection) will require flexibility, some comfort with uncertainty, and a willingness to take a different route to our goal than we'd planned.

There's great freedom in letting go of expectations. This allows us to develop a sense of trust in the notion that each of us is right on schedule, exactly where we are supposed to be—moving, creating, and growing as fast as we are supposed to be. Whether we see results or not, we keep moving forward. "Progress is not measured in miles, it is measured in inches," urges Walsch. "Everything is rolling out exactly as it needs to. Rest easy and be at peace. Life is working its magic even as you take your very next breath."[460]

> "Progress is not measured in miles, it is measured in inches," urges Walsch. "Everything is rolling out exactly as it needs to. Rest easy and be at peace. Life is working its magic even as you take your very next breath."

The Gifts of Gratitude

Perfectionists can be consumed by negativity. Fear of failure, obsession with flaws, and a faithful concentration on errors, inadequacies, and shortcomings edges us up against anxiety, depression, and hopelessness—if not smack-dab in the middle of all three. At times, we get overcommitted, overloaded, and stressed out enough to compromise our physical well-being, mental health, relationships, and self-care routines.

Fortunately, we have a wonderful tool for redirecting our thinking away from all this negativity and fear. Even if it's only for a moment, making a conscious decision to shift our focus to the *good* in our lives can ground us in a far better frame of mind. Deliberately acknowledging what we have going for us—from concrete conveniences, comforts, beauty in our environment, and caring people that enrich our lives to the inner guidance, dreams, inspirations, perspective, and our ability to learn from our experiences—can have a powerful and positive impact on our social and emotional lives, career, health, and sense of contentment.[461]

Unfortunately, if we grew up having our complaints and concerns dismissed with comments about how lucky we were to have what we had (or that things weren't worse), gratitude may not appear quite as helpful as it truly can be. "When I was a kid, gratitude was used like a drug to distract us from feelings of sadness, anger, disappointment, or want," one contributor shared. "It took me a long time to realize that all feelings are legitimate, that I could have a desire or feel a negative feeling and still be grateful for what I had or how good I had it. The two were not mutually exclusive."

No, not hardly. But scarcity models teach us to mistrust happiness and prosperity, leaving some of us afraid of enjoying what we have, waiting for the other shoe to drop if things are going a little too well. "We learned not to want," this contributor continued. "Receiving was hard, unless I felt I had struggled for it. I didn't feel that I deserved what I had if it didn't cost me somehow."

Learning to receive—and understand that deservingness is not the same as feelings of entitlement—becomes part of the healing mission. "I accept that my way doesn't work," admits Luria. "I decide that instead of focusing on doing and achieving, I'm going to look for the many ways that life gives me little treats without me doing a thing, without lifting a finger." Exhaustion helped Luria realize "that if everything good that comes my way [always depends on] my efforts, then I'm never going to get to the finish line . . ."

Healing asks us to trust that we are getting both the lessons *and* the blessings we need—and to appreciate the gifts in both. "The more you praise and celebrate your life, the more there is in life to celebrate," claims Oprah Winfrey. "The more you complain, the more you find fault, the more misery and fault you will have to find."[462] For those of us expecting to finally be happy after we meet the right mate, buy the big house, lose those last five pounds, or get our novel (or song or quilt or report) just right, let's ask ourselves how satisfied we felt with our previous accomplishments.

> "If we do not feel grateful for what we already have, what makes us think we'd be happy with more?"

"If we do not feel grateful for what we already have, what makes us think we'd be happy with more?"[463] Author Robert Holden warns, "Beware of Destination Addiction . . . a preoccupation with the idea that happiness is in the next place, the next job and with the next partner. Until you give up the idea that happiness is somewhere else, it will never be where you are."[464]

Healing also asks us to trust the outcomes of our efforts, even though many worthwhile tasks offer no immediate payoffs, or even solid evidence of their impact or value. This is tough for those of us used to getting a gold star because so much of the impact we have on the world is never rewarded, reported, or even visible. We may never know how we've changed or touched a life. In fact, the people whose lives we influence might "wake up," move forward, or stop hurting themselves, for example, with no memory of their interaction with us or any awareness of how our influence changed them for the better. So we learn to live with not knowing and without acknowledgment, but somehow trusting that our best efforts are never, ever wasted.

For the ultimate message of gratitude and optimism, consider samurai poet Mizuta Masahide's lines, "Barn's burnt down. Now I can see the moon."[465] Okay, I'll admit that despite generally being a glass-half-full kind of person, I'm not quite there yet. Aviator Martin Pigg reports that this quote "resonated so strongly because it reminded me that what's needed most in challenging times is the courage to look for beauty and meaning amidst the rubble. Because even in the midst of what we perceive as disastrous, there are opportunities on the other side of every challenge we face." He continues, "It's easy to give up, to tell ourselves that what's happened means the end of our dreams. But that attitude is not worthy of us and our purpose for being on this planet. My message to you is this: Look Up. See the beauty and magic of your life. Know that you arrived on this planet with all of the courage and faith you need to turn tragedy into triumph."[466]

Practical Strategies for Practicing Gratitude

In the United States, Canada, and a few other spots on the globe, we set aside one day a year for giving thanks for the blessings of the previous year. However, gratitude is more than an idea to drag out and dust off for the holidays. A worthwhile tool for shifting perspective and priorities, grounding us in present time, and creating a positive change in our frame of mind, even a few seconds of gratitude practice can help pull us out of the negative vortex perfectionism can create. Here are a few ideas to get started. Wishing you all good things, always, as well as the mindfulness to notice.

+ Make a list of conveniences, merchandise, or services available to you today that did not exist when you were growing up, or even ten or fifteen years ago.

+ Take a walk and notice five new things you've never noticed before.

+ Identify five people who have touched your heart in a profound or unique way. Describe what they've done.

+ List ten gifts of service you could give now. Remember that "gifts" do not have to cost any more than a smile!

+ Write about what you would do if you knew you absolutely could not fail.

+ If you have a question or problem currently challenging you, write it down before you go to bed. Note the kind of images and information that come to you in your dreams and throughout the following day or days.

+ Write about past wishes, wishes you made at different stages in your life. Which ones came true? Bonus: identify examples of abundance that already exist in your life.

+ Describe ways that you are creative. What are some new ways you can express your creativity?

+ Ask your close friends to remind you of three examples of significant growth or personal development in you that they have observed and admired in the last five or ten years.

+ Describe three of the most significant or satisfying accomplishments of your life. Then go back and do the same for the past year, the past month, and the past twenty-four hours.

+ Make a collage of images that represent your most positive personal attributes.

+ Describe how your life is better today than it was at some time— or various times—in the past. [467]

CHAPTER 17

Connecting with Others

When business professors Tiziana Casciano and Miguel Sousa Lobo examined characteristics of employees that affected hiring decisions and choice of work partners, they focused their research on two criteria—competence and likability. No one was surprised when everyone chose the people who were high on both scales. "Things got a lot more interesting though, when people faced the choice between competent jerks and lovable fools."

Most managers insist on competence, stating that they can put aside their hostility toward an obnoxious person who can get the job done. However, in practice "personal feelings played a more important role in forming work relationships . . . than evaluations of competence." In fact, they described feelings toward coworkers as a "gating factor," noting that competence is irrelevant for people who are strongly disliked. "By contrast, if someone is liked, his colleagues will seek out every little bit of competence he has to offer."

These findings were consistent throughout their study. "Generally speaking, a little extra likability goes a longer way than a little extra competence in making someone desirable to work with."[468]

Although Casciano and Lobo's research didn't mention perfectionism, I think it's fair to say that this trait, whether describing an employee or a boss, could lean some of us toward the "jerk" column. "Perfectionists can be annoying," notes Greenspon, "either when they are pressuring others to be perfect or when they engender inferiority feelings in others by their high standards."[469] This observation can certainly apply to personal relationships as well, so let's look at a few things we can do to maintain the best possible connections with the important people in our lives.

Starting with Self

It may seem a little strange to bring up the issue of self-care in a chapter on relationships, but the truth is, a relationship is only as healthy as the individuals in it. If we don't believe we are worthy of being treated well, we're just as likely to miss out on the respect and consideration we would like. The tools we use here include things like modeling self-respect, setting and maintaining boundaries, valuing what we see in the mirror, and making constructive choices on our own behalf.

"Friendship with one's self is all-important," advised Eleanor Roosevelt, "because without it one cannot be friends with anyone else in the world."[470] This is where it starts: a comfort in our own skin, an acceptance and appreciation of ourselves before we offer these gifts to others. It is then that we can find places where we feel accepted and wanted—as is. "Fitting in and belonging are not the same thing," Brené Brown cautions. "In fact, fitting in is about assessing a situation and becoming what you need to be to be accepted. Belonging, on the other hand, doesn't require us to change who we are; it requires us to *be* who we are."[471]

Relating to people is not about conforming to their idea of who we should be. "Every woman should claim herself before she deeply shares her heart with another," writes Courtney Walsh. "She must be able to look into the mirror and be at peace with her own reflection. This doesn't mean she will see perfection or miss areas that she may want to improve. But she can hold her own gaze and say: 'I see you. I claim you for love. I honor you.'"

Walsh acknowledges that this will not be easy: "At first she will cringe. She will hear all the critical voices of perfection, doubt, and demand listing her flaws and faults. Then she will relax and sigh and weep at her own heart shine. Knowing that it is not about eyes or lips or hair or skin. That it is about the sadness, the yearning and the mystery, the grace and the fear . . . the stranger and friend that is peering back at her asking only to be seen and loved. Cherished and nourished."

Claiming this beauty is a source of great power, Walsh continues: "She is unstoppable. Not because she is confident or cheerful or appealing or pleasing. Not because she is bold or determined or persistent. But because she has become safe in her own tender-loving gaze. She has let herself come fully home."[472]

Another meme making the rounds cautions, "At your absolute best, you still won't be good enough for the wrong person. At your worst, you'll still be worth it to the right person."[473] True love and friendship will not demand a hair transplant or a boob job, a fancy car or college degree. In fact, conditional offers that rest on superficial requirements make great filters for weeding out people who are likely to keep us jumping through hoops that will probably never fully satisfy them.

"Don't waste your time, money, energy, and love on someone who is unappreciative and brings heartache into your life," cautions self-development activist Bryant McGill. "Everyone may deserve love, but not everyone deserves your love."[474] Physician Charles F. Glassman adds, "Before you discover your soul mate, you must first discover your soul." He advises, "Rather than a soul mate, strive for a soulful relationship. That is one in which both partners do not need each other. Lasting, happy, soulful relationships are not needy ones."[475]

"Love isn't a state of perfect caring," claims the late television host, minister, and everyone's favorite neighbor Fred Rogers. "It is an active noun like 'struggle.' To love someone is to strive to accept that person exactly the way he or she is, right here and now."[476] So before we commit to head-over-heels, let's make sure we are valued for the amazing work-in-progress we bring to the party. If we're already in a relationship with someone who gets that, let's add our appreciation to the top of our gratitude list. And if not, well, fortunately there are a few things we can do to increase the odds of getting those needs met.

Control Issues and Power Dynamics

"Years ago, I was taking an older relative out for dinner," recalls a survey respondent. "I was hungry and open to pretty much anything that resembled food, so I asked what she was up for. 'I don't know,' she mumbled. I threw out a few options but could not persuade her to commit to a preference. With no information to go on—other than her apparent willingness to leave the decision up to me—I pulled into the first decent-looking place we passed. Of course, she wasn't happy with whatever she ordered. Her only real success that night was in how well she set herself up to play Victim."

Control issues come in all sorts of disguises, and passivity can be just as manipulative as aggression. This seems to be an issue in all sorts of relationships, from our most intimate to encounters with total strangers. In my work with parents and educators, the topic of power struggles always seems to wind up at the top of the list of concerns they want to discuss and resolve. No surprise there. But it turns out that most of us are not much better at dealing successfully with control issues when it comes to working and living with other adults.

If we want to be part of healthy, mutually respectful relationships (and who doesn't?), we need to talk a bit about the idea of *win-win*. This term was first coined in the 1920s by human relations and management pioneer Mary Parker Follett. It was used initially in the business world, where clients and consumers tend to be far more likely to, say, sign a contract or buy a product when they believe that their needs are being respected and accommodated. In more mainstream applications, the concept generally refers to efforts to meet the needs of all individuals involved in some sort of interaction or negotiation.[477] Unfortunately, as attractive as win-win outcomes would appear, the intentions and behaviors to execute these outcomes are still relatively uncommon.

Communications consultant Diane Rheos attributes our destructive, win-lose traditions to a system in which we define power "as being about an ability to control others," one that presumes that only some people have access to this commodity. She notes that our hierarchical thinking has brought about a need for expertise—proof that we have earned the right to our power—and for competition, which suggests that we can only win if we beat out others, or make them lose.[478] For a perfectionist who needs to be "at the top," being competitive and controlling may seem to be a given, regardless of the costs, but it's hell on relationships.

Gilbert looks at this concept through a different lens, seeing power in individuals who are simply doing what they want to be doing with their life. "Power doesn't have to be fierce," she explains. "It doesn't have to be aggressive or combative or cocky. It doesn't have to tear anything down. It doesn't have to be in your face. It doesn't have to be a moment of fist-pumping victory. It doesn't have to be expensive or monumental. It doesn't have to make the world explode."

In fact, she suggests that "the deepest kind of power doesn't have much to do with anyone else at all. Nothing to do with status, nothing to do with reputation, nothing to do with winning. No, true power comes from standing in your own truth and walking on your own path. That's it."[479] Despite her orientation to a more traditional context, Rheos would appear to agree. "Authentic power has nothing to do with control, or holding a specific title. Authentic power is an ability to freely and fully express who you came here to be."[480]

> True power comes from standing in your own truth and walking on your own path.

Unfortunately, the majority of our role models typically fall at extreme ends of a continuum in which someone is "losing" on either end. Perhaps the most obvious are the bullies and the bulldozers, the ones who take care of themselves without regard for other people's needs. They can be corrosively critical, dismissive, intimidating, or just plain mean. They need to win and feel entitled to do so at the expense of the other person's ideas, expertise, confidence, or dignity. These tactics are reinforced by their apparent effectiveness—keeping others too frightened or insecure to challenge them.

On the other end of the spectrum are the passive and compliant folks who surrender their own needs to accommodate others. Since self-sacrifice is often applauded by family, cultural, and religious institutions, it's an easy habit to adopt, and many of us do so early on. These people can be agreeable and helpful, although they can also be passive-aggressive and resentful. By putting everyone else's needs ahead of their own, they usually get to look good and earn approval. But self-abandonment

> Self-abandonment also offers a ticket to self-righteousness, feelings of helplessness, and a self-perception of victimization, which can likewise promote guilt, fear, and feeling the need to care-take in others.

also offers a ticket to self-righteousness, feelings of helplessness, and a self-perception of victimization, which can likewise promote guilt, fear, and feeling the need to care-take in others. So these tactics, too, have their payoff.

Oddly, both approaches are about manipulation and control, and in both forms of interaction, someone has to lose. Growing up with either or both of these models can present obstacles when we attempt to take care of ourselves in relationships with others in a win-win configuration that consider the needs of all parties involved. The goal is learning to run down the middle, getting what we want with a minimum of conflict or inconvenience for others. This means identifying and expressing our needs or desires, sticking up for ourselves, and still being considerate of other people. Despite the lack of models and familiarity, when we deliberately attempt to consider and accommodate the needs of everyone involved, we'll know we're on track for establishing relationships with possible win-win outcomes.[481]

> When we deliberately attempt to consider and accommodate the needs of everyone involved, we'll know we're on track for establishing relationships with possible win-win outcomes.

Finding Our Voice, Drawing the Line

In the all-or-nothing context of a win-lose reality, the concept of "standing up for yourself" is likely to conjure images of aggression and defensiveness. Indeed, the only alternative will seem to appear as letting people walk all over us. Even the word assertive, recommended as the preferable, win-win option, will often summon a combative or belligerent connotation. However "true assertiveness always takes into account the thoughts and feelings of others," advises clinical psychologist Leon F. Seltzer.[482]

Once again, we don't have many models (or much cultural support) for asking for what we want, so many of us have actually lost touch with our true desires, much less the confidence or skill for expressing them. Seltzer recommends clarifying our perspective without self-righteously explaining the superiority of our position or defensively seeking to discredit or reject an unfavorable impression someone else might have about us.[483] "Come from a place of desire—not obligation," suggests Andra Brosh. "When you are trying to learn how to set boundaries and say no you will be forced to really ask yourself what you want and need. This may be something you have never considered before, so it will seem selfish and weird at first. Make choices as opposed to fulfilling obligations. There are always things you have to do, but you are always choosing."[484]

This can be especially challenging for perfectionists. We learn to silence our desires and needs when stating them draws fire from people we look to for approval. We stay safe by keeping people happy. Drawing our identity from our value to others, we suppress anything that might compromise the roles we've learned to play. "People pleasers tend to have a hard time expressing themselves openly and honestly," Brosh affirms. "It's scary to share your feelings when you think they will cause conflict or drive the other person away." Nonetheless, "rocking the boat, and upsetting the status quo is a natural and healthy part of growing in your relationships," she adds.[485]

Especially in dealings with inconsiderate, controlling, critical, pushy, invasive, competitive, or negative people, I heartily recommend a good boundary for letting people know what we want—and how they can get what *they* want. (This tool also comes in handy with people who are dismissive, indifferent, or not conscious that we might want a say in how things are going.) Unlike rules, demands, reactive criticism, or pleas for respect, boundaries allow us to clearly, proactively express our needs, preferences, and tolerances without attacking or making others wrong.

> I heartily recommend a good boundary for letting people know what we want—and how they can get what *they* want. Unlike rules, demands, reactive criticism, or pleas for respect, boundaries allow us to clearly, proactively express our needs, preferences, and tolerances without attacking or making others wrong.

Boundaries can be expressed as statements or direct requests, often sharing the conditions under which others can get their needs met: "I want to finish this project before I take another one on." "Let's go someplace with vegetarian options (or great burgers)." "I'll be happy to finish this report, as soon as you send me the data I need." For hard-core people pleasers, even these statements can sound harsh. But this is an effective technique for owning our power in a way that respects others' need for the same.

Boundaries let us off the hook for constantly explaining ourselves —a sign of approval-seeking if I ever saw one. They allow us to ask for guidance, instruction, or the working conditions we might require by connecting our successes to a payoff for the person we're addressing.

They do not attempt to make others responsible for our feelings or rely on people's concern for our emotional well-being to change the way they interact with us. They offer positive incentives, stated as promises (not threats), letting people know when, and under what conditions, they are welcome to play in our sandbox. And while boundaries don't always assure that we'll get others to back off or respect our wishes, they will make us seem less vulnerable as we continue to stand up for ourselves.[486]

We can take drastic measures when our sanity and self-protection become important enough. Years ago, I met a woman whose grown children kept showing up on her doorstep with their kids and possessions. When her children showed little inclination to get back out on their own, the mom finally sold her house and bought a one-bedroom place, so "moving home" was no longer an option.[487] Few boundaries will require such extreme measures, but the process for inspiring respect is pretty much the same even when the stakes are much smaller.

"Learn to say no," says Brosh. "The word no has a negative connotation most of the time, but it's actually a way to set a boundary. Even a toddler uses the word no to differentiate his sense of self. It's hard to say no, and sometimes we can't, but drawing the line in the sand when we need to is a healthy practice, and it lets other people know our limits."[488] Scher points out, "For every no you say, you are actually saying yes to countless other things. For example, when you say no to another late night at work, what are you actually saying yes to? Time with your family? Time for healthier food or exercise? More sleep? Your new assignment is to find the yes's and not focus on the no's. It will be almost impossible to see them as a negative once you do this."[489]

Following Through
Despite Resistance and Opposition

For perfectionists who have spent years conforming things like their appearance, relationships, personality, and career choices to the expectations of others, shifting into unfamiliar self-care behaviors can provoke a bit of backlash. "If we suddenly start setting boundaries, with a history of none or few, it's quite possible that our efforts will be greeted with very little enthusiasm from the people we've been so faithfully serving!" Teversham cautions. "If we'd been people-pleasing all our lives, it can be a shock to those around us. Go gently."[490]

People do what works and and our loved ones, friends, and work associates can become rather put off when familiar expectations and reactions no longer work for them. We need not be surprised at what will feel like attempts to undermine our healing. "I knew I'd made a huge breakthrough when my father called me a bitch," reported one contributor. Another shared, "My mother kept calling me asking if I was sick. Apparently saying no is a sign of disease in our family."

I am often asked the big Abandonment question when I bring up self-care issues in my seminars: "What if I start taking care of myself and people leave?" they ask. And as much as I would like to reassure them that people will be thrilled to discover that they can no longer manipulate and bully these individuals, the truth is, a few may well move on to more malleable pastures. "If you've been a pleaser for a while, then the people in your life will be used to it," states Brosh. "Some will automatically respect your new way of relating, but others will resist it. If there are people who simply cannot accept your limits and boundaries, then you might want to rethink these relationships. Some relationships work for a reason, but the reason isn't always healthy."[491]

I've known people who have cut—and grieved—their losses and ended up creating space for the respectful and loving relationships they deserved. We've got no guarantees, but I can swear that minimizing contact with people who bring us down, hold us back, or limit our aspirations is actually a good thing. It's kind of like having a big social garage sale, where we finally realize that we've outgrown certain friendships, while others are cluttering our lives, maybe even making us sick. "Don't change, someone will like you. Be yourself and the right people will like and love the real you."[492] If we're creating a vacuum, there's a good chance that it will now fill up with A-list material.

Connecting with Others

Working from home offers some incredible benefits. I get to decide on my hours, wear whatever I want, and not bother with rigid schedules, commutes, or even makeup. On the down side, I'm always at work. We deliberately bought a house with a big, separate area downstairs—a place I could actually leave and shut the door behind me when I was done. These good intentions were eventually undermined by a wireless network that turned the entire house into office space. Although more comfortable and convenient in many ways, this also means that any time I'm in the house, I am, effectively, at work.[493]

Building my business has required a tremendous amount of time and work, and trying to juggle the various tasks involved in the setup, management, and creative ventures, was keeping me tied up with work from morning until late at night. No matter how much I'd get done, there was always so much more I needed to do. Even with an incredibly supportive, understanding (and independent) husband, I was starting to feel the strain. I absolutely had to learn to just stop—sometimes forcing myself away from my desk when I was in the middle of something, enjoying the work, and making progress—or I'd end up a stranger in my own home.

It doesn't take long to start feeling a bit of distance and disconnection creep into any relationship that isn't being nourished. Perfectionists can get so caught up in efforts to look good and perform well that the importance of positive, caring relationships may not even register. "When an individual is caught up in the bondage of perfectionist striving, that person is likely to be less interested in developing a healthy, mutually satisfying marriage and more interested in chasing the elusive rabbit in his or her own head," shares psychologist and lifestyle researcher Shauna Springer.

Further, when perfectionists believe that they need to "be strong and in control of their emotions," Springer notes that they are likely to conceal feelings of fear, inadequacy, insecurity, and disappointment, even from those closest to them. This limits emotional intimacy, and may explain why people in relationships with perfectionists "often comment on their partner's emotional unavailability."[494]

Showing up in our own imperfect glory can encourage others to drop their walls and deceptions. "I know that as I have let go of being perfect, I have become much more honest, more real, more vulnerable, more humble, and more connected to people around me," admits Rheos. "I am willing to talk about things I didn't before, I am willing to actually ask for help and let others support me. I am happier, more compassionate, and more willing to allow others to not be perfect either!"[495]

Fucarino sees the connection between happiness and having strong, healthy connections with others. "Nurture social relationships," she advises. "A lonely person is a miserable person." She reminds us to always make time for our family, friends, and significant other.[496] This may be ridiculously obvious, but it's far too easy to run out the day, not to mention our energy, barely having made time for a meaningful conversation. Recognizing this need and making these connections a priority are important steps to healing relationships that have been starved by perfectionism. The next step requires us to look at the quality of these associations, making sure that the behaviors and beliefs this disorder can evoke does no harm to them.

Showing Kindness and Appreciation

Balancing our social needs will require some of us to let go of the idea that we have to do everything ourselves. Learning to delegate is a huge challenge for many perfectionists because it requires an appreciation, or at least a certain degree of tolerance, for the fact that someone else may do things differently that we do, and maybe not exactly the way we'd like. So self-acceptance is only a part of the equation. Accepting others—which involves appreciating different beliefs, approaches, habits, and ideas—is another necessary part of the healing prescription.

While we need skills for taking care of ourselves, this door swings both ways, and many of us also have to learn to connect with others in a manner that honors their needs for belonging, success, worth, power, and dignity. Edberg encourages us to "Set human standards for everyone. Everything and everyone has flaws, and things don't always go as planned."[497] As we learn to ask for what we need, this task may compel us to examine agendas we have for people in our lives and become willing to drop them in favor of accepting people for who they are. It's one thing to want people to put the cap back on the toothpaste, and quite another to expect them to love opera, be a morning person, or aspire to becoming (or marrying) a doctor, for example.

Accepting and appreciating people—as is—does not mean lowering standards or settling for poor quality. Especially if we have an opportunity to guide their growth (a child or employee, for example), this just means starting where they are and encouraging improvement and new skills. In any relationship, expecting or demanding perfection is a recipe for stress, conflict, and alienation. "There's a clear distinction between insisting on perfection and encouraging and helping others to perform and be their best," observes Staak, who also emphasizes the value of trial and error and embracing failure and imperfections as a path to success.[498] Similarly, Schoen cautions that demanding perfection breeds mediocrity. Lack of tolerance for differences, flaws, and different ways of seeing, feeling, and operating "suffocates the potential for innovation and creativity."[499]

For those of us who grew up hearing sayings like, "You can catch more flies with honey than you can with vinegar," the takeaway was meant to advocate for the effectiveness of persuading with kindness over attempting to bully people to do what we want with rude demands or threats. Marketing guru Peter Shankman advises businesses that "If you go the extra mile by treating people nicely, they will be loyal customers—rabidly so." (He also maintains that the opposite is true: angry customers can become ex-customers in a moment.) He favors admitting mistakes and going out of our way to win over an irate customer. "There is no greater lover than a former hater," he says.[500]

Most people respond well to empathy and understanding. When we meet someone for the first time, let's make an effort to push ourselves to see beyond superficial first impressions—the judgment, the desire to dismiss or label. Everyone carries stories, including talents, desires, joys, fears, losses, and pains that we can barely begin to imagine. Can we consciously shift to seeing people with our hearts, opening to connections with a Soul we'll never know from that first, quick glance?

Let's make a commitment to speak kindly of people, focusing our feedback, whenever possible, on their assets, efforts, progress, or improvement. Let's acknowledge other people's contributions and keep our egos in check. "It's amazing what you can accomplish if you don't care who gets the credit."[501] I know few people who would complain of getting too much recognition or appreciation. I think it's easy to assume people know we love and value them. Let's learn to share these feelings without any expectations for a specific response.

We live in a world where we are, to various degrees, dependent on one another. We need people to help us take care of our health, our cars, our homes. We need people to teach our children and help us with our taxes. We need people to maintain the inventory of things we wish to purchase. And most of us need people for social contact, emotional support, and romantic involvement. Our ability to interact positively with one another contributes in a big way to the quality of our lives.

Healthy Interdependence and Letting Go

On her list of things to give up in order to be happy, Sauvic includes needing to be right and needing to be in control, and the tendency toward criticism and blame.[502] Any one of these can tank a relationship, as well as the goodwill needed to make one work or keep it going. I've seen people willing to lose friends, alienate family members, and even risk job security by insisting on being right in ways that backed others into a corner, demeaned them, or made them wrong. Anyone who has been on the receiving end of an exchange like this knows how damaging (and emotionally exhausting) it can be.

I suspect we'll all have experiences where just knowing we're right will be enough. Let's recognize them when they come up. We don't need to die on every hill. There are ways to correct people who are doing something incorrectly or give negative feedback without being hurtful or derisive. But seeking satisfaction over a difference of opinions or points of view is not likely to end well. We can acknowledge their frustration or anger without agreeing with their opinion, and, often times, a potential skirmish will just fizzle out there. (Changing the subject afterwards is a handy way to disengage before tensions escalate.)

Even if we are in a position of authority where our responsibilities include giving feedback and information to guide the development or performance of others, we are likely to encounter some resistance to suggestions that would require significant changes in beliefs or behaviors. It's hard to change long-held patterns that have protected us, even if we are unhappy with the results or afraid of the potential outcomes of not changing. Especially in a peer relationship—that is, where we are not someone's parent, teacher, boss, or supervisor—we want to tread lightly on the advice-giving, even if we are asked.

When we start hearing "Yeah, but . . ." in response to any suggestion we've been invited to make, it's a good sign that we're dealing with people who are committed to hanging on to beliefs and behaviors they're not ready to question or change. Keep pushing and we'll come off as invasive and controlling. There are a lot of people who just like to complain, and if we've been fixers and helpers all our lives, it could be very challenging to not get sucked into one fruitless conversation after another. Sometimes acceptance requires us to just let people be where they are and try to keep off that particular topic, knowing that they may never change the things they are complaining about.

Healthy interdependence requires healthy and clear boundaries. "Be there for others, but never leave yourself behind," writes author Dodinsky.[503] We can listen and model, reflect and acknowledge, ask questions and offer encouragement—and we can do this without taking responsibility for other people's problems. "When faced with senseless drama, spiteful criticisms, and misguided opinions, walking away is the best way to stand up for yourself. To respond with anger is an endorsement of their attitude," he adds.[504] Stepping out of the role of rescuer allows us to support others without getting enmeshed in other people's issues or assuming ownership of problems that are not ours to resolve. Sometimes, the best way for us to help someone is to just let go, get out of the way, and move forward on our own path—knowing that our success and confidence will carry more weight than any advice we could offer.[505]

> Forgiving them doesn't make their actions acceptable, but it does absolve us from carrying around the weight of the damage they've done.

And while we're at it, let's brush up on our forgiveness skills, which life strategist Rhonda Britten describes as "a willingness to get over what you think should have happened and an acceptance of the reality of what actually happened."[506] People make mistakes. People can be thoughtless and self-absorbed and deliberately hurtful. Forgiving them doesn't make their actions acceptable, but it does absolve us from carrying around the weight of the damage they've done.

"Replaying a painful memory over and over in your head is a form of self-abuse," writes Jerose.[507] It can be hard to stay objective when we're feeling irritated or offended, but consider how much more peaceful our lives will feel if we can instead believe that most oversights are the result of forgetfulness or some old, unresolved wound that has nothing at all to do with us. Just knowing that we don't have to take things personally can help us deal with difficult people without getting upset or feeling like there is something wrong with us. Let's assume it's not intentional, even when it is.[508]

"Don't hold grudges," advises Fucarino. "Why let anyone who has wronged you have power over you?"[509] We don't need to stay in relationships with toxic people, but hanging on to the wrong they've done keeps us attached to their toxicity. Nonetheless, if they have gone to the trouble of making amends and have deliberately become more loving and respectful, all the more reason to let go of past hurts and hang on to the person—and the possibilities their efforts present.

Table 17.1. Healthy Versus Unhealthy Relationships [510]

Do you have people in your life who leave you feeling happy and uplifted? Or do you feel drained, agitated, angry, or resentful when you've spent time with them? Use the following list to compare two very different types of relationships.	
Healthy relationships are not one-sided. Both people benefit from knowing each other.	In unhealthy relationships, one person always seems to give a lot more than the other.
Healthy relationships are based on mutual respect. (Teasing is perceived by the recipient as playful, even affectionate.)	In unhealthy relationships, people ridicule one another, gossip or spread rumors, or act mean to one another. ("Teasing" is more likely to come out as an insult or putdown; perceived as hurtful.)
Healthy relationships allow each other to grow and change.	Unhealthy relationships are threatened when one person grows or changes.
Healthy relationships are not possessive.	Unhealthy relationships are threatened by other people.
Healthy relationships nourish you and add to your life.	Unhealthy relationships leave you feeling empty and drained.
Healthy relationships involve people who accept you for who you are.	Unhealthy relationships require you to act the way someone else wants you to be in order to be accepted.
Healthy relationships allow you to have your feelings.	Unhealthy relationships only accept certain feelings.

Table 17.1. Healthy Versus Unhealthy Relationships *(continued)*

Healthy relationships respect differences.	Unhealthy relationships demand conformity.
Healthy relationships are safe and secure.	In unhealthy relationships, trusts are broken, secrets are shared, and confidentialities are betrayed.
In healthy relationships, both people are committed to the relationship.	In unhealthy relationships, only one is.
Healthy relationships are not about power or status.	Unhealthy relationships look to take advantage of another person's social standing in order to improve their own.

Deepak Chopra suggests, "Think about someone in your life who leaves an open space for you to be yourself. No one is more valuable. I would rather have a pillar of trust in my life than a pillar of strength."[511]

CHAPTER 18

Moving Forward: Mind and Body

Few things would please me more than being able to offer up a cure for perfectionism, especially an easy one. As I mentioned previously, I think a more realistic (and potentially effective) approach would be to work toward becoming more aware of how this disorder affects us, and doing what we can to decrease the frequency and intensity of its impact on our lives.

The good news is that there are many ways to reach this goal, including a wide range of remedies that can help us shift our thinking and change our physical responses to stress and anxiety. Different contributors reported finding strength and comfort in a variety of healing traditions and resources, many benefitting from a mixed bag of modalities. So while it may require a bit of exploration, whatever feels safe and supportive will probably be a good choice.

The *other* good news is that change is possible. Educator Martha Kaufeldt reminds us that we can reorganize the wiring in our brain,

We can reorganize the wiring in our brain, building new brain cells and networks with changes in behavior, environment, emotions, and thinking.

building new brain cells and networks with changes in behavior, environment, emotions, and thinking. "It's empowering to know that the more you stimulate those connections, the stronger they will become," she says. "New connections practiced over time become automatic. This is great news for those who want to make big changes in their lives."

The bad news is, the process can hurt like hell. "All change is hard at first, messy in the middle, and gorgeous at the end," says leadership expert Robin Sharma.[512] Nobody likes the "hard" and "messy" parts, but sometimes it's harder and messier to try to stay where we are, frantically trying to elude change. Although many of the suggestions in this chapter are easy, relaxing, and fairly painless, modifying deeply ingrained, long-term habits can back us into corners we've managed to avoid for a long time. Stripping away the masks we've relied on to protect us is no easy feat.

"All change is hard at first, messy in the middle, and gorgeous at the end."

Given the differences in our experiences, sensitivities, and the ways in which we express our perfectionism, this journey will vary among individuals with the courage to undertake it. Let's stay open to different approaches, because even small changes can trigger big shifts. A quick-fix prescription would be dandy, but I think actual healing requires a bit of exploration to discover what resonates best and will prove most effective over time, sometimes undertaking a variety of paths to identify what feels right for us.

Sometimes a Rugged Journey

Many of the suggestions that follow offer do-it-yourself remedies, and many of these can offer an effective and immediate shift in our day and frame of mind. However, the structures on which perfectionistic beliefs and behaviors are built generally go so deep and so far back that they will be hard to get to—much less rebuild—without some fairly intensive personal work. For most of us, getting real and getting well will not be an easy intellectual exercise. "Most perfectionists find that insight into the nature of their difficulties is not sufficient for change," cautions Burns.[513]

Teversham agrees, finding it "quite a challenge to just drop this behavior by merely being aware of it. I find plenty of inner work necessary in order to get the little child inside feeling safe enough to make his or her own mistakes and let it be okay." Likewise, blogger Sam Watts notes, "You can't transform by simply hearing a description of what the end result is like, any more than you can read the menu instead of eating the meal and feel that your hunger is truly satisfied. If you're going to wake up, and to really apprehend just what it means to be integrated, whole, and ordinary in the most profound sense, you need to embark on the journey of disintegration first."[514]

And no, that's not much fun, but getting to a place where perfectionism isn't holding our life hostage will probably mean digging around in the muck of our past for a bit, which is never easy. This experience may not be necessary for everyone, and I'd never push anyone to "disintegrate," even with a great deal of support and the prospect of a healthy reintegration on the other side. But I can't write about healing strategies and not mention this process because4 at some point, people who want to get serious about extricating themselves from destructive patterns in their lives may need to walk through this fire. (I would absolutely recommend having someone—a therapist or support group, for example—to be there for anyone willing to take this step, or for anyone already in a desperate, dark place.)

Sometimes our lives can just seem to unravel. It may be a crisis, illness, loss, or some other major life change that pushes us to confront demons we have fought to keep hidden, or we may just reach a point where we simply don't have the juice to keep up the deception any longer. The meaning we have given to our life seems to collapse, and we enter what some traditions refer to as the dark night of the soul—a potentially transformational journey that, according to author and spiritual teacher Eckhart Tolle, can likewise resemble "what is conventionally called depression."[515]

Experiencing the death of our ego's notion of who we are and the loss of security we once found in old ways of thinking can provoke uncertainty, hopelessness, fear, and loss. None of our old tricks are working for us. Our mind isn't buying our version of truth and reality any more. "You are meant to arrive at a place of conceptual meaninglessness," says Tolle. "Or one could say a state of ignorance—where things lose the meaning that you had given them, which was all conditioned and cultural." As painful as this may sound, I also believe that some part of us must be hungry enough to discover the truth of who we are for this door to open. It might help to remember that as traumatic as this transformation (or "dying") can be, Tolle notes that "nothing real has actually died . . . only an illusory identity."[516]

There's a saying that often shows up in therapy and recovery circles that says, "The only way out is through." Writer and coach Robin Amos Kahn reports, "The first time I heard that I thought, 'Damn! I don't want to go through this. I want to go around it, over it, under it. I want to sleep through it, wake me up when it's over, fast forward me to happy days are here again."[517] But, as Watts observes, "Disintegration is necessary because up until the point of setting out on a path to awakening, you feel an intuitive sense of being a separate being in a world which is simultaneously familiar and foreign to you. This sense of separateness becomes utterly unbearable."[518] Or think of it this way: "For a seed to achieve its greatest expression, it must come completely undone," says Cynthia Occe. "The shell cracks. Its insides come out and everything changes. To someone who doesn't understand growth, it would look like complete destruction."[519]

Some days, it will feel like the pain will never end, like the world will never make sense again, and anyone who wants to run and hide will certainly be in good company. "You can, if you want, try to avoid the pain—drinking, drugs, sleeping, lying, stealing, cheating, shopping, sleeping around, eating gallons of ice cream, bags of potato chips, staring at the television, gambling," Kahn confirms. "You can do any or all of those things, but sooner or later the grief you are avoiding will show up in a meltdown, a pile of debt, another divorce, an illness, an accident, or any number of other possibilities."[520]

The true test will be in our willingness to go through this process without our usual anesthesia. "You have to find your raw, unconditioned tenderness and vulnerability and refuse to cover it over," advises Watts. "You must allow life to touch you. The type of surrender that is the expression of true courage is a willingness to experience whatever comes, eyes wide open, unflinching. This is what allows the disintegration process to complete itself. This is not the end of the pain, but it is the end of the old way of relating to it."[521] (One contributor noted that depending on the symptoms and experiences different people will encounter, sometimes medication will be required to function or even survive. This is an important distinction from self-medicating to numbing ourselves out.[522])

"Any treatment that works requires you to initially tolerate signifi-cant anxiety and ultimately befriend the awareness of personal imper-fection," cautions Springer.[523] For perfectionists who have invested so much in looking good and avoiding pain, this whole idea of getting real—*really* real—can introduce us to levels of vulnerability we've been protecting for a long time. But as Lamott notes, "After ten years of being sober, with huge support to express my pain and anger and shadow, the grief and tears didn't wash me away. They gave me my life back! They cleansed me, baptized me, hydrated the earth at my feet. They brought me home, to me, to the truth of me."[524] Tolle describes the potential outcome as a kind of rebirth or awakening into a deeper sense of purpose and connectedness, one that is no longer based on deception or mental constructs.[525]

Peeling back the layers of illusion, copping to whatever we've been defending, or sitting in a place of not knowing can be excruci-ating. "The first thing I tell myself is that 'dark nights of the soul' is a productive part of the cycle," reflects educator Kristie Norwood. "It feels awful [but] I often find that if I stop fighting it and just allow the pain, it passes quicker."

I've known many people who have come back from some pretty dismal, desperate places, places with little hope or promise, and ended up experiencing their greatest successes, connections, and happiness. No guarantees, but we never really know what tomorrow will bring. Nonetheless, I do want to suggest that there *is* light at the end of the tunnel, even if for much of the "dark night" experience, we may not be able to see it. But as the old saying goes, "If it feels like you're going through hell, keep moving."[526] It won't be like this forever.

Reaching Out

Perfectionists aren't great at asking for help. Needing assistance implies frailty and imperfection. "We become afraid to admit that we are hurting and struggling, because we fear that we will be seen as weak. And we can't be weak," writes educator and culture critic Josie Pickens. "How does one share her struggles with mental illness when she's convinced the world that she is strong, when she has somehow become an example to others?"[527] This is the burden of deception.

The fact is, human beings *are* imperfect, and sometimes we're weak and in pain. Trying to maintain the illusion that we are exempt from this reality is grueling, self-defeating, and frankly crazy-making. Even if we have no problem asking others to help us take care of our car, teeth, or taxes, when it comes to getting support for the things that are hurting us emotionally, socially, and psychologically, we somehow get a little squeamish about admitting that we can't do it alone.

All of us need help from time to time. "The real tragedy of reaching for perfectionism isn't that you fail to reach it, but that you fail to reach out to the people around you," observes Spencer.[528] This fear limits our access to genuine growth and healing and, more significantly, can subject us to the unfiltered influence of distorted thinking, fears, and self-loathing in the absence of a clarifying reflection and reality check. "We all go through these crises and feel like it

only happened to us," says Norwood. "When I reach out to someone
and they say, 'Oh yeah, I remember going through something like
that,' I feel relieved because I know it's just part of the process."

This validation can sometimes be enough. "When my husband
died, I had a group of friends who were available 24/7," reports air-
port security worker Judy Heck. "Having those special people who
were there 100 percent for me was crucial for my mental health.
The dark nights were a little brighter because of them." Optometrist
Kathy Hayes describes a friend who survived a very difficult work
situation by looking at loving, encouraging texts from her husband
throughout the day. "She said it got her through [this transition]."

"Ask for help" advises Luria. "Ask for easy stuff and ask for big,
stupid, outlandish stuff. The worst that can happen is someone will
say no, and that's really not as bad as it sounds." Nearly all perfectionists could use a lesson or two in simply receiving—which connects to old deservingness issues—whether offers of help or a simple
compliment. We are so used to showing our not-needy face to the
world that we even have trouble accepting help when it's offered.
Luria invites us to stop saying "No, that's okay," or "No, I've got it,"
any time someone offers to give us a hand. "Just say 'Yes, thank you,'"
instead, she suggests.

We also need to recognize when we need more than a friend's ear.
Pickens cautions, "Your girlfriends, as well-meaning and supportive
as they are, have their own Superwoman capes to throw off, and they
honestly don't know the answers either. Seeing a mental health professional to confide in and ask direction from can mean the difference
between life or death—for real, for real."[529] Yes, cost can be an issue.
Fortunately, there are free and low-cost options listed online and are
often available through employers, religious institutions, community
organizations, health care facilities, or schools in most communities.

And many free recovery programs and groups can help directly or with possible referrals.[530]

For anyone who's been living behind a mask, once the façade starts to crumble, the need for professional help can become critical for simply helping us hold our lives together. Systems engineer Dennis Mutchler shares, "When I finally reached the point where I knew that I would have to tell my wife that I was gay, I realized that I would have to blow up everything in my life and then put it back together again." After years of trying to figure things out on his own, Mutchler realized that the pressure was taking its toll. "I really felt that if I didn't do something, I would be seriously ill or dead due to the stress and anxiety."

Never having been to a therapist before, he was surprised that during the first session, he "sat there and talked for two and a half hours—a lot of that time in tears." Over the course of the next several months, the therapist helped him work through this transition and identify what he needed to do. Mutchler also confided in a couple close friends who assured him that he could tell people and not lose them as friends. "That eliminated one of the big fears that I had—that I would end up alone."

Which brings us back to the coping strategies we developed to prevent rejection and abandonment in the first place, and why we may need help dismantling them. Ann Smith talks about the early stages of healing, when perfectionists begin to identify what's not working in their lives and give it a name. This step "brings some relief from the guilt and shame of struggling alone." It also assures patients that they did not "get this way" all by themselves and that the compulsive pattern of perfectionistic behavior, which had served them well, "no longer makes sense." Smith notes that, although talking and listening to others in group settings can challenge perfectionists, she also asserts that they "benefit greatly from reaching out for support and take a giant leap forward when they begin to share with other imperfect people."[531]

A professional therapist or counselor can mirror a more realistic middle-ground view back to us when we start thinking of ourselves in black-and-white terms. This is especially important after we've gone through some tough times and feel like we'll never get our mojo back. "Sometimes all it takes to get things rolling in the wrong direction is one or two setbacks," says Leman. "We begin to see ourselves as losers," subject to forces that are aligned against us, which set us up for feelings of "defeat and futility."[532] A good therapist or group can keep us from getting stuck there, and help us find what we need to start moving forward again.

Oh, and if the thought of self-harm or suicide starts looking attractive, even if for a second, pick up the phone and reach out for help—immediately.[533] Problems nearly always turn out to be temporary ones. There are silver linings everywhere and even great losses can lead to positive connections and solutions we can't imagine right now. "Remember that you always have options," remind Adderholdt and Goldberg. "You can correct mistakes. You can change your mind. You can switch directions from a dead-end road to a positive alternate path. You can rack up failures and still be a success . . . The only time you don't have options is when you're not around to exercise them."[534]

Screening and Disengaging

Refusing to reach out because we're afraid of looking weak, needy, and imperfect is only one factor in our resistance. If our past efforts to seek help have left us feeling burned, betrayed, or abandoned, we're likely to resist asking for support because we anticipate similarly pointless or painful outcomes. (Remember, perfectionists are really good at assumptions and generalizations.)

Being at our most vulnerable can indeed expose us to opportunistic people who see our crisis as an opportunity to impose their opinions or agendas, feed their need for superiority by blaming or criticizing, or minimize or dismiss our feelings to protect themselves from our pain (or from feeling responsible for fixing our situation). So the times we need these connections the most end up being the times we are inclined to do so the least. Rather than shutting down, how about developing a bit of discretion when it comes to the people we might want to approach instead? Because, as Brené Brown cautions, when we reach out to the wrong people, "they can easily become one more piece of the flying debris in an already dangerous storm."[535]

When I'm feeling shaky, frightened, hopeless, or lost, I may not know exactly what I need, but I've gotten pretty clear about what I *don't* need. For example, if I trust people enough to open up, I don't need them to cheer me up, distract me, or compete with me by turning the conversation around to their problems. I don't want to hear how good I have it and for heaven's sake, please hold off on any sentence that starts with "You're lucky . . ."

I don't want advice or pity, nor do I need anyone to own my feelings for me. I don't need to be fixed and I don't need others to feel responsible for fixing me. I definitely don't want to hear about how I got myself into this mess or how I've disappointed people, nor do I want to have to defend or explain why something is bothering me. These filters really narrow down the field because these are default (if non-supportive) responses that most of us know all too well.[536] I don't need all my friends to understand these requirements or be able to honor them, but when I'm in pain and need to connect with someone, I'm going to reach out to the ones who can.

Sometimes, what really, really helps is just having someone who can hold a space for me to just be where I am at the moment. Someone who can listen, someone who can tolerate my sadness, anger, confusion, fear, or regret without taking those feelings on or freaking out because of them. (The last thing I need is to have to care-take someone else when I'm struggling.) So while part of my journey has been about learning how to ask for these things, I also have to pay attention to responses that compound my stress, and to recognize—and avoid—non-helpful attempts to help.

We are *all* entitled to this level of support. If our friends have the skill and willingness to provide what we need, that's great. But this is often where a trained and caring professional will be a lifesaver. (Likewise for a therapy group that operates by these or similar protocols.) Not all will be a good match, but let's give it a bit of time. Watch the temptation to bail. Is there a genuine threat or lack of safety happening? Are things moving faster than we can handle them with the level of support available? Or are we just getting nervous about getting too close to things we don't want to face?

Even day-to-day, non-crisis interactions deserve similar consideration. Let's get very selective about who benefits from the gifts of our time and energy, and start shrugging off even lifelong connections when we realize that they are sapping a bit too much of either. "I've never regretted leaving a job where the stress and negativity were costing me my sanity and health," said one contributor. "Same thing with distancing myself from friends who always pulled me down. That just gave me time to meet new people and make stronger, more meaningful connections." McGill reminds us, "There is a difference between giving up and strategic disengagement."[537] Or as Toni Morrison suggests, "You wanna fly, you got to give up the shit that weighs you down."[538]

Let's also monitor our exposure to the news and social media, making friends with the fast forward, mute, block, delete, or unfriend buttons available to us. People and experiences have an impact on our energy and goodwill and it's hard to inoculate ourselves against constant negativity. "When we are on a true journey of embodying our Soul and being of service in our own unique

> People and experiences have an impact on our energy and goodwill and it's hard to inoculate ourselves against constant negativity.

way, we are invited to let go of everything that does not make us feel like a true authentic Self," says guide for personal transformation Polona Somrak.[539]

And for those of us who have been told that our spirit is a little too bright, maybe that's the signal to turn it up even brighter and keep shining it on. This may prove to be a great way to screen out the people who are put off or unsettled by who we are. Trust that the ones who stay around are the ones worth keeping.

When We Really Need Help

+ Resist the urge to isolate. The times we need to reach out the most are usually the times we want to reach out the least.

+ Be proactive. The best time to prepare for a crisis is when we're not in the middle of one. Make a list of available community services and crisis or suicide hotlines—phone numbers and addresses, including national emergency numbers in case you're not at home. Keep a copy on your phone, at home, and in your car.

+ We all need "safe" connections in our lives, so include a list of trusted friends or family members on your list. "Be honest with your close friends, even if it's just one person," advises former medical social worker Nancy Knickerbocker. Be careful to choose someone you believe will be able to listen without judging or advising, someone who doesn't have agendas for how you should feel or act. Let at least one person know what's been going on, preferably before you're in full crisis mode.

+ Even if cost of treatment is an issue, Knickerbocker says, "there are so many self-help groups out there that you can reach out and get support." Open 12-step meetings welcome anyone who wishes to attend. There are no fees or signing in, nor is there a requirement to talk. Even if you're not an alcoholic, there are meetings for workaholics, codependents, and people with eating disorders— which will cover a pretty big segment of the perfectionist population. There are also meetings for people who live with alcohol and substance abusers.

+ If addiction (to any substance or behavior) is an issue, consider dealing with this problem as a good starting point. While I suspect that it really doesn't matter where we jump into this loop, I do believe that it's hard to heal something we're constantly trying to numb or cover up.

+ Allow people who want to help to be there for you. Nobody is strong all the time, and you don't have to do this alone.

+ If the person you call isn't available, or if it doesn't feel like you're able to connect in the way you need at that moment, *call someone else*. Keep calling until you find someone who has what you need. (Understand that people have their own stresses, and if you happen to catch them at a time that they can't be there for you in the way you'd like, don't take it personally. Cut them some slack and try the next number on your list.)

+ Get out of your physical environment. A change of scenery can help you get out of your head. Licensed professional counselor, Loretta Maase, suggested that there are times when going to a movie or a good walk can also help shift perspective and reduce stress.

+ Breathe. Feel your feet connected to the ground. Lie down and listen to soft, soothing music. Stretch. Do whatever you can to get your physical body out of panic mode. (It's not a bad idea to learn some of the calming techniques before you need them.)

+ Help someone. Get out and do something for another person. It doesn't have to be any more heroic than holding a door or smiling. Offer a brief, generic compliment if you feel like talking. Even a simple gesture can shift the focus from your situation for a bit, and may even help pull another person out of a space worse than the one you're in.

+ If you call an emergency number and need more help than you're getting (or are advised that you can't get in for an appointment for several weeks), Alfano advises claiming to be a "danger to self or others," to get help immediately.

+ Let's be careful about easy access to quick fixes. Changing long-held beliefs and behaviors is the goal, and achieving this goal takes time, often more than we want to give it. We may have to look around and try several different approaches, but please, let's not settle for treating the symptoms alone.[540]

Going Within

As previously noted, change—the really effective, lasting healing we seek—rarely happens overnight. Even flashes of insight, realizations, and epiphanies demand some time for us to quietly process and internalize what we can learn from them. Perfectionists are so good at being busy that simply sitting and being quiet (and—*gasp!*—unproductive) for a few minutes feels like some creepy form of cheating.

The amount of recognition and rewards some of us have gotten for living our life at a full gallop reinforces a pace that few human bodies can sustain for long. Throw in a potential encounter with the scary aspects of our emotional and psychological lives, which we've been dodging for years, and it's a wonder that any of us manage to come

> More "doing" is not the answer. So I want to mention the value of taking some time to just *be*—quiet, alone, deliberately not *doing*.

up for air at all. More "doing" is not the answer. So I want to mention the value of taking some time to just *be*—quiet, alone, deliberately not *doing*. This can be incredibly uncomfortable and unfamiliar for perfectionists, so here are a few suggestions that might help.

"Become a master of the pause," urges Rechtschaffen, "whether saying grace before a meal or taking a few quiet unrushed breaths before a meeting or phone call. Find pause breaks during your day to reset to a relaxed rhythm. Listen to some classical or peaceful music. Learn to shift your rhythm instead of being caught in high speed all the time."[541] Somrak recognizes the need for silence "to hear the whispers of our Soul and the calling of our Spirit Self," and the solitude we need to connect with this guidance.[542]

Cameron likewise notes, "An artist must have down time, time to do nothing."[543] Unfortunately, in perfectionist-speak, the word "nothing" generally connotes only doing two or three things at once, or maybe doing something not especially productive like playing computer games or scrolling through social media for hours on end. (I'm guilty of both, and while these activities may be relaxing and enjoyably distracting, they are not the same as *reflective inactivity*— disconnected from people and devices, distractions, and noise.) "Almost everything will work again if you unplug it for a few minutes," observes Lamott, "including you."[544]

Because of our conditioning, some of us may actually need to add "take a break to do absolutely nothing" to our to-do list, so we'll have something to check off when we're done. We start wherever we are, and if we need to turn "doing nothing" into a task to get to it, I'm hardly in a position to object. We need time to decompress and recharge, and many of us won't make time for things that aren't on our calendar or lists. Creating time to disconnect and be alone with our thoughts is far more important than how we get there.

There are several ways to make this work. Norwood extols the benefits of being outside. "I once camped outside for a whole year. I had just made it through a life-altering illness and I was lost. Being out in nature brought me home to myself." Even a little fresh air can be a tremendous shot in the arm, and being in pretty much any kind of nature, whether strolling along a beach, walking up desert hills, or hanging out in an urban park, can put a whole different spin on our thoughts and attitude.

For some of us, going within takes a more tactile route. Journaling has been a way for me to process experiences, identify problems, explore solutions, and over time, discern patterns and changes in my beliefs, attitudes, and behaviors. For more than five decades, my journal has served as an anchor, pressure valve, and "portable psychiatrist," especially helpful in grounding me when I've gone through crises and major turning points in my life. (Although most entries are fairly mundane and occasionally sporadic, during especially difficult periods of my life, I could fill an entire 120-page, college-ruled notebook in a week or two.)[545]

Primary teacher Pamela Victoria Garrett recounts that after growing up amid abuse and addiction, "the best thing I ever did was start a co-journal with my best friend. I would keep the journal for a week, write everything I was feeling in it and any questions I might want

> We need time to decompress and recharge, and many of us won't make time for things that aren't on our calendar or lists. Creating time to disconnect and be alone with our thoughts is far more important than how we get there.

answered but didn't necessarily want to talk about out loud." Her friend would do the same. "We talked, sure, but this was our way of communicating about the huge deep, dark stuff you keep to yourself. I've never felt so free in communicating. It really got me through some dark times." Mutchler also kept a private blog as well as a hand-written diary. "The process of putting my thoughts on paper was more intimate because I tended to express my feelings there easier than online [where] I was slightly more guarded. But the process of writing was the thing that helped."

While journaling has, at times, offered me a sort of salvation, I recognize that it may not be an attractive or appropriate option for everyone. Some contributors swear by drawing, doodling, or mind-mapping (to visually organize thoughts and information), for example. Playing a musical instrument, knitting, spinning wool, fixing something that's needed attention, or other forms of crafting, for example, offer alternative kinesthetic outlets and can be a great way to ground emotional agitation.

Among her recommendations for therapeutic strategies for per-fectionists, Adderholdt includes creative visualization, describing the process as "picturing changes in behavior in one's mind as a step toward changing that behavior."[546] Often practiced as a meditation to imagine multiple aspects of achieving a certain goal or performance level, we can also create specific, concrete visual images to help us conceptualize positive outcomes we desire.

"When I was going through treatment for advanced cancer, I cre-ated a vision board to remind me of my goal—to regain my health and vitality," recalls writer Elizabeth Schoch. "I used uplifting pictures I cut from magazines and also encouraging phrases." Propping up her vision board so she could see it from her bed as she was recovering from surgery, she also taped encouraging messages and quotes around her bed. Currently in remission, Schoch recalls, "I made a decision to heal, and my vision board and quotes helped me get there."

Having made a number of vision boards or collages with images of things I wanted to achieve or create in my life (or sometimes things for which I was grateful), I see great value in this process. Over the years, I've gotten a lot more selective about what I add to the mix. Choose carefully. The hammock on a beautiful beach is a healthy image for me to crave, though the images of young, tall, and impossibly thin women have (fortunately) lost their allure—now replaced with photos of healthy, fit, strong, happy women much closer to my age and build.

Knickerbocker expresses concern about the degree to which technology has created a sense of disconnection for so people, many of whom lack the skills or experience for reaching out and connecting with others. She also sees "a tremendous spiritual punch" in mental health crises. In her current work as a quality assurance specialist in the medical field, Knickerbocker claims to live "in a world governed by precision." She balances the demands and stresses of her job "with meditation, spiritual readings, and connections with friends she can talk with about things that matter."

The idea of "going within" is not a one-time trick, nor is it only for times of crisis. In fact, I believe that the time we take to sit quietly without thoughts, feelings, and aspirations can help keep frantic feelings of overwhelm at bay. Patience will be a tremendous asset here. Martha Kaufeldt encourages her seminar participants "to use the phrase 'not yet.' It's such a hopeful thought. It says you will get there—you just aren't there *yet*." These words can be especially helpful when we slip into black-and-white thinking, questioning our adequacy or feeling like a failure. Shifting our thinking to "not yet" leaves a lot of doors open. Kaufeldt asserts that we can find great comfort and empowerment from the assurance of knowing that we are on our way.

Talking It Out

My first venture into a therapeutic environment consisted primarily of conversations with a counselor who gave me a safe place to confront what wasn't working in my life. Initially, I believe I was looking for ways to make other people responsible for these problems. But doors gradually opened and lights started coming on, revealing how my patterns of thinking, expecting, and interacting—what I'd always seen as normal and *right*—might be playing a part.

Facing the outcomes of beliefs we've held onto most tenaciously is where many of us are most tempted to cut and run. But these conversations, especially in a trusting relationship with someone who can gently nudge us from destructive patterns and errors in reasoning, can eventually lead us to thinking in terms of things being black or not-black, rather than black or white.[547]

There are dozens of approaches to psychotherapy in which talking with a trained practitioner or group will, over time and with a good match, result in positive, functional alternatives to more familiar harmful patterns in our behaviors, beliefs, compulsions, thoughts, or feelings.[548] During this process, we may be challenged to question what we have held as our truths, gain new perspectives, and release or transform ideas that are no longer relevant, helpful, or true. We may begin to identify the fears against which we've been defending,

There are dozens of approaches to psychotherapy in which talking with a trained practitioner or group will, over time and with a good match, result in positive, functional alternatives to more familiar harmful patterns in our behaviors, beliefs, compulsions, thoughts, or feelings.

depersonalize what is beyond our control, and start to recognize the ways in which perfectionism is, and has been, working to our disadvantage.[549]

Therapeutic techniques might include things like exposure therapy (to gradually develop a tolerance for flaws and imperfections), response prevention (to stop engaging in perfectionistic behaviors), communication training (to identify patterns of judging, criticizing, or attempting to control others), examining the evidence (to confirm or disprove perfectionistic beliefs), changing cognitive processes (to alter perceptions, beliefs, or wishes that result in anxiety or depression), bibliotherapy (using content and characters in books to facilitate recovery), distress tolerance, emotional regulation, managing self-talk, learning self-acceptance and self-compassion, or learning to identify and set priorities.

Further, changing verbal patterns by using believable coping statements like "It's okay to make mistakes" or "It's okay if some people don't like me" can help, as can shifting fixed-mindset phrases like "I can't do this" to growth-mindset language: "I haven't been very successful with this but I could improve with help and practice." And Beck recommends monitoring thoughts and jotting down self-critical judgments, recording comments and thoughts that say, "I'm a loser, I'm stupid, I'm ugly." She advises that "that process alone may decrease the intensity and frequency" and suggests noting when and where these feelings occur to try to identify and modify patterns.[550]

Finally, I'd like to briefly mention the potential benefits of working with others in a group setting. Sharing our stories, especially our secrets, can lift an enormous burden, although listening and hearing other people's experiences can be even more reassuring and validating. One contributor found that a 12-step group for children of alcoholics offered her an opportunity "to be around others whose parents were toxic." She relates that she felt very lonely about being voluntarily estranged from her family of origin, "like it meant something was wrong with me." Attending meetings confirmed that "there are plenty of other folks who are right there with me, but I didn't know that for a long time." Plus, she added, "There's a *lot* for perfectionists to learn from those meetings."

Descriptions and recommendations of specific programs exceed the scope of this book; however, according to psychologist Bruce Wampold, the type of therapy is far less of a factor in the effectiveness of the treatment than the patient's faith in the treatment's effectiveness, the therapist's ability to understand and communicate with the patient, and the quality of a collaborative, trusting relationship between the practitioner and the patient (or what he calls the "therapeutic alliance").[551] In other words, the connection is key.

Beyond the Analytical

Some perfectionists identify so strongly with the image we project that breaking through the deception, which can feel very real, may require strategies that go beyond intellectual discourse and left-brain oriented exercises. "Perfectionists can be smart, manipulative, and tricky," noted one contributor. "We know how to play the game and say what we think other people want to hear."

If we're not fully satisfied with the progress we're making in our talk therapy work (or not comfortable pursuing that route), we have a variety of alternative modalities we can explore or add to help us reach our recovery goals. Many of these therapies employ sensory approaches involving touch, pressure points, deep tissue massage, creative expression, eye movement, music and sound, or our responses to different scents or colors, for example.

These body-oriented approaches can do an end-run past our cognitive and verbal defenses, cutting to the core of our issues. "I recommend feeling therapies where people can cry and don't remain in their heads, intellectualizing issues endlessly," shared Joanna Folino, a professor of theatre, film, and literature. "I tend to hold pain in my body, so whatever works to move it out physically eventually leads to psychic healing as well."

Multidimensional or combination-type approaches look at factors such as our early history, belief systems, and behaviors, along with our physiological symptoms and even cultural influences. A number of contributors shared successes they had using a variety of healing strategies, integrating body work, energy work, and relaxation techniques (with or without traditional cognitive approaches) to balance thoughts and emotions, reduce fear, desensitize responses to traumatic memories, and directly access stress and survival centers of the midbrain without the more rational, analytical frontal lobes getting in the way.[552] Although not necessarily designed to target perfectionism, any therapy that touches on this disorder, including its origins or effects, is probably worthy of consideration.

I'm a fan of mixing it up from time to time, and have tried various types of cognitive and somatic therapies—those related to the body as separate from the mind. I can vouch for my experience with a handful of the hundreds of remedies available, including the progress or success I've had with them at various points in my own journey. We each have our own combination of belief systems, traumas, and defenses to work through, and what has brought relief and healing to me may not be

> We each have our own combination of belief systems, traumas, and defenses to work through, and what has brought relief and healing to me may not be an ideal mix for anyone else.

an ideal mix for anyone else. The point of including these sections is to encourage some exploration so that we can each find the path (or combination of paths) that will work best for us. Any road that feels safe and leads to something we would define as healing is a good road.

Shifting Out of Stress: Moving Around, Tuning It Down, Lending a Hand

A friend of mine is a recovering bulimic who still struggles with exercising compulsively. Not surprisingly, we met at the gym years ago. I thought of her as soon as I started to process what I want this section to say because while exercise and movement are important healing remedies for anyone in a human body, they can easily fall into the *abuse* and *addiction* columns for some perfectionists. So let me be clear: I'm not talking about better ways to sculpt our abs or slim our thighs. This is about exercise, movement, and relaxation as healing modalities, that is, ways to bring a degree of balance and grounded-ness to our physical and psychological lives.

This is a tricky topic, simply because of the number of perfectionists who struggle with food and body image issues. One self-proclaimed food addict recalls, "At the same time that I was learning to medicate my emotions with excess food, I was developing a fear and loathing of gym class." He recalls how the shame of being the fattest kid in class and, naturally, the last one called for teams has hounded him throughout his life. "When it comes to overeating and underexercising, I find that perfectionistic thinking can fuel me to act out with both of these behaviors," he says, using them as excuses to "not bother" since he can't perform either perfectly.[553]

So let's be careful here. This is about disengaging from destructive patterns, not creating new ones. "In my quest for perfection, I feel that my own acceptance of my uniqueness has only occurred after much reflection on the time spent chasing the impossible," reflects education specialist in palliative medicine Venita Kaye. "Healthy meals and exercise are essential for me, not to achieve 'skinniest,' but to be healthy in mind, body, and spirit."

We all need to move. Having been the kid who would much rather stay inside to read or color than go out for recess, this whole exercise thing has always taken me way out of my comfort zone. But as an educator, I know my brain works better when I move. Even a few minutes' walk can clear my head and get my thinking (and writing) unstuck. And as far as stress management goes, I've walked into a yoga or dance fitness class feeling wound up and crazy and walked out laughing and back to my old, good-natured self.

Although my default activities will probably always be more sedentary—not that knitting or beading or spinning aren't incredibly grounding and relaxing—I'm well aware that this body feels better when given the chance to stretch, walk, dance, or swim on a fairly regular basis. When I start sliding into old perfectionistic habits, getting lost fixing details nobody will ever see, writing in circles and losing track of what I'm trying to say, or spending way more time on a task than it deserves, that's when it's time to walk away from whatever I'm doing—and move.

Stretching—especially after sitting far too long as I've been working on this book—improves concentration and blood flow and increases oxygen to every part of my body. Even a short walk around the corner can get the left and right sides of my brain talking to one another, which shifts me to from detail obsessions to a big-picture perspective, rendering creative and cognitive tasks a little easier when I come back to my work.[554]

"Exercise releases 'happy hormones' that reduce stress," says Reid. "Exercise is a way to keep fit and healthy lengthening your life span."[555]

We don't need to go to a gym, although I have thankfully found some that are welcoming, accepting, and non-competitive—a much safer experience than some of us remember from school. Despite my occasional skepticism about it never being too late (for me) to start something new in this arena, I discovered a dance class at age fifty-nine where I didn't have to be especially good but somehow got better the more I went, and I always manage to have fun.[556]

Fortunately, if dancing or group activities don't appeal, there's always a good walk. Go fast, go slow, five minutes, a couple hours. Just move. Neuroscientist Andrew Tate claims that walking makes us more creative and increases productivity. It doesn't seem to matter if we're using a treadmill or walking outdoors. "A simple walk outside can aid your creative brain if you find yourself stuck at a desk and unable to elicit the next bright spark. Instead of sitting, waiting for inspiration to strike, head outside for five minutes and see if the extra blood flow can get the creative juices flowing."[557] Walking with the specific intention of appreciating the beauty in nature, listening for different sounds around us, or looking for a variety of colors, shapes, and textures can get us out of our head, distance us from obsessions, and shift us into a space of gratitude and calm.[558]

As specific exercise programs go, yoga came up on a lot of people's lists as a way to slow down the frenetic pace of daily life. I would have to agree. Years ago, yoga helped me stop smoking (mostly because I started feeling really dumb lighting up after an hour of conscious deep breathing). More recently, even in classes where the only pose I could do with any degree of competence required little more than lying on the floor, I *still* felt better after the class. Yoga has also been used successfully with children with behavioral problems and attention deficit hyperactivity disorder (ADHD), as well as with combat veterans with post-traumatic stress disorder (PTSD), so let's consider the therapeutic possibilities for perfectionists as well.[559]

Any relaxation technique can help. "Meditating silences your mind and helps you find inner peace," writes Fucarino. "You don't have to be a zen master to pull it off. Happy people know how to silence their minds anywhere and anytime they need to calm their nerves."[560] A student prone to panic attacks suggests working to break the cycle of thinking about the same fear over and over. He recommends relaxation breathing, even for a few minutes, cold water on the wrist or back of the neck, and remembering, "This too shall pass."[561]

Eric Katz offered suggestions for students prone to anxiety and stress. He included relaxation breathing and muscle relaxation, drinking water to ensure hydration and manage stress better, exercising or even eating spicy food as a source of endorphin release, taking a warm bath or shower, and avoiding caffeine and nicotine, which can increase anxiety. He also recommended taking a break from the stressful situation and moving to another spot or room. Also on his list was listening to music, drawing, writing, or hanging out with your pet.[562]

Social worker Debra Sugar offered another angle. "One word: laugh! Laugh at a dumb TV show, or a silly joke, or your own foibles —it doesn't matter what. Just find something that makes you laugh at least a little bit every day!" Kristie Norwood, who is a certified Laughter Yoga instructor (and who has one of the best laughs of anyone I've ever known), includes laughter on her list of helpful remedies as well. Learning how to lighten up and not take ourselves, or our imperfections, so incredibly seriously is a pretty good idea for anyone with perfectionistic tendencies.

Other contributors weighed in with a wide range of ideas for healing. Special education teacher Tabitha Hall's "lifesaving formula" includes avoiding snacks, alcohol, negative people, and too much TV.

She also recommends exercising, interacting with others, and some sort of artistic expression. Cramer suggests music to soothe the soul, connect with memories, and express past and current feelings.[563] (I personally find music a great companion for workouts and on walks, often keeping me motivated and moving longer than I would have lasted otherwise.)

Finally, I'd like to add helping others to this list. Sometimes the best way to get out of our own head and disconnect from our problems and stress is by doing service for others. I add this with caution, as many perfectionists confuse helping with self-sacrifice. That said, service can be as simple as making time to truly listen to another human being.

Validating someone else's experience can be a generous and wonderful gift. Retired family therapist Stan Davis found that young people who had been mistreated by their peers confirm the benefits of hearing from others that the mean behavior was inappropriate and wrong. This validation confirmed that the person who had been targeted was not deserving of the mistreatment—a very welcome and much-appreciated message for anyone who's been on the receiving end of harassment or abuse.

"Do for others what you want for yourself," encourages Reid. "Helping someone else will give you a feeling of satisfaction and worthiness. Besides we all could do with a helping hand at times. Be that person."[564] Good advice for us all, perfectionists or not, especially if we give graciously without any expectation of recognition, results, or reward. Giving of our imperfect selves—a kind word, courteous gesture, or a genuine smile—can change the world. And it can connect us to the humanness and need for connection in us all. "No one can measure the effects of a single act of giving," said scholar Taitetsu Unno, "for its repercussions are beyond our limited imagination."[565]

Starting Now

Every day we are given offers us certain choices about our priorities and attitudes, what we're going to do with our time, thoughts, and energy. Photographer Suzanne Sagmeister offers this pointer: "You can spend your life worrying about what you look like, or you can throw love around like glitter at a three-year-old's art party. The choice is yours." Where is our focus and sense of purpose—even just for today? "Mother Teresa didn't walk around complaining about her thighs," Sagmeister adds. "She had shit to do."[566]

As do we all. Let's be remembered for something besides having the cleanest house or the best hair or the highest grades in our class. We are so much more than that, no matter how others judge us. "Don't allow other people to tell you that you're too old or . . . you're not smart enough," advises clinical neuropsychologist Mario Martinez. "Those are admonitions that have nothing to do with who you are. It has to do with the [people] who are shaping or shaped who you are." Based on his work with people around the world who have lived to and past 100 years old, he believes, "The present is never too late to make changes."[567]

So can we please stop chasing perfection? It doesn't exist, won't last when we think we've found it, and will create all sorts of problems for us along the way. Help is available. Change is possible, as is self-acceptance and the kind of love that doesn't take away from who we are or came to be.

> Let's be remembered for something besides having the cleanest house or the best hair or the highest grades in our class. We are so much more than that, no matter how others judge us.

> "The present is never too late to make changes."

"When all is said and done, I'll know I lived my life well. Not because I was kind or wise or good-hearted or right or holy or perfect. But because I was whole, real, honest, open, and willing to grow and to share my true heart with the world," writes Courtney Walsh.

"That's why I came. That's why I stay. That's how I want to be remembered. Not as the best person. Just as the best me."[568]

That's the goal. That is why we're here.

> "That's why I came. That's why I stay. That's how I want to be remembered. Not as the best person. Just as the best me."

NOT

Poem by Erin Hanson[569]

You are not your age,

Nor the size of clothes you wear.

You are not a weight,

Or the color of your hair.

You are not your name,

Or the dimples in your cheeks,

You are all the books you read,

And all the words you speak,

You are your croaky morning voice,

And the smiles you try to hide,

You're the sweetness in your laughter,

And every tear you've cried,

You're the songs you sing so loudly,

When you know you're all alone,

You're the places that you've been to,

And the one that you call home,

You're the things that you believe in,

And the people that you love,

You're the photos in your bedroom,

And the future you dream of,

You're made of so much beauty,

But it seems that you forgot,

When you decided that you were defined,

By all the things you're not.

NOTES

I n the two years during which I was exploring the various topics
that appear in this book, I discovered an enormous amount of
material through various sources. Books, magazines, and printed
journal articles offer stable reference information. So does the information contributed by individuals in interviews, surveys, and personal conversations. (To streamline the size of this project, their
names have been listed in the acknowledgments rather than adding
their contributions to the footnotes.)

Unfortunately, because of the ever-changing nature of the Internet, it is possible that the URL that yielded a valuable piece of information for me may change or no longer be available at some point
in the future. I do want to assure you that all website addresses were
accurate and working at the time this manuscript was submitted.

Chapter 1: "What's Wrong with Perfectionism?"

1 Paul Hewitt, quoted in Etienne Benson, "The Many Faces of Perfectionism." Posted
November 2003 (Vol. 34, No. 10, print page 18) on the *American Psychological Association*
website *http://www.apa.org/monitor/nov03/manyfaces.aspx*.

2 Alfred de Musset, quoted on Paul Hewitt's *Perfectionism and Psychopathology Lab* website
http://hewittlab.psych.ubc.ca/.

3 Thomas Greenspon, "'Healthy Perfectionism' Is an Oxymoron," *Journal of Secondary Gifted
Education*, Prufrock Press (Vol. 11, No. 4): 197-208. Posted on the *Davidson Institute* website.
No date, *http://www.davidsongifted.org/db/Articles_id_10486.aspx*.

4   Anne Lamott, Facebook post, May 12, 2014. *https://www.facebook.com/AnneLamott/posts/485327 514930230?fref=nf*.

5   Craig Ferguson. Quote from an interview on August 8, 2014 on his television program, *The Late Late Show with Craig Ferguson* (CBS).

6   Penelope Trunk, "Perfectionism Is a Disease. Here's How to Beat It." Posted on Penelope Trunk's website, Oct. 19, 2010. *http://blog.penelopetrunk.com/2010/10/19/bnet-column-perfectionism -is-a-disease-beres-how-to-beat-it/*.

7   F. Forrester Church, quoted in Lata Jagtiani, "The Trap of Perfectionism." Posted June 26, 2002 on the *Boloji* website. *http://www.boloji.com/index.cfm?md=Content&sd=Articles&ArticleID= 3218;* also quoted in Kelly Ann Haker, "The Ultimate Price for Perfection: The Relationship Between Suicidal Ideation and Perfectionism." Posted Oct. 10, 2008, on the *Vanderbilt University* website. *http://healthpsych.psy.vanderbilt.edu/2008/PerfectionismSuicide.htm*.

8   Christine Carter, "Perfectionism Is a Disease." Posted August 30, 2008 on the *Greater Good* website *http://greatergood.berkeley.edu/raising_happiness/post/perfectionism_is_a_disease*.

Chapter 2: The Culture of Perfectionism

9   Kimbriel Dean, "The Culture of Perfectionism: How It Affects You." Blog on the *Ignite. me* website. Posted Apr. 26, 2013, *http://ignite.me/articles/culture/the-culture-of-perfectionism-how-it -affects-you/*.

10 Although most of the clips I've seen have involved women, male models are subjected to the same "improvements." Model CJ Richards compares Photoshop enhancements to special effects in movies. And while admitting "that society would be better off without retouching" (including a reference to the "mental disorders and eating disorders" he has seen), he recognizes this trend as a way of life. "So accept it and know that this is actually a real person underneath all of the computerized effects that they're adding in," he says. Quoted in Rebecca Adams, "Male Model On Photoshop: 'You Understand That This Isn't Real . . . So Accept It.'" *http://www.huffingtonpost.com/2014/01/23/male-model -photoshop_n_4650816.html*.

11 Jean Kilbourne, "Killing Us Softly 4: Advertising's Image of Women." On the *Upworthy* website *http://www.upworthy.com/5-minutes-of-what-the-media-actually-does-to-women-8?c=bw1*.

12 Monica Ramirez Basco. *Never Good Enough: Freeing Yourself from the Chains of Perfectionism*. (New York: The Free Press, 1999): 10.

13 Laura Willard, introduction to 37-second video showing an example of this transformation on the *Upworthy* website. *http://www.upworthy.com/see-why-we-have-an-absolutely-ridiculous- standard-of-beauty-in-just-37-seconds?c=ufb1*.

14 Franchesca Ramsey, "These 4 regular guys put on designer underwear, and I'm officially sold. Fashion industry? Take note." Posted on the *Upworthy* website. *http://www.upworthy .com/these-4-regular-guys-put-on-designer-underwear-and-im-officially-sold-fashion-industry-take-note*. "This photo series shows what men's underwear ads might look like if they featured 'regular' bodies."

15 "Human Ken Doll Goes Under the Knife for 113th Surgery." Article on *Inside Edition* website. Posted April 29, 2013, *http://www.insideedition.com/headlines/6243-human-ken-doll-goes-under -the-knife-for-113th-surgery*. This individual has spent $150,000 on muscle implants and facial reconstruction.

16 "Man Undergoes Extensive Plastic Surgery to Look Like Justin Bieber, Spends $100,000 in 5 Years." Posted Oct. 19, 2013, on *Huffington Post* website *http://www.huffingtonpost.com/2013/10 /19/plastic-surgery-justin-bieber-100k_n_4128563.html.*

17 Stephan Rechtschaffen, "Five Tips to Help You Stop Rushing." Blog on the *Huffington Post* website, courtesy of the Omega Institute. Posted Aug. 11, 2013, at *http://www.huffingtonpost. com/omega-institute-for-holistic-studies/live-in-the-moment_b_3684291.html.*

18 "How to Stay Stressed." Tips from a bookmark distributed by De Anza College, Cupertino, CA. Blog on Jane Bluestein's website. Posted May 5, 2013, *http://janebluestein.com/2013/ how-to-stay-stressed/.*

19 Julia Cameron, *The Artist's Way* (New York: Jeremy P. Tarcher/Putnam Books, 1992), 166.

20 Liesel Teversham, *No Problem: The Upside of Saying No.* (Fish Hoek, South Africa: Kima Global Publishers, 2013), 11. From unpublished manuscript shared prior to publication.

21 Elicia Brown, "A Woman's Guide to Reducing Stress: Being Imperfect is Perfectly Fine." Posted Spring 2012 on the *Jewish Women* website *http://www.jwmag.org/page.aspx?pid=3258#sthash. sBooMZLm.dphs.*

22 David D. Burns, "The Perfectionist's Script for Self-Defeat," *Psychology Today* (Nov. 1980): 34–52.

23 Sandra Aamodt, "Why Dieting Doesn't Usually Work." TED Talk filmed June 2013. *http://www.ted.com/talks/sandra_aamodt_why_dieting_doesn_t_usually_work?utm_content=awesm-publisher&awesm=on.ted.com_boNxZ&utm_medium=on.ted.com-facebook-share&utm_source=facebook. com&utm_campaign=#t-707613.*

24 Basco, 78–81.

25 Burns, "The Perfectionist's Script for Self-Defeat."

26 Haven Daley and Hillel Italie, "Actor Apparently Committed Suicide." Robin Williams quoted in article in *Albuquerque Journal,* Aug. 12, 2014, p. A4.

27 Vince Lombardi quote posted on the *Brainy Quote* website. *http://www.brainyquote.com/quotes/ quotes/v/vincelomba385070.html.*

28 Jim Carrey, "Jim Carrey's Secret of Life Inspiring Message." Published June 14, 2014 on *YouTube. https://www.mum.edu/whats-happening/graduation-2014/full-jim-carrey-address-video-and-transcript/* Also Jim Carrey, "Transcript of Full Commencement Address by Jim Carrey." Presented May 24, 2014 at the Maharishi University of Management and posted on their website.

29 FQXi Forum. Description of video by Xiangjun Shi posted Spring 2014 on the *Foundational Questions Institute* website. *http://fqxi.org/community/forum/topic/2144.*

30 Xiangjun Shi, "Why Do I Study Physics?" Video posted 2013 on Xiangjun Shi's website. *http://www.xiangjunshi.com/film.html.* Text appears on *Jesus, Jazz, and Buddhism* website *http:// www.jesusjazzbuddhism.org/why-study-physics.html.*

31 Osho (Chandra Mohan Jain). Quote posted on the *Goodreads* website. *https://www.goodreads. com/quotes/487326-your-whole-idea-about-yourself-is-borrowed.*

Chapter 3: Reality as Defined by the Media

32 Information compiled from the following resources: James L. Baughman, "Television Comes to America, 1948–1957." Posted on the *Illinois Periodicals Online* website (Northern Illinois University); previously published in *Illinois History* (March 1993): 42. *http://www .lib.niu.edu/1993/iby930341.html;* also Bill Genzel, "Television," posted 2007 on the *Wessels Living History Farm* website. *http://www.livinghistoryfarm.org/farminginthe50s/life_17.html;* also Norman Herr, "Television and Health." Television statistics posted (2007 copyright) on *The Sourcebook for Teaching Science* website. *https://www.csun.edu/science/health/docs/tv&health. html;* also Tomi Ahonen, "Digital Divide: Global Household Penetration Rates for Technology," posted Jan. 26, 2011 on the *Bright Side of News* website. *http://www.brightsideofnews. com/2011/01/26/digital-divide-global-household-penetration-rates-for-technology/.* Note: Wikipedia statistics show a slight decline in recent years, which likely reflects an increase in the number of people getting their digital content on digital devices. "Television in the United States." Posted on *Wikipedia* website, last updated Aug. 9, 2014. *http://en.wikipedia.org/wiki/ Television_in_the_United_States.*

33 David Hinckley, "Americans Spend 34 Hours a Week Watching TV, According to Nielsen Numbers." Posted Sept. 19, 2012, on the *New York Daily News* website *http://www. nydailynews.com/entertainment/tv-movies/americans-spend-34-hours-week-watching-tv-nielsen-numbers-article-1.1162285.*

34 Genzel; also Baughman.

35 With soap operas being the obvious exception here.

36 Julie Chen, quoted in "Julie Chen Reveals She Got Plastic Surgery to Look Less Chinese: See the Before and After Pictures." Article by Allison Taketa, posted Sept. 12, 2013 on the *Us Weekly* website. *http://www.usmagazine.com/celebrity-news/news/julie-chen-reveals-she-got-plastic-surgery-to-look-less-chinese-see-the-before-and-after-pictures-2013129.* This is not an exclusive U.S. phenomenon. A tiny blurb in *Time Magazine* (Aug. 25, 2014): 19, reported on the firing of "all employees over the age of 35 at India's national public radio," allowing that "some may be allowed to stay, provided they pass a test indicating that they don't sound 'too mature and boring.'"

37 David Wong, (Jason Pargin), "5 Ways Modern Men Are Trained to Hate Women." Posted March 27, 2012, on the *Cracked.com* website *http://www.cracked.com/article_19785_5-ways-modern -men-are-trained-to-hate-women.html.*

38 A 2006 study showed that "92 percent of boys and 61 percent of girls aged 13 to 16 have been exposed to pornography online." Youth worker Maree Crabbe, "believes schools need to play a bigger role in teaching kids media savviness so they can recognize the difference between reality and screen. Early exposure to porn can be very harmful to kids, shaping their sexual expectations." Quoted in "Sex Education: Where Are Your Children Getting It?" Blog on *Kidspot Parent Exchange* website. Posted Oct. 9, 2013, at *http://parenting. kidspot.com.au/sex-education-child-getting/.*

39 Donna Bowater, "Pornography Is Replacing Sex Education." Posted Dec. 16, 2011, on *The Telegraph* website *http://www.telegraph.co.uk/education/educationnews/8961010/Pornography-is-replacing-sex-education.html*

40 Debby Herbenick, "Pornography Is No Substitute for Sex Ed." Posted Nov. 11, 2012 on *The New York Times* website. *http://www.nytimes.com/roomfordebate/2012/11/11/does-pornography-deserve-its-bad-rap/pornography-is-no-substitute-for-sex-ed.*

41 KB (kbcreativelab), "Porn Sex vs. Real Sex: The Differences Explained with Food." You-Tube video posted Jul. 29, 2013, *http://www.youtube.com/watch?v=q64bTNEj6KQ&oref=http%3 A%2F%2Fwww.youtube.com%2Fwatch%3Fv%3Dq64bTNEj6KQ&has_verified=1.*

42 Meredith Thomas, "New Short Film Centrefold Tackles the Ethics of Labiaplasty." Posted Jul. 20, 2012 on the *Wellcome Trust* website, *http://blog.wellcome.ac.uk/2012/07/20/new-short-film-centrefold-tackles-the-ethics-of-labiaplasty/;* also Rowena Davis, "Labiaplasty Increase Blamed on Pornography." Posted Feb. 26, 2011, on *The Guardian* website. *http://www.theguardian.com/ lifeandstyle/2011/feb/27/labiaplasty-surgery-labia-vagina-pornography.* Note: I've been getting ads for male enhancement products for as long as I've had an Internet connection, this despite having a female name and dozens of spam filters in place.

43 Think of some of the nastiness you see in some consumer reviews, for example. Or consider the shame-based "educational campaigns" that attack individuals who are already "struggling and desperate for love and belonging" in a misguided effort to curb obesity or teenage pregnancy as described by Brené Brown, "Public Shaming is a Better Example of 'If it Feels Good, Do it' than Teen Pregnancy". Blog on Brené Brown's website. Posted Mar. 20, 2013, *http://brenebrown.com/2013/03/20/2013320meuitdwaubpgr9qt1xanm3fwwaosjo/*

44 Information compiled from the following resources: "How Many TV and Radio Stations Are There?" Federal Communications Commission data posted May 16, 2011 on the *Benton Foundation* website. *http://benton.org/node/65435;* also "List of Countries by the Number of Television Broadcast Stations." Post updated August 6, 2014 on the *Wikipedia* website. *http://en.wikipedia.org/wiki/List_of_countries_by_number_of_television_broadcast_stations.* (There are now thousands of broadcast, satellite, cable, and Internet-protocol television stations worldwide.) Megan Geuss, "On Average, Americans Get 189 Cable TV Channels and Only Watch 17." Posted May 6, 2014, on the *ars technica* website. *http://arstechnica.com/business /2014/05/on-average-americans-get-189-cable-tv-channels-and-only-watch-17/.* (Over the six years reported, American viewers watch 17 stations out of their cable package offerings. In 2014, the average U.S. home got 189 channels, up from 129 in 2008.) Wayne Schmidt, "How Much Commercial Length Has Grown Over the Years." Posted on Wayne Schmidt's website. *http://www.waynesthisandthat.com/commerciallength.htm.* Also Herr.

45 Hollie McKay, "Are Out-of-Control In-Theater Commercials Driving Away Moviegoers?" Posted Jan. 19, 2012, on the *Fox News* website. *http://www.foxnews.com/entertainment/2012/01/19/ are-out-control-in-theater-commercials-driving-away-moviegoers/;* also Dorothy Pomerantz, "Movie Theater Advertising is Here to Stay." Posted Nov. 30, 2010, on the *Forbes* website. *http:// www.forbes.com/sites/dorothypomerantz/2010/11/30/movie-theater-advertising-is-here-to-stay/.*

46 "Types of Media." Posted 2014 on the *SparkNotes* website. *http://www.sparknotes.com/us-govern-ment-and-politics/american-government/the-media/section1.rhtml.*

47 This is especially true for fashion magazines. (In 2007, Vogue included 727 ads in its 840-page September issue.) But 50% of a recent craft magazine and 33% of a computer maga-zine were devoted to advertising, and a prominent news weekly had about 20% of its pages covered with ads. Also Tatiana (The Anonymous Model), "In *Vogue*: Things I Learned from the September Issue, *September Issue* Trailer." Posted Jun. 25, 2009 on the *Jezebel* website. *http://jezebel.com/5302363/in-vogue-things-learned-from-the-september-issue-september-issue-trailer.*

48 Kilbourne.

49 Alva Noë, "The New Perfectionism: Why Can't We Just Be Ourselves?" Blog on the *NPR* website. Posted Mar. 17, 2013, *http://www.npr.org/blogs/13.7/2013/03/15/174413119/the-new-perfectionism-why-cant-we-just-be-ourselves.*

50 Gail Dines, quote posted on the *Raw for Beauty* website. *http://rawforbeauty.com/blog/if-tomorrow
    -women-woke-up-and-decided-they-really-liked-their-bodies-just-think-how-many-industries-would-go-
    out-of-business-dr-gail-dines.html.*

51 Tess Munster, "Your Size Doesn't Define You." Posted Feb. 21, 2014, on the *Huffington
    Post* website, *http://www.huffingtonpost.com/tess-munster/your-size-doesnt-define-you_b_4832960.html
    ?ncid=edlinkusaolp00000009.*

52 David Wong, (Jason Pargin).

53 Brené Brown. *The Gifts of Imperfection* (Center City, MN: Hazelden, 2010), 67.

54 Alva Noë, "Are You Overwhelmed? You Don't Have to Be." Blog on the *NPR* website. Posted
    Mar. 1, 2013, *http://www.npr.org/blogs/13.7/2013/03/01/173216644/are-you-overwhelmed-you-dont
    -have-to-be*

55 Tim Jordan. "The Miley Cyrus Culture." Posted August 29, 2013 on Tim Jordan's website,
    http://drtimjordan.com/2013/08/29/the-miley-cyrus-culture/.

56 Kilbourne.

57 Jordan. Note: I would be willing to bet that a similar activity conducted with boys of this
    age (or older) would paint a similarly unrealistic picture.

Chapter 4: Risk and Vulnerability

58 Alice D. Domar and Alice Lesch Kelly. *Be Happy without Being Perfect: How to Break Free from
    the Perfection Deception* (New York: Crown Publishers, 2008), p. 20. The authors reference an
    1829 bestselling book called *The Frugal Housewife* with a message advising women that "they
    were responsible not only for their families' well-being, but also for the welfare, morality,
    and success of the entire nation."

59 Liz Lenz, "How to Raise a Kid Who Isn't Whiny and Annoying." Posted May 9, 2013
    on the *Huffington Post* website, *http://www.huffingtonpost.com/lyz-lenz/how-to-raise-a-kid-who-isnt-
    whiny-and-annoying_b_3248085.html?utm_hp_ref=fb&src=sp&comm_ref=false.* Pinterest "is a social
    network that allows users to visually share, and discover new interests by posting (known
    as "pinning" on Pinterest) images or videos to their own or others' boards (i.e., a collec-
    tion of "pins," usually with a common theme) and browsing what other users have pinned
    . . . allowing you to share your tastes and interests with others and discovering those of
    likeminded people." Andy Meng, *"What Is Pinterest and How Does It Work?* Posted Jan. 20,
    2014, on the *Infront Webworks* website. *http://www.infront.com/blogs/the-infront-blog/2014/1/20/
    what-is-pinterest-and-how-does-it-work.*

60 Dean.

61 Ann W. Smith, "The Never Enough Syndrome: Overt and Covert Perfectionism," *Counselor
    Magazine* (June 2013): 10–14. Temperament is described as "an individual's behavioral style
    and characteristic emotional response" which forms "the biological and emotional founda-
    tions of personality." John W. Santrock, *A Topical Approach to Lifespan Development* (New York:
    McGraw-Hill Higher Education, 2011): 343.

62 Marilyn Price-Mitchell, "Are You Raising a Perfectionist?" Blog on *Roots of Action* website.
    No post date, *http://www.rootsofaction.com/are-you-raising-a-perfectionist/.*

63 Melinda Beck, "Inside the Minds of the Perfectionists." Article on the *Wall Street Journal*
    website. Posted Oct. 29, 2012, *http://online.wsj.com/article/SB10001424052970204840504578*

85802751238578.html; also Michael C. Pyryt, "Helping Gifted Students Cope with Perfectionism," *Parenting for High Potential* magazine (July 2009): 10-14. Also available on the *Davidson Institute* website: *http://www.davidsongifted.org/db/Articles_id_10459.aspx;* also Ann Smith, "The Never-Enough Syndrome," 10-14.

64 Ann Smith, "The Never-Enough Syndrome," 11.

65 Adapted from Jane Bluestein, *Creating Emotionally Safe Schools* (Deerfield Beach, FL: Health Communications, Inc., 2001): Chapter 4: Fear, Stress, and Learning; also Brynn Carter, "A Problem with Threat," previously available on the *Parents' Learning Group* website, 2013. Content confirmed in correspondence.

66 Daniel Goleman quoted in Shel Horowitz, "Emotional Intelligence: How to Stop Amygdala Hijackings." Posted 2014 on the *UMassAmherst* website. *http://www.umass.edu/fambiz/articles/values_culture/primal_leadership.html.*

67 Horowitz.

68 Daniel Goleman, "Higher Suicide Risk for Perfectionists." Posted May 1, 1996 on *The New York Times* website. *http://www.nytimes.com/1996/05/01/us/higher-suicide-risk-for-perfection ists.html;* also Haker; also Jagtiani; also Rick Nauert, "Perfectionism Linked to Suicide." Posted Sept. 26, 2014 on the *PsychCentral* website. *http://psychcentral.com/news/2014/09/26/ perfectionism-linked-to-suicide/75399.html;* also "Perfectionism is a Bigger than Perceived Risk Factor in Suicide." Posted on the *York University* website (no date). *http://news.yorku. ca/2014/09/25/perfectionism-is-a-bigger-than-perceived-risk-factor-in-suicide-york-u-psychology-expert/* The online article refers to the following study: Flett, Gordon, Paul Hewitt, and Marnin Heisel, "The Destructiveness of Perfectionism Revisited: Implications for the Assessment of Suicide Risk and Prevention of Suicide." American Psychological Association, *Review of General Psychology* (2014, Vol. 18, No. 3): 156–172.

Chapter 5: Safe and Secure

69 Saul McLeod, "Maslow's Hierarchy of Needs." Published 2007, updated 2014, on the *Simply Psychology* website. *http://www.simplypsychology.org/maslow.html;* also William G. Huitt, "Maslow's Hierarchy of Needs." Published 2007 on the *Educational Psychology Interactive* website. *http://www.edpsycinteractive.org/topics/conation/maslow.html;* also Kendra Cherry, "Hierarchy of Needs." Published on the *About (Education)* website. *http://psychology.about.com/od/ theoriesofpersonality/a/hierarchyneeds.htm.*

70 Ann W. Smith, *Overcoming Perfectionism: Finding the Key to Balance and Self-Acceptance.* (Deerfield Beach, FL: Health Communications, Inc., 2013): 22.

71 Kendra Cherry, "What Is Attachment Theory?" Posted (c. 2014) on the *About* website (psychology). *http://psychology.about.com/od/loveandattraction/a/attachment01.htm.*

72 Linda Graham, "The Neuroscience of Attachment." Posted (c. 2014) on Linda Graham's website. (First presented as a Clinical Conversation at the Community Institute for Psychotherapy, Fall 2008.) *http://lindagraham-mft.net/resources/published-articles/the-neuroscience-of -attachment/.*

73 Cherry, "What Is Attachment Theory?"

74 Ann Smith, *Overcoming Perfectionism,* 24.

75 Potential problems included depression, anxiety, and eating disorders. Cherry also notes the possibility that "oppositional-defiant disorder (ODD), conduct disorder (CD), or post-

traumatic stress disorder (PTSD) frequently display attachment problems, possibly due to early abuse, neglect, or trauma." Reactive Attachment Disorder (RAD) is also included as an extreme and rare outcome in which a child is unable to form attachments (or might form attachments inappropriately). Resources include Cherry; also "Attachment Parenting." Post last modified Sept. 21, 2014, on the *Wikipedia* website. *http://en.wikipedia.org/wiki /Attachment_parenting;* also Mayo Clinic Staff. "Reactive Attachment Disorder." Posted July 10, 2014 on the *Mayo Clinic* website. *http://www.mayoclinic.org/diseases-conditions/reactive-attachment-disorder/basics/definition/con-20032126;* also "Reactive Attachment Disorder." Post last modified Sept. 13, 2014, on the *Wikipedia* website. *http://en.wikipedia.org/wiki/Reactive _attachment_disorder.*

76   Melinda Smith, Joanna Saisan, and Jeanne Segal. "Attachment Issues and Reactive Attachment Disorder: Symptoms, Treatment, and Hope for Children with Insecure Attachment." Last updated Oct. 2014 on the *Help Guide* website. *http://www.helpguide.org/articles/secure -attachment/attachment-issues-and-reactive-attachment-disorders.htm.*

77   "Still Face" experiments conducted at Harvard's Child Development Unit demonstrate that when a parent stops responding to or interacting with the infant, the parent's withdrawal of attention resulted in an immediate stress response from the child. Attempts to re-engage the parent included repeating facial expressions and body movements that had previously elicited a positive, caring response; crying and making screeching sounds; and "[losing] control of their posture because of the stress that they're experiencing." Quoting Edward Tronick, director of Harvard's Child Development Unit. "Baby's Reaction to Mom's 'Still Face' Reveals Another Form of Abuse." Video of Edward Tronick, posted Oct. 18, 2014 on the *San Francisco Globe* website. *http://sfglobe.com/?id=16299&src=share_fb_ new_16299.*

78   Ann Smith, *Overcoming Perfectionism,* 24.

79   Quote from The Children's Centre Polesworth posted Oct. 31, 2014, on Elizabeth Jarman for Families Facebook page. *https://www.facebook.com/563198060360604/photos/a.563737883639 955.144923.563198060360604/98309853503721 9/?type=1&theater.*

80   This outcome is similar to children who grow up with authoritarian parents and teachers who are more likely to issue commands than offer choices.

81   Perri Klass, "Are You Overprotecting Your Child?" Posted (copyright 2014) on the *Parenting* website. *http://www.parenting.com/article/are-you-overprotecting-your-child.*

82   Anna Quindlen, "The Good Enough Mother." From the Feb. 21, 2005 issue of *Newsweek* (pages 50–51). Posted Feb. 20, 2005, on the *Newsweek* website. *http://www.newsweek.com/good -enough-mother-122059.*

83   L. Kevin Chapman, "Control: The Red Flag of Family Anxiety," posted Dec. 24, 2011, on the *Psychology Today* website. *http://www.psychologytoday.com/blog/the-color-anxiety/201112/ control-the-red-flag-family-anxiety;* also John Rosemond, "Parental Anxiety Breeding Anxious Kids," posted Oct. 25, 2014, on the *Buffalo News* website. *http://www.buffalonews.com/columns/ john-rosemond/john-rosemond-parental-anxiety-breeding-anxious-kids-20141025.*

84   "Anxious Kids, Anxious Parents." Interview by the Book Brigade with Reid Wilson and Lynn Lyons posted June 23, 2014, on the *Psychology Today* website. *http://www.psychologytoday .com/blog/the-author-speaks/201406/anxious-kids-anxious-parents.*

85   Klass.

86 Klass.

87 Miriam Adderholdt and Jan Goldberg. *Perfectionism: What's Bad About Being Too Good* (Minneapolis, MN: Free Spirit Publishing, 1987).

88 "Newsweek Cover: The Myth of the Perfect Mother." News release posted Feb. 13, 2005 on the *PR Newswire* website. *http://www.prnewswire.com/news-releases/newsweek-cover-the-myth-of-the-perfect-mother-54038797.html*.

89 Quindlen, "The Good Enough Mother."

90 Sandra Levy, "A New Generation of Dads Juggle Work and Childrearing." Posted June 27, 2014, on the *Healthline* website. *http://www.healthline.com/health-news/dads-taking-on-more-childcare-responsibilities-062714#1*.

91 Quindlen, "The Good Enough Mother"; also Katy Read, "Mommy Madness." Posted Feb. 23, 2005, on the *Salon* website. *http://www.salon.com/2005/02/23/warner_12/*. This article focused on pressures on women; however, other resources and contributors agree with Hara Estroff Marano's assessment that *"both mothers and fathers are working more hours and feeling very stressed (and loaded with guilt, too)."* Hara Estroff Marano, "Rocking the Cradle of Class." Article on the *Psychology Today* website. Posted Sept. 1, 2005, *http://www.psychologytoday.com/articles/200508/rocking-the-cradle-class*. (Italics added.)

92 Judith Warner, quoted in Read.

93 Quindlen.

94 From "Pressure for Perfection." Transcript of the *Dr. Phil* show featuring Phil McGraw, Nov. 4, 2009.

95 "Pressure for Perfection."

96 John O'Sullivan, "The Race to Nowhere in Youth Sports." Posted Oct. 20, 2014, on the *Steve Nash Youth Basketball* blog. *http://stevenashyb.wordpress.com/2014/10/20/the-race-to-nowhere-in-youth-sports/*

97 In some instances, going to the extreme of disowning the child and, in one case, formally mourning as though the child had died. Unconditional love doesn't come with conditions.

98 Adderholdt and Goldberg.

99 Quote shared by Lynne Lang. This quote also appears as I used it in James Martin, "Clinical Counseling: The Trap of an Unlived Life." Posted Oct. 9, 2014, on the *Ruidoso News* website. *http://www.ruidosonews.com/ruidoso-news/ci_26696728/clinical-counseling-trap-an-unlived-life* as well as several other sources. However, other sources cite the following as Jung's quote: "Nothing has a stronger influence psychologically on their environment and especially on their children than the unlived life of the parent." (Included in a list of Carl Jung's quotes on *The Quotations Page* website. *http://www.quotationspage.com/quotes/Carl_Jung*).

100 Bluestein, Jane. "Children at Risk," *Dr. Bluestein's Book of Handouts*. (Albuquerque, NM: I.S.S. Publications, 2015), 25.

101 Marano.

102 Marano.

103 Noë, "Are You Overwhelmed?"

Chapter 6: Shaping Our Reality

104   Greenspon.

105   Elizabeth Gilbert, "Beware of Tribal Shame." Posted Apr. 10, 2015, on Elizabeth Gilbert's Facebook page. *https://www.facebook.com/GilbertLiz/posts/806653502750100:0.*

106   Andra Brosh, "5 Ways to Start Pleasing Yourself Before Pleasing Others," on the *Purpose-Fairy* website, posted August 12, 2013 at *http://www.purposefairy.com/65718/5-ways-to-start-pleasing-yourself-before-pleasing-others/*

107   Greenspon.

108   Gilbert, "Beware of Tribal Shame."

109   James T. Webb,"Dabrowski's Theory and Existential Depression in Gifted Children and Adults." Originally presented at The Eighth International Congress of the Institute for Positive Disintegration in Human Development, Aug. 7, 2008. Available on the Davidson Institute website at *http://www.davidsongifted.org/db/Articles_id_10554.aspx.*

110   Quoted in Catherine Newman, "Creating Creative Kids," *FamilyFun* Magazine (Oct 2013): 74. Authors such as John Naisbitt, Thomas Friedman, and Daniel Pink have commented on the need for creativity, randomness, right-brain thinking, and strong interpersonal skills for social and economic success in a post-industrial society.

111   Jean Van't Hut, "Make Art." Quoted in *FamilyFun* Magazine (Oct. 2013): 80.

112   Karen Benke,"Write About Anything." Quoted in *FamilyFun* Magazine (Oct. 2013): 80.

113   The DSM-IV (Diagnostic and Statistical Manual of Mental Disorders) now classifies symptoms such as "questioning authority, negativity, defiance, argumentativeness, and being easily annoyed" under the diagnostic criteria for Operational Defiant Disorder (for children and adults), according to an article concerned with free thinking, resisting the status quo, and nonconformity representing the presence of a mental illness. Andrew, "Is Free Thinking a Mental Illness?" Posted Oct. 8, 2010 on the *Off the Grid* website. *http://www.offthegridnews.com/how-to-2/is-free-thinking-a-mental-illness/.*

114   Marano.

115   Sarah Koppelkam,"How to Talk to Your Daughter About Her Body." Posted July 30, 2013 on the *Huffington Post* website, *http://www.huffingtonpost.com/sarah-koppelkam/body-image_b_3678534.html.*

116   Basco, 12–13. Basco notes that the "superstar" could also be an older brother or sister.

117   Adapted from Bluestein, *Creating Emotionally Safe Schools* (Deerfield Beach, FL: Health Communications, Inc., 2001), 142–144. These are the primary dysfunctional or harmful traditions that increase the likelihood of perfectionism. Other traditions, including reactivity (versus proactivity) and win-lose power dynamics (versus win-win interactions), seem to be have less influence in this instance.

Chapter 7: Building Our Identity

118   Jane Bluestein, "Picking Up the Pieces: Reclaiming Our Essence." Blog on Jane Bluestein's website. Posted Dec. 23, 2012, at *http://janebluestein.com/2012/picking-up-the-pieces/.*

119   Denis Mareschal and Paul C. Quinn, "Categorization in infancy." *Trends in Cognitive Science* (Vol. 5, No. 10, Oct. 2001): 443. Posted on the USCD website: *http://crl.ucsd.edu/courses/bdp1/Readings/Mareschal_infant_categor.pdf.*

120 Robin Marantz Henig, "Your Adult Sibling May Be the Secret to a Long, Happy Life." Posted Nov. 27, 2014, on the *NPR* website. *http://www.npr.org/blogs/health/2014/11/27/366789136/your-adult-siblings-may-be-the-secret-to-a-long-happy-life?fb_ref=Default&fb_source=message.* Note: Family patterns of superficial identity and comparison, pigeonholing children (even with apparently positive labels) is included in the list of family patterns and adult behaviors of children at risk. (Bluestein, *Dr. Bluestein's Book of Handouts*, 26.)

121 Jane Bluestein, "Guidelines for Reinforcing Cooperation." Posted Nov. 19, 2012, at *http://janebluestein.com/2012/guidelines-for-reinforcing-cooperation/.*

122 Carol Dweck in "The Effect of Praise on Mindsets." *YouTube* video published on Sept. 26, 2013, at *http://www.youtube.com/watch?v=lp5FvxnCoEw.* Similar results were also reported in Dweck's paper, "Caution— Praise Can Be Dangerous," PDF on the *American Federations of Teachers* website (Spring 1999), *http://www.aft.org/pdfs/americaneducator/spring1999/PraiseSpring99.pdf* and "The Perils and Promises of Praise," article on the *ASCD* website (Oct. 2007, Vol. 65, No. 2: Early Intervention at Every Age): 34–39, *http://www.ascd.org/publications/educational-leadership/oct07/vol65/num02/The-Perils-and-Promises-of-Praise.aspx.*

123 Dweck, "Caution— Praise Can Be Dangerous."

124 Dweck, "The Effect of Praise on Mindsets," also Dweck, "Caution— Praise Can Be Dangerous;" also Dweck, "The Perils and Promises of Praise."

125 Dweck, "The Perils and Promises of Praise." This research leads to a rather sticky issue: Looking through the filter of Dweck's research, we might want to consider the implications of labeling kids as gifted and talented—especially given the rather limited tools and definitions we typically use to identify these children. To what degree are we inadvertently building perfectionists by assigning these kids labels and expectations they need to satisfy? How willing are we to challenge *all* children, recognizing and encouraging effort to build a love of learning and a growth mindset, regardless of the gifts each child displays?

126 Ann Smith, "The Never-Enough Syndrome," 14.

127 Miriam Adderholdt, "Perfectionism: What's Bad About Being Too Good?" Handout packet to accompany presentation for North Carolina Council for Exceptional Children, Feb. 3, 2011.

128 Jennifer Santos Madriaga, "Three Magic Words You Should Say Today." Posted Nov. 26, 2013, on the *PurposeFairy* website. *http://www.purposefairy.com/67021/3-magic-words-you-should-say-today/*

129 Price-Mitchell.

130 Burns, "The Perfectionist's Script for Self-Defeat."

131 The word "parent" can apply to any primary adult or caregiver in a child's life, here and throughout this book.

132 Karyl McBride, "The Legacy of Distorted Love." Posted Oct. 13, 2014, on the *Psychology Today* website. *http://www.psychologytoday.com/blog/the-legacy-distorted-love/201410/do-you-feel-not-good-enough.*

133 Jane Bluestein, "What's Wrong with I-Messages? Problems with a Popular Formula." Posted Jan. 14, 2013, on Jane Bluestein's website. *http://janebluestein.com/2013/whats-wrong-with-i-messages/.*

134 McBride, "The Legacy of Distorted Love."

135 First-born children are often characterized as the family caretakers and of course, in many cases, this turns out to be true. As the oldest sibling, I can personally relate to having played this role in the family, as did several other first-born contributors. However, this was not always the case. A number of other individuals I interviewed who fit this description included several women who were the only (or oldest) girl in the family and, in one case, a last-born child who was significantly younger than her siblings.

136 Adderholdt and Goldberg.

137 Reported in Lawrence M. Kutner, "Living in Deep Fear of an A-Minus," *The Salisbury Post* (Feb. 12, 1989): 30.

138 Teversham, 8–9.

Chapter 8: Through the Looking Glass: Living in a Distorted Reality

139 Martin M. Antony and Richard P Swinson. *When Perfect Isn't Good Enough: Strategies for Coping with Perfectionism* (Oakland, CA: New Harbinger Publications, Inc., 2009), 2.

140 Sources include Pavel Somov, "4 Types of Perfectionism," last reviewed July 9, 2011, on the *Psych Central* website. *http://blogs.psychcentral.com/mindful-living/2010/07/4-types-of-perfectionism/;* also Haker; also Smith, "The Never-Enough Syndrome," 10–14; also Kevin Leman, *Why Your Best is Good Enough.* (Grand Rapids, MI: Revell Books, a division of Baker Publishing Group, 2010), *http://assets.bakerpublishinggroup.com/processed/book-resources/files/Excerpt_9780800787943. pdf* 14.; also "Perfectionism," article posted on the *Out of the Fog* website. *http://outofthefog.net /CommonBehaviors/Perfectionism.html;* also Tammy Fuller, "Are You a Frustrated Perfectionist?" Posted Jan. '10, 2010, on the *Craving Fitness* website. *http://cravingfitness.org/physical-fitness/ frustrated-perfectionist/.* Basco also uses the terms "inwardly focused perfectionist" and "outwardly focused perfectionist" in Basco, 2.

141 "Stinking Thinking." Definition posted on the *Cambridge Dictionary* website. *http://dictionary. cambridge.org/us/dictionary/british/stinking-thinking.*

142 David Burns, "The Top 10 Types of 'Stinkin' Thinkin'."" Posted on the *Psyche Central* website. *http://psychcentral.com/lib/the-top-10-types-of-stinkin-thinkin/0001o.*

143 "Stinking Thinking: When Negative Thinking Becomes Harmful." Posted on the *Alcohol Rehab* website. *http://alcoholrehab.com/addiction-recovery/stinking-thinking/.* Note: Although this site is geared to individuals struggling with alcohol and substance abuse, note that the thinking patterns of perfectionists share many similar characteristics to the thinking patterns of alcoholics and substance abusers.

144 "Perfectionism." Definition found on the *Merriam-Webster Dictionary* website. http://www. merriam-webster.com/dictionary/perfectionism; also the Dictionary app on my laptop, Version 2.2.1 (156), (c) Apple, Inc., 2005–2011. The term is also referred to as black-and-white thinking, "splitting," or dichotomous reasoning.

145 "Perfectionism." Posted in 2007 on the *University of Illinois at Urbana-Champaign Counseling Center* website, *http://counselingcenter.illinois.edu/brochures/perfectionism.*

146 David Burns, "The Top 10 Types of 'Stinkin' Thinkin'.""

147 Elizabeth Scott, "Perfectionistic Traits: Do These Sound Familiar?" Posted June 3, 2014, on the *About Health* website. *http://stress.about.com/od/understandingstress/a/perfectionist.htm.*

148 Adderholdt and Goldberg.

149 Les Parrott, *Shoulda, Coulda, Woulda: Live in the Present, Find Your Future* (Grand Rapids: MI: Zondervan, 2003), 64.

150 Burns, "The Perfectionist's Script for Self-Defeat."

151 Amy Wilson, "The Cost of Perfection," article posted Jan. 1, 2000. *http://www.psychology today.com/articles/200001/the-cost-perfection;* also Jane Bluestein, *Parents, Teens and Boundaries: How to Draw the Line* (Deerfield Beach, FL: Health Communications, Inc., 1993), 25–28; also Tara Parker-Pope, "Go Easy on Yourself, a New Wave of Research Urges," posted Feb. 28, 2011, on the *New York Times* website, *http://well.blogs.nytimes.com/2011/02/28/go-easy-on-yourself-a-new-wave-of-research-urges/?_php=true&_type=blogs&_r=0.*

152 Burns, "The Perfectionist's Script for Self-Defeat."

153 Jagtiani, (referencing Burns's work).

154 John Tagg, "Overgeneralization." Posted (c) 1996 among Tagg's "Reflections on Learning" on the *Palomar College* website. *http://daphne.palomar.edu/jtagg/overgeneralization.htm.*

155 Antony and Swinson, 51, 53.

Chapter 9: Living on the Dark Side: A Tendency Toward Negativity

156 Cameron, *The Artist's Way*, 120.

157 Posted on Facebook on Nov. 15, 2014, by Steve Bluestein, author of *It's So Hard to Type with a Gun in My Mouth* and his play, *Rest in Pieces.*

158 Burns, "The Top 10 Types of 'Stinkin' Thinkin'.'" Burns also cites "discounting the positive" as a separate cognitive distortion, but since this involves a similar type of filtering, I've chosen to include it in this section.

159 Jon Acuff, "Three People You Need to Ignore Online." Blog post on Michael Hyatt's website. Posted, July 19, 2013, *http://michaelhyatt.com/ignore-people-online.html.*

160 Antony and Swinson, 50.

161 Jagtiani.

162 Benson.

163 Hendrie Weisinger and Norman Lobsenz, *Nobody's Perfect* (New York: Warner Books, 1981), 237. Quoted in Patricia A. Schuler, "Voices of Perfectionism: Perfectionistic Gifted Adolescents in a Rural Middle School." National Research Center on the Gifted and Talented, 1999. Posted on the *Neag Center for Gifted Education and Talent Development, University of Connecticut* website. *http://www.gifted.uconn.edu/nrcgt/reports/rm99140/rm99140.pdf,* page 8.

164 Miriam Adderholdt, "Perfectionism and the Gifted Adolescent." Chapter in *Understanding the Gifted Adolescent: Educational, Developmental, and Multicultural Issues,* edited by Marlene Bireley and Judy Genshaft (New York: Teachers College Press, 1991); also Adderholdt and Goldberg.

165 Adderholdt, "Perfectionism and the Gifted Adolescent."

166 Adderholdt, "Perfectionism: What's Bad About Being Too Good?" Handout packet.

167 Cloe Madanes, "The 14 Habits of Highly Miserable People: How to succeed at self-sabotage." Posted Nov. 18, 2013, on the *Alternet* website, *http://www.alternet.org/personal-health/14-habits -highly-miserable-people.*

168 Adderholdt and Goldberg.

169 Scott, "Perfectionistic Traits."

170 Carolyn Gregoire, "14 Signs Your Perfectionism Has Gotten Out of Control." Updated Nov. 25, 2013, on the *Huffington Post* website. *http://www.huffingtonpost.com/2013/11/06/why-perfectionism-is-ruin_n_4212069.html*

171 Study by Michael Mahoney et al. reported in Burns, "The Perfectionist's Script for Self-Defeat."

172 Luminita Sauvic, "5 Ways to Let Go of Your Inner Critic and Let the Real You Shine." Posted Dec. 10, 2013, on the *PurposeFairy* website, *http://www.purposefairy.com/67323/5-ways-to-let-go-of-your-inner-critic-and-let-the-real-you-shine/*.

173 Margie Warrell, "Afraid of Being 'Found Out'? How to Overcome Impostor Syndrome." Posted April 3, 2014, on the *Forbes* website. *http://www.forbes.com/sites/margiewarrell/2014/04/03/impostor-syndrome/*.

174 Lauren Martin, "6 Reasons Why Beautiful Women Are Also Insecure Women." Posted Dec. 30, 2014, on *Elite Daily* website. *http://elitedaily.com/women/make-beautiful-women-insecure/893913/*

175 Glennon Doyle Melton. *Carry On, Warrior: Thoughts on Life Unarmed* (New York, NY: Scribner, 2013), 15.

176 Lauren Martin.

177 Antony and Swinson, 58.

178 Iyanla Vanzant. Quote posted on the *BrainyQuote* website. *http://www.brainyquote.com/quotes/authors/i/iyanla_vanzant.html;* also quoted in Warrell.

179 Warrell.

180 *University of Illinois at Urbana-Champaign Counseling Center.*

181 Neeta Patel, "Coping With Failure Is as Important as Coping With Success." Updated June. 5, 2013, on the *Huffington Post* website. *http://www.huffingtonpost.co.uk/neeta-patel/coping-with-failure_b_2818657.html*

182 Leman, *Why Your Best is Good Enough*, 20. Note: Leman makes this comment with regard to what he calls "defeated perfectionists," however I believe this description would apply far more broadly.

183 Parrott, 132.

184 This condition is sometimes referred to as the impostor phenomenon or fraud syndrome. "The Impostor Syndrome." Posted on the *Caltech Counseling Center* website. *https://counseling.caltech.edu/general/InfoandResources/Impostor;* also "Impostor Syndrome." Posted on the *Wikipedia* website (last modified Jan. 11, 2015). *http://en.wikipedia.org/wiki/Impostor_syndrome.*

185 Parrott, 132.

186 Ann Smith, "The Never-Enough Syndrome," 12.

187 Warrell.

188 Maya Angelou, quoted in Warrell.

189 Rachel Maddow quoted in David Dobbs, "Rachel Maddow Gets Depressed." Posted April 2, 2012, on *Wired* website. *http://www.wired.com/2012/04/rachel-maddow-gets-depressed/*.

Chapter 10: Establishing Our Value

190 Jessica Ortner, quote posted on Jessica Ortner's website: *http://jessica-ortner.com.*

191 "Atelophobia." Wikipedia entry (as posted on August 11, 2014). *http://en.wikipedia.org/wiki/Atelophobia.*

192 Brené Brown, *The Gifts of Imperfection*, 55, 39.

193 Kristalyn Salters-Pedneault, "What is Shame?" Updated June 19, 2014 on the *About* website. *http://bpd.about.com/od/glossary/g/shame.htm.*

194 Michael Lewis, quoted in "Shame." Posted on the Wikipedia website, last modified Oct. 18, 2014. *http://en.wikipedia.org/wiki/Shame.* Original source: *Shame: The Exposed Self* (New York: Free Press, 1992), 10.

195 Gilbert.

196 Salters-Pedneault.

197 John Bradshaw, *Bradshaw On: The Family.* (Deerfield Beach, FL: Health Communications, Inc., 1990), 2–3.

198 Brené Brown, "Public Shaming."

199 Includes material from Parrott, 133–134; also Julia Cameron, *The Vein of Gold: A Journey to Your Creative Heart.* (New York: Jeremy P. Tarcher/Putnam Books, 1996), 141; also Scott, "Perfectionistic Traits"; also John Bradshaw, *Healing the Shame that Binds You* (Deerfield Beach, FL: Health Communications, Inc., 1988); also Robert Subby, *Lost in the Shuffle: The Codependent Reality* (Deerfield Beach, FL: Health Communications, Inc., 1987); also Brené Brown, *The Gifts of Imperfection*, 41; also Richard Winter, "Perfectionism: The Road to Heaven—or Hell?" L'Abri Papers #RW01 (© 1990–2008), posted on the *L'Abri* website *http://www.labri. org/england/resources/05052008/RW01_Perfectionism.pdf.*

200 "Perfectionism." *University of Illinois at Urbana-Champaign Counseling Center.*

201 Ibid.

202 Dean.

203 Thomas Greenspon, quoted in afterword of Trudy Ludwig, *Too Perfect.* (Toronto, ON: Tricycle Press, 2009).

204 John Tagg, "Emotional Reasoning." Posted (c) 1996 among Tagg's "Reflections on Learning" on the *Palomar College* website. *http://daphne.palomar.edu/jtagg/emotion.htm*

205 Quoted in "14 Signs Your Perfectionism Has Gotten Out of Control." Updated Nov. 25, 2013 on the *Huffington Post* website. *http://www.huffingtonpost.com/2013/11/06/why-perfectionism-is-ruin_n_4212069.html.*

206 Richard Winter.

207 Adderholdt, "Perfectionism and the Gifted Adolescent," 68.

208 Sherie Venner, "The Shocking Truth About Making Mistakes." Blog on *Sherie Venner's* website. Posted, Aug. 28, 2012, *http://sherievenner.com/2012/shocking-truth-making-mistakes/.*

209 Steve Kamb, "Two Words that Will Level Up Your Life." Posted Feb. 13, 2014, on the *Nerdfitness* website, *http://www.nerdfitness.com/blog/2014/02/13/two-words-that-will-level-up-your-life.*

210 "I Want to Be Perfect. I Need to Be Perfect." Reasons for needing to be perfect listed on a blog at *http://theperfectionproject.tumblr.com/myreasons.78.*

211 Adderholdt, "Perfectionism: What's Bad About Being Too Good?" Handout packet. Note: This list bears a troubling resemblance to the cruel and repressive "poisonous pedagogy," rules and beliefs of unhealthy adult-child systems proposed by Alice Miller. The overlap is especially strong in many perfectionists' buy-in to values like obedience, orderliness, and the control of feelings and desires. See Alice Miller, *For Your Own Good: Hidden Cruelty in Child-Rearing and the Roots of Violence* (New York: Farrar, Straus and Giroux, 2002), 59; also,

Jane Bluestein, "Rules and Beliefs of Unhealthy Systems," posted Nov. 26, 2012, on Jane Bluestein's website. *http://janebluestein.com/2012/rules-and-beliefs-of-unhealthy-systems/*.

212   Chick Moorman and Thomas Haller. *The Abracadabra Effect: The 13 Verbally Transmitted Diseases and How to Cure Them* (Bay City, MI: Personal Power Press, 2015). From the introduction as seen in prepublished manuscript.

213   Theodore Roethke quoted in Priscilla Gilman, "In Praise of Imperfection." *More.com* (May 2014): 128.

214   Brené Brown, *The Gifts of Imperfection*, 56.

215   Cameron, *The Artist's Way*, 120.

216   Madriaga.

217   Greenspon.

218   Teversham, xii.

219   Teversham, 10.

220   Christine Kane, "The Recovering Perfectionist's Guide to Productivity and Success." Posted 2011 on the *Consistently Great* website *http://consistentlygreat.com/the-recovering-perfectionists-guide-to-productivity-success/*.

221   Marc Chernoff, "10 Painfully Obvious Truths Everyone Forgets Too Soon." Posted Jan. 29, 2014, on the *Marc and Angel Hack Life* website *http://www.marcandangel.com/2014/01/29/10-painfully-obvious-truths-everyone-forgets-too-soon/*.

Chapter 11: The Perfect Sabotage

222   Antony and Swinson, 61.

223   Jennifer Buchanan, "Perfectionism." Slide show created for a graduate class taught by Miriam Adderholdt; also "Perfectionism," *University of Illinois at Urbana-Champaign Counseling Center*.

224   Adderholdt and Goldberg.

225   Kris Ward, "The 5 Root Causes of Self Sabotage and How to Untangle Them." Posted Jan. 9, 2014, on the *PurposeFairy* website, *http://www.purposefairy.com/67319/the-5-root-causes-of-self-sabotage-and-how-to-untangle-them/*.

226   Kane.

227   Jeff Goins, "Overcoming Perfectionism: Stop Going Around in Circles." Posted on Jeff Goins's website (copyright 2014). *http://goinswriter.com/overcoming-perfectionism/*.

228   Joseph Ferrari, quoted in Adderholdt and Goldberg.

229   Cameron, *The Artist's Way*, 119.

230   Scott, "Perfectionistic Traits."

231   James Victore. "Ferk Perfuction." Video posted Jan. 12, 2015, on Chase Jarvis's Facebook page. *https://www.facebook.com/video.php?v=10152574634805978&set=vb.58624920977&type=2&theater*.

232   Eric Jaffe, "Why Wait? The Science Behind Procrastination." Article appearing in *The Observer* (Vol.26, No.4 April, 2013), posted on the *Association for Psychological Science* website. *http://www.psychologicalscience.org/index.php/publications/observer/2013/april-13/why-wait-the-science-behind-procrastination.html*.

233   Adderholdt and Goldberg.

234 Scott, "Perfectionistic Traits."

235 Alyce P. Cornyn-Selby, quoted in Ward.

236 Alina Larson, "Are You a Procrastinator?" Posted on the *Guideposts* website. *http://www.guide posts.org/personal-growth/self-knowledge-are-you-procrastinator.*

237 "Procrastination/Time Management." Posted on the *University of Oregon* Testing and Counseling website. *http://counseling.uoregon.edu/TopicsResources/StudentSelf-Help/ProcrastinationTime Management.aspx;* also Lisa Rivero, *The Smart Teens' Guide to Living with Intensity* (Scottsdale, AZ: Great Potential Press, 2010), 77; also Gregoire.

238 Jaffe.

239 Rivero, *The Smart Teens' Guide to Living with Intensity*, 79.

240 Winter.

241 Fuller.

242 Comment following post by Jeff Goins.

243 Carol Dweck, "The Perils and Promises of Praise."

244 Burns, "The Perfectionist's Script for Self-Defeat."

245 Kane. It's worth noting that studies of athletes showed less-skilled players "reported greater difficulty in recovering from mistakes and were more likely to set perfectionistic standards," and were more likely to obsess about (and panic over) past mistakes. (Burns, "The Perfectionist's Script for Self-Defeat.")

246 Kane.

247 Burns, "The Perfectionist's Script for Self-Defeat."

248 Rechtschaffen.

249 Nisha Naik, "Overcoming Perfectionism: Good Enough Really Is Good Enough!" Blog on the *One Move Forward* website. Posted Sept. 6, 2012, *http://www.onemoveforward.com/2012/09/06/ overcoming-perfectionism/.*

250 Scott, "Perfectionistic Traits."

251 Victore.

252 Jennifer Bostic, "Giving Up Perfect." Blog on *The Ordinary Chaos* website. Posted Apr. 30, 2013, *http://theordinarychaos.com/giving-up-on-perfect/.*

Chapter 12: The Perfect Relationship: Power and Perfectionism

253 There is a great deal of power in neediness and helplessness, as well as in allowing ourselves to be subjugated or victimized, as this gives us access to excuses, self-righteousness, and blame.

254 Victore.

255 Vanzant quote.

256 Henrik Edberg, "Let Go of Perfectionism: 7 Powerful Tips That Will Help You." Posted on *The Positivity Blog, http://www.positivityblog.com/index.php/2010/06/24/let-go-of-perfectionism -7-powerful-tips-that-will-help-you/.*

257 Beck, "Inside the Minds of the Perfectionists."

258 Winter.

259   Carrey, "Jim Carrey's Secret of Life Inspiring Message."

260   Teversham, ix.

261   Ward.

262   Adapted from Jane Bluestein, "Making Someone Wrong: What Does That Really Mean?"
      Posted April 23, 2014, on Jane Bluestein's website. *http://janebluestein.com/2014/making-someone-wrong/*.

263   Basco, 2-3.

264   eHarmony Staff. "What 'All-or-Nothing' Says About You." Posted on the *eHarmony* website.
      http://www.eharmony.com/dating-advice/about-you/what-all-or-nothing-says-about-you/#.VKGyyBCA.

265   Alan Entin, quoted in *Psychology Today* staff. "The Perfectionist's Flawed Marriage," posted
      May 1, 2003, on the *Psychology Today* website. *http://www.psychologytoday.com/articles/200002/the-perfectionists-flawed-marriage*.

266   Quoted in Edberg, "Let Go of Perfectionism."

267   Ann Smith, "The Never-Enough Syndrome," 13. Smith includes these characteristics in
      describing Overt Perfectionists.

268   Miriam Adderholdt, "The Effects of Perfectionism Upon the Self Concepts of Undergrad-
      uate Women at the University of Georgia." Doctoral dissertation, University of Georgia,
      Athens, 1984.

269   Paraphrasing author Harold J. Smith, quoted on the *Goodreads* website. *https://www.goodreads.com/quotes/183818-more-people-would-learn-from-their-mistakes-if-they-weren-t*.

270   Gregoire.

271   Sheri Staak, "The Pitfalls of Perfection." Blog on Sheri Staak's website. Posted Mar. 12,
      2013, *http://sheristaak.com/the-pitfalls-of-perfection/*.

272   Scott, "Perfectionistic Traits."

273   Marc Schoen quoted in Sheri Staak, "The Pitfalls of Perfection." Blog on Sheri Staak's
      website. Posted Mar. 12, 2013, *http://sheristaak.com/the-pitfalls-of-perfection/*.

274   Staak.

275   Emmie Martin, "4 Ways Perfectionists Ruin Their Careers." Posted Aug. 18, 2014 on the
      Business Insider website. *http://www.businessinsider.com/being-a-perfectionist-ruins-your-career-2014-8*.

276   Miriam Adderholdt (quoting work of Schreiber and Herman), "The Effects of Perfection-
      ism Upon the Self Concepts of Undergraduate Women at the University of Georgia."

277   *Psychology Today* staff. "The Perfectionist's Flawed Marriage."

278   Jagtiani.

279   Kevin Leman, *Why Your Best Is Good Enough*, 18.

280   eHarmony Staff. Note: Winter suggests that chronic indecision also gives a perfectionist
      a semblance of control over their fate. (Winter.)

281   Wong.

282   Robin Korth. "My 'Naked' Truth." Posted July 12, 2014, on *The Huffington Post* website *http://www.huffingtonpost.com/robin-korth/sex-over-50_b_5563576.html?ncid=fcbklnkushpmg00000063*.

283 Lauren Slayton, "What's Your Excuse for Not Looking Like Maria Kang?" Posted on the *Huffington Post* website, Dec. 30, 2013, *http://www.huffingtonpost.com/lauren-slayton/whats-your-excuse-for-not_b_4414068.html.*

284 Brené Brown, "Public Shaming . . ."

285 Susan Heitler, "How Contempt Destroys Relationships." Posted Mar. 4, 2013, on the *Psychology Today* website. *https://www.psychologytoday.com/blog/resolution-not-conflict/201303/how-contempt-destroys-relationships.*

286 Adapted from Jane Bluestein, *The Parent's Little Book of Lists: Do's and Don'ts of Effective Parenting* (Deerfield Beach, FL: Health Communications, Inc., 1997), 96–99

Chapter 13: The Perfect Stress for Body and Mind

287 Susanna Grover, excerpted and condensed from a more elaborate description of this process detailed in e-mails sent through March 2, 2015.

288 "Stress and Anxiety." Posted Nov 13, 2014, on the *Scripps* website. (Reviewed by: Fred K. Berger, MD, Addiction and Forensic Psychiatrist, Scripps Memorial Hospital, La Jolla, CA. Also reviewed by David Zieve, MD, MHA, Isla Ogilvie, PhD, and the A.D.A.M. Editorial team.) *https://www.scripps.org/articles/1405-stress-and-anxiety.*

289 Jennifer Drapkin, "The Pitfalls of Perfectionism." Posted Sept. 1, 2005, on the *Psychology Today* website. *https://www.psychologytoday.com/articles/200509/the-pitfalls-perfectionism.*

290 Victoria Maxwell, "The Vicious Triangle of Perfectionism, Anxiety & Depression." Posted Jan. 19, 2012, on the *Psychology Today* website. *https://www.psychologytoday.com/blog/crazy-life/201201/the-vicious-triangle-perfectionism-anxiety-depression.*

291 Kathariya Mokrue, "Perfectionism Leading to Anxiety." Posted Sept. 19, 2013, on the *Huffington Post* website. *http://www.huffingtonpost.com/kathariya-mokrue-phd/effects-of-perfectionism-_b_3950430.html.*

292 Brené Brown, *The Gifts of Imperfection,* 108.

293 Gregoire.

294 Amelia Hill, referencing Carol Platt Liebau's book, *Prude: How the Sex-Obsessed Culture Damages Girls* in "Today's Girls Prefer to Look Sexy Rather Than Be Clever." Posted Dec. 8, 2007, on *The Guardian* wbsite. *http://www.theguardian.com/uk/2007/dec/09/books.politicsphilosophyandsociety.*

295 Lisa Hinkelman, from seminar presentation and notes, "What's Going On for Girls and How Can We Help Them?" presented Jan. 10, 2015, at the Corwin Author Consultant Conference, Thousand Oaks, CA.

296 Jamie Varon, "17 Annoying Things Girls Who Care More About Being Smart Than Being Pretty Understand." Posted Dec. 11, 2014, on the *Thought Catalogue* website. *http://thought catalog.com/jamie-varon/2014/12/17-annoying-things-girls-who-care-more-about-being-smart-than-being-pretty-understand/.*

297 Lauren Martin. "Ladies, The Smarter You Are, The More Likely You Are to Be Single." Posted July 22, 2014 on the *Elite Daily* website. *http://elitedaily.com/women/intelligent-women-likely-single/678309/.*

298 Ann Smith, "The Never-Enough Syndrome," 11.

299   John Spencer, "Why Perfectionism Is a Career-Killer." Posted on John Spencer's website. *http://www.spencerideas.org/2015/03/why-perfectionism-is-career-killer.html.*

300   Anna Quindlen, *Being Perfect.* New York: Random House, 2009. (Quotes also available at *http://www.goodreads.com/work/quotes/106493-being-perfect.*)

301   Teversham, 55–56. Moorman and Haller also describe the "'Make Me Psychosis" as one of their "verbally transmitted diseases" that are "continually affecting our physical, emotional, and mental health, both as individuals and as a society." (*The Abracadabra Effect*, introduction.)

302   Shelly Bullard, "How to Stop Medicating with Men." Posted Oct. 8, 2012, on the *Mind-BodyGreen* website, *http://www.mindbodygreen.com/0-6375/How-to-Stop-Medicating-with-Men.html*

303   Katherine Muller, quoted in Melinda Beck, "Silencing the Voice That Says You're a Fraud." Posted June 16, 2009, on the *Wall Street Journal* website. *http://online.wsj.com/news/articles/SB124511712673817527.*

304   Beck, "Silencing the Voice That Says You're a Fraud."

305   Alistair Ostel, quoted in Wilson. Note: Ostel's studies involved British headteachers (school principals), although he cautions that the risks of absolutist (all-or-nothing) thinking occurs across jobs and personality types.

306   Taryn Brumfitt quoted in Erica Williams Simon, "The Story Behind One of the Best Before-And-After Photos I've Ever Seen." Video of Taryn Brumfitt, Founder of Body Image Movement, posted on the *UpWorthy* website, *http://www.upworthy.com/the-story-behind-one-of-the-best-before-and-after-photos-ive-ever-seen?c=fea.*

307   Chris Tognotti, "Yes, Men Struggle With Body Issues, Too: Here's My Story." Posted April 29, 2014, on the *Huffington Post* website. *http://www.huffingtonpost.com/bustle/positive-body-image-_b_5193674.html.* Note: Chris writes from the perspective of a man who has dealt with body and weight issues since childhood.

308   Nina Bahadur, "If 'Real Men' Posed in Underwear Ads." Posted July 1, 2014 on the *Huffington Post* website. *http://www.huffingtonpost.com/2014/07/01/real-mens-bodies-underwear-ads_n_5543693.html.*

309   Nicky Hutchinson and Chris Calland quoted in Joanna Moorhead, Children Start Dieting as Young as Ten." Posted May 7, 2012 on *The Guardian* website. *http://www.theguardian.com/education/2012/may/07/body-image-anxiety-primary-school-pupils.*

310   Chris Calland, quoted in Moorhead.

311   Claire Bates, "A Quarter of Children Under Ten Diet Because They Think They Are Overweight and Face Bullying Taunts, Shocking Survey Finds." Posted Jan. 5, 2012, on the *Daily Mail* website. *http://www.dailymail.co.uk/health/article-2082500/A-quarter-children-10-diet-think-overweight-face-bullying-taunts-shocking-survey-finds.html.*

312   Katy Winter, "What Would You Change About Your Body?" Posted Nov. 4, 2014, on the *Daily Mail* website. *http://www.dailymail.co.uk/femail/article-2820169/What-change-body-Moving-video-shows-children-add-super-power-adults-just-want-fix-flaws.html.*

313   Chris Calland, quoted in Moorhead.

314   Adderholdt and Goldberg.

315   Ellie Krieger, "Stop Using These Words When You Talk About Food." Published May 25, 2015 in the *Albuquerque Journal*, C2. Krieger also included "detox" and "skinny" in her list, noting that this "morally judgmental" language shows food in a negative, harmful light, and likewise promotes unhealthy thinking and behaviors.

316 Antony and Swinson, 248.

317 "Eating Disorder Statistics." Posted 2015 on the *National Association of Anorexia Nervosa and Associated Disorders* website. *http://www.anad.org/get-information/about-eating-disorders/eating-disorders-statistics/*

318 "Pro-ana." Definitions posted between 2003 and 2007 on the *Urban Dictionary* website, *http://www.urbandictionary.com/define.php?term=pro-ana.* Note: Other eating disorders, such as compulsive overeating, are not part of the pro-ana movement. Also, Joanne Eglash, 'Thin-spiration' Sites Promote Anorexia, Bulimia, and Other Eating Disorders," posted August 2, 2013, on the *Examiner* website at *http://www.examiner.com/article/thinspiration-sites-promote-anorexia-bulimia-and-other-eating-disorders.*

319 "Eating Disorder Statistics." Only 5 percent of women have body types that naturally reflect those we see in advertisements.

320 Taryn Brumfitt, "Dear Maria Kang . . . this is my excuse (for not having a body like yours) Posted Nov. 29, 2013, on the *Body Image Movement* website, *http://bodyimagemovement.com.au/dear-maria-kang-this-is-my-excuse/.* Brumfitt promotes "reverse progress fitness," encouraging women to love their bodies at any size. Also, "Australian Mom Lashes Back at the 'Fit Mom.'" *Good Morning America* interview from Dec. 17, 2013, available on *YouTube* (published Dec. 26, 2013). *https://www.youtube.com/watch?v=OHK4QA3YPEQ;* also Andrea Wurtz-burger, "Everything You Need to Know About the 'Reverse Progress' Fitness Movement." Published (*Redbook,* Healthy Living) May 21, 2014, on the *Yahoo* wbsite. *https://www.yahoo.com/music/bp/everything-know-reverse-progress-fitness-movement-174800442.html.*

321 Gregoire.

322 Chernoff, "10 Painfully Obvious Truths Everyone Forgets Too Soon."

323 Cameron, *The Artist's Way,* 120.

324 Lynn Collins, "Help! My Child's Having a Feeling." *Families in Recovery* (Vol. 11, Issue 2, 1991): 8-9; also Jane Bluestein, "Non-Supportive Responses to Avoid: Yes, These Really Do Make Things Worse." Posted May 7, 2013, on Jane Bluestein's website. *http://janebluestein.com/2013/non-supportive-responses-to-avoid/.*

325 Quoted in Sarah Hepola, Interview with Anne Lamott: "We Stuffed Scary Feelings Down and They Made Us Insane." Posted Nov. 3, 2014, on the *Salon* website. *http://www.salon.com/2014/11/04/anne_lamott_we_stuffed_scary_feelings_down_and_they_made_us_insane/.*

326 Collins, 8-9; also Bluestein, "Non-Supportive Responses to Avoid."

327 Jane Bluestein, "Talking with . . . Grace Slick." *Families in Recovery* (Vol. II, Issue 1, 1991): 15.

328 Marc Chernoff, "8 Things Unhappy People Refuse to Admit." Posted August 29, 2013, on the *Marc and Angel Hack Life* website, [*http://www.marcandangel.com/2013/08/29/8-things-unhappy-people-refuse-to-admit/.*

329 Adderholdt and Goldberg.

330 Melinda Smith and Jeanne Segal, "Cutting and Self-Harm: Self-Injury Help, Support, and Treatment." Post last updated Dec. 2014 on the *Helpguide* website. *http://www.helpguide.org/articles/anxiety/cutting-and-self-harm.htm.*

331 Jeanie Lerche Davis, "Cutting and Self-Harm: Warning Signs and Treatment." Posted on the *WebMD* website. *http://www.webmd.com/mental-health/features/cutting-self-harm-signs-treatment.*

332 Smith and Segal.

333 Melton, *Carry On, Warrior*, 14–15; also Glennon Doyle Melton, "About Glennon." Bio posted on Melton's website. *http://momastery.com/blog/about-glennon/*.

334 "Perfectionism is a bigger than perceived risk factor in suicide." Note: The statistic for U.S. suicides is consistent with the 2013 number reported in "Facts and Figures (Suicide)." Posted on the *American Foundation for Suicide Prevention* website (copyright 2015). *https://www. afsp.org/understanding-suicide/facts-and-figures*.

335 Drapkin.

336 Haker.

337 Haker. Haker also notes that "suicidal ideation is distinguished from suicidal behavior in that it includes the both the thought and desire to die as well as the actual action toward taking one's life. . . . It is estimated that for every successful suicide there are 25 attempts made; as a result, nearly 400,000 people are treated in the hospital for self-inflicted wounds every year, which unquestionably makes suicide a public health concern."

338 Melissa Dahl, "The Alarming New Research on Perfectionism." Posted Sept. 30, 2014, on the *New York Magazine* website. *http://nymag.com/scienceofus/2014/09/alarming-new-research-on-perfectionism.html*.

339 Eric Metcalf, "Perfectionism and Suicide Risk: How to Help." Posted Dec. 8, 2014 on the *Addiction Treatment Magazine* website. *http://www.addictiontreatmentmagazine.com/addiction-news/ mental-health/perfectionism-suicide-risk-help/*.

340 Dahl.

341 David Conroy, quote posted Aug. 12, 2014, as a tweet on Don Tapscott's account. *https:// twitter.com/dtapscott/status/499201539744219136*. Note: Conroy's statement actually starts with the comment, "Suicide isn't chosen." However, given the deliberate nature of a perfectionist's suicide, I have a hard time reconciling this notion with the precision, planning, and commitment described in the literature, and have decided to omit this part of the quote in this context.

342 Dahl.

343 Metcalf.

Chapter 14: Living with Perfectionism

344 Victoria Maxwell.

345 Alysa Landry, "Navajo Weaver Shares Story with Authentic Rugs." Article on the *Native American Times* website. Posted Mar. 16, 2009, *http://www.nativetimes.com/archives/22/1217-navajo -weaver-shares-story-with-authentic-rugs*.

346 Harry Benally and Harold Carey. "Navajo Rug Guide." Posted on the *Navajo Arts* website. http://navajo-arts.com/navojo-rugs.html.

347 Krishna Kumari Challa, "Science and Art—Perfection and Imperfection." Posted on the *Sci-Art* website May 26, 2010. *http://kkartlab.in/profiles/blogs/science-and-art-perfection*.

348 "Islamic Art." Posted on *Wikipedia*, modified Aug. 28, 2014. *http://en.wikipedia.org/wiki/Islamic_art*.

349 Elicia Brown.

350 "Wabi-sabi." Image posted on *Reference for Woodworking* website, 2011. *http://referenceforww2. tumblr.com/image/6547460506*

351 "Wabi-sabi." Definition and description on Wikipedia. *http://en.wikipedia.org/wiki/Wabi-sabi.*

352 Zo Newell, "Kintsugi as Yoga: Filling the Cracks with Gold." Posted June 23, 2012 on the *Elephant Journal* website. *http://www.elephantjournal.com/2012/06/kintsugi-as-yoga-filling-the-cracks -with-gold-zo-newell/.*

353 Benally and Carey.

354 Julia Cameron, *The Vein of Gold: A Journey to Your Creative Heart* (New York: Jeremy P. Tarcher/ Putnam Books, 1996), 191.

355 Challa.

356 Marc Schoen, "Is Perfection Worth Striving For?" *Spirit* magazine (March 2013).

357 Goins.

358 Richard Morgan, "A Thousand Cuts." Posted Dec. 12, 2014 on *The New Yorker* web page. *http://www.newyorker.com/culture/culture-desk/paper-cutouts;* also Hannah Kohl, "Hannah Kohl Papercuts." Posted 2014 on *A Thousand Tiny Snips* website. *http://www.athousandtinysnips.com.*

359 Nathan Barry, "Self-Doubt and Launch Stats." Posted May 28, 2013 on Nathan Barry's website. *http://nathanbarry.com/self-doubt-launch-stats/.*

360 Jean Rhys, quote posted on *Goodreads* website. *https://www.goodreads.com/quotes/137048-all-of- writing-is-a-huge-lake-there-are-great.* With thanks to Betty Carlson.

361 Pyryt, 10–14. Also available on the *Davidson Institute* website: *http://www.davidsongifted.org/db/ Articles_id_10459.aspx.*

362 Dean.

363 "Perfectionism." *University of Illinois at Urbana-Champaign Counseling Center.* Note: Leman uses terms like "pursuers (or seekers) of excellence" with similar ways to distinguish these indi- viduals from perfectionists. Kevin Leman, *The Birth Order Book* (Ada, MI: Revell, a division of Baker Publishing Group, 2009), 120–121.

364 Edberg, "Let Go of Perfectionism."

365 Includes suggestions from Teversham, 3–12; also Polona Somrak, "The Soul Navigator." Blog on the *Ascension Pioneers* website. Posted May 17, 2013, *http://ascension-pioneers.org/ articles/588-the-soul-navigator.html;* also Antony and Swinson, 64–77; also Leman, *The Birth Order Book,* 120–121.

Chapter 15: Being Your Biggest, Baddest Self

366 Author unknown. "Twenty Dollars." Story posted on the *Inspiration Speak* website. *http:// www.inspirationpeak.com/cgi-bin/stories.cgi?record=33.*

367 Kute Blackson, "What Other People Think of You is None of Your Business." Posted Aug. 26, 2013, on Kute Blackson's web page. *http://kuteblackson.com/blog/?p=1235.*

368 Ted Rubin, quote posted June 2, 2013, on Ted Rubin's website. *http://tedrubin.com/your-value- doesnt-decrease-based-on-someones-inability-to-see-your-worth/.*

369 Maria Rivera, quoted on *Search Quotes* website. *http://www.searchquotes.com/quotation/ Sometimes_people_try_to_expose_whats_wrong_with_you,_because_they_cant_handle_whats_right _about_y/465886/.*

370 Michael W. Kraus, "The Power to Be Me." Article on *Psychology Today* website. Posted Jan. 26, 2012, in "Under the Influence," *http://www.psychologytoday.com/blog/under-the-influence/201201/the-power-be-me.*

371 Luminita Saviuc, "9 Reasons Why You Should No Longer Care About People's Approval," on the *PurposeFairy* website, posted April 22, 2012 at *http://www.purposefairy.com/5212/9-reasons-why-you-should-no-longer-care-about-peoples-approval/*; also Luminita Saviuc, "15 Things You Should Give Up to Be Happy." Blog on *PurposeFairy* website. Posted May 30, 2011, *http://www.purposefairy.com/3308/15-things-you-should-give-up-in-order-to-be-happy/.*

372 Steve Jobs, quote posted July 19, 2014, on the Shift of the Ages Facebook page. *https://www.facebook.com/shiftoftheages/photos/a.10151121301348951.448044.165116518950/10152240188588951/?type=1&theater.*

373 Ralph Waldo Emerson, quote posted on Goodreads website. *https://www.goodreads.com/quotes/876-to-be-yourself-in-a-world-that-is-constantly-trying.*

374 Ernest Hemingway, quoted in Martha Beck, "Heartbreak Academy: How to Make It Through." Posted Feb. 17, 2013, on Martha Beck's website. *http://marthabeck.com/2013/02/heartbreak-academy/.*

375 Ashkay Dubey, quote posted on the *Goodreads* website. *https://www.goodreads.com/quotes/828232-healing-doesn-t-mean-the-damage-never-existed-it-means-the.*

376 Robert Frost, quote posted on the *Big Think* website. *http://bigthink.com/words-of-wisdom/robert-frost-on-defining-yourself.*

377 "Is Pride a Bad Thing?" Comments posted on the *Debate* website at the time of this writing show a 50-50 split in the responses, with remarks associating pride with sin, deceit, insecurity, prejudice, and a sense of superiority. (The numbers shifted slightly after I weighed in on pride's behalf.) *http://www.debate.org/opinions/is-pride-a-bad-thing.*

378 Ashleigh Brilliant, quote posted on the *Goodreads* website. *https://www.goodreads.com/book/show/657266.I_May_Not_Be_Totally_Perfect_but_Parts_of_Me_Are_Excellent.*

379 Courtney E. Martin, quote posted on Goodreads website. *https://www.goodreads.com/quotes/891245-you-know-what-s-really-powerfully-sexy-a-sense-of-humor.*

380 Image and text on Christina Huffington, "Subversion, Clothing Brand, Awesomely Redefines 'Dress for Your Shape' on Facebook." Blog on *Huffington Post* website. Posted April 22, 2013, *http://www.huffingtonpost.com/2013/04/22/dress-for-your-shape_n_3131220.html.*

381 Courtney Walsh, posted Oct. 2, 2013, on Courtney Walsh's Facebook page. *https://www.facebook.com/147516272002947/photos/a.534309606656943.1073741826.147516272002947/534309586656945/?type=1&theater*; also in e-mail correspondence. Walsh's posts appear on her website at *http://www.courtneyawalsh.com*, as well as on her blog at *http://scribechickie.blogspot.com*; used with permission.

382 James K. A. Smith, "Secure Your Own Mask First." Posted May 24, 2013 on the *Cardas Daily* website. *http://www.cardus.ca/blog/2013/05/secure-your-own-mask-first.*

383 Adapted from Jane Bluestein, *The Win-Win Classroom* (Thousand Oaks, CA: Corwin Publishing, 2008), 259.

384 Larry Eisenberg, quoted on the *ThinkExist* website. *http://en.thinkexist.com/quotation/for_peace_of_mind-resign_as_general_manager_of/254137.html.*

385 Alina Tugend quoted in Elicia Brown.

386 Blackson.

387 Chiara Fucarino, "22 Things Happy People Do Differently." Posted Oct. 31, 2012 on the *Successify!* website. *http://successify.net/2012/10/31/22-things-happy-people-do-differently/*.

388 Rechtschaffen.

389 Melissa McCreery, "The Hidden Hungers Quiz." Posted on the *Too Much on Her Plate* website. *http://www.toomuchonherplate.com/docs/biddenbungersquiz.pdf*. Note: She includes the hunger for rest, stress relief, emotional ease, self-compassion, along with self-care and me-time, noting that "one unfed hunger can actually lead to more hunger in the other areas."

390 Kristin Neff, quote posted on Kristin Neff's website. *http://self-compassion.org*.

391 Kristin Neff quoted in Tara Parker-Pope, "Go Easy on Yourself, a New Wave of Research Urges." Posted Feb. 28, 2011, on the *New York Times* website, *http://well.blogs.nytimes.com/2011/02/28/go-easy-on-yourself-a-new-wave-of-research-urges/?_php=true&_type=blogs&_r=0*.

392 Susan W. Berry, quote posted Feb. 20, 2015, on the Evolved Eating Facebook page. *https://www.facebook.com/evolvedeating/photos/pb.387375795971.-2207520000.1426189254./10153148315250972/?type=3&theater*.

393 Beck, "Silencing the Voice That Says You're a Fraud."

394 Teversham, xii.

395 Chick Moorman and Thomas Haller, "Making a Mistake in Front of Your Class." Posted March 20, 2015, on Jane Bluestein's website. *http://janebluestein.com/2015/making-a-mistake-in-front-of-your-class/*.

396 Thomas Carlyle, quote posted on the *Quoteworld* website. *http://www.quoteworld.org/quotes/2409*

397 Aaron Lazare, quoted in Trudy Ludwig, *Sorry* (Berkeley, CA: Tricycle Press, 2006), in afterword.

398 Dale E. Turner, quote posted July 28, 2013, on the Positivity Vibrations Facebook page. *https://www.facebook.com/Positivity.Vibrations/photos/a.95130334336.76396.93061444336/10151726338114337/?type=1&permPage=1*.

399 Jinny Ditzler, "Appreciate Your Success." Posted Nov. 30, 2009, on the *Best Year Yet* website. *https://bestyearyet.wordpress.com/2009/11/30/appreciate-your-success/*.

400 Warrell.

401 Sauvic, "5 Ways to Let Go of Your Inner Critic and Let the Real You Shine."

402 Warrell.

403 Adderholdt and Goldberg.

404 Ann Smith, "Am I Good Enough Yet? Yes You Are!" Article on *Psychology Today* website. Posted Nov. 10, 2010, *http://www.psychologytoday.com/blog/healthy-connections/201011/am-i-good-enough-yet-yes-you-are*.

405 Ditzler.

406 Kathy Manning, quoted in Elicia Brown.

407 Lisa Rivero, *A Parent's Guide to Gifted Teens: Living with Intense and Creative Adolescents* (Scottsdale, AZ: Great Potential Press, 2010), 78.

408 Amy B. Scher, "5 Ways to Overcome Feeling Overwhelmed." Blog on *PurposeFairy* website. Posted Mar. 6, 2013, *http://www.purposefairy.com/10430/5-ways-to-overcome-feeling-overwhelmed/*.

409 Drapkin.

410 "Perfectionism." *University of Illinois at Urbana-Champaign Counseling Center.*

Chapter 16: Developing Psychological Strength

411 Glenn Capelli, "Leading Learning: The Art, Science, and Craft of Teaching." Podcast posted Jan. 26, 2013 on Jane Bluestein's website. *http://janebluestein.com/2013/leading-learning-with-glenn-capelli/.*

412 "Kaizen." Wikipedia entry. Modified Jun. 19, 2013, *http://en.wikipedia.org/wiki/Kaizen*

413 Warrell.

414 Marvin Marshall, *Discipline Without Stress, Punishment or Rewards* (Los Alamitos, CA: Piper Press, 2001), 180.

415 Although this quote has been widely attributed to both Winston Churchill and Abraham Lincoln, this site references a 1953 book about public speaking by this author as the "earliest first match." "Success Is Going from Failure to Failure Without Losing Your Enthusiasm: Winston Churchill? Abraham Lincoln? Apocryphal? Anonymous?" Posted June 28, 2014, on the *Quote Investigator* website. *http://quoteinvestigator.com/2014/06/28/success/.*

416 Neale Donald Walsch. Quote posted on *Brainy Quote* website. *http://www.brainyquote.com/quotes/quotes/n/nealedonal452086.html*

417 Spencer.

418 Warrell.

419 Ken Davis, "A Disease That Can Stop You from Living." Posted May 31, 2012 on Ken Davis's website. *http://www.kendavis.com/commentary/a-disease-that-can-stop-you-from-living/#more-2838.*

420 George Burns, quote posted on *Brainy Quote* website. *http://www.brainyquote.com/quotes/quotes/g/georgeburn121344.html.*

421 Author unknown. Quote posted on the *Get Organized Wizard* website, Oct. 31, 2012. *http://www.getorganizedwizard.com/blog/2012/10/when-you-stumble-make-it-part-of-the-dance/.*

422 Zig Ziglar, quoted in Kevin Kruse, "Zig Ziglar: 10 Quotes That Can Change Your Life." Posted Nov. 28, 2012, on the *Forbes* website. *http://www.forbes.com/sites/kevinkruse/2012/11/28/zig-ziglar-10-quotes-that-can-change-your-life/*

423 Henry Ford, quoted on the *Brainy Quote* website. *http://www.brainyquote.com/quotes/quotes/h/henryford121339.html.*

424 Winston Churchill, quoted on the *Think Exist* website. *http://thinkexist.com/quotation/success_is_not_final-failure_is_not_fatal-it_is/150143.html.*

425 Ken Robinson, "How Schools Kill Creativity." Filmed Feb. 2006 for TED website. *https://www.ted.com/talks/ken_robinson_says_schools_kill_creativity.*

426 David Burns, quoted in BJB, "Aim for Success, Not Perfection," posted Feb. 19, 2008, on the *Between the Lines* blog. *http://voicesfromloysville.blogspot.com/2008/02/aim-for-success-not-perfection.html.*

427 Moorman and Haller, "Making a Mistake in Front of Your Class."

428 Wendy Webb, "Why You Should Reward Employees for Failures." Posted March 10, 2015 on the *National Federation of Independent Businesses* website. *http://www.nfib.com/article/why*

-you-should-reward-employees-for-failures-bizhelp-68279/?utm_campaign=BR&utm_source=Facebook&utm_medium=Social.

429   Adda Birnir, "The True Meaning of 'Fail Harder.'" Posted July 19, 2013, on the *Skillcrush* website. *http://skillcrush.com/2013/07/19/the-true-meaning-of-fail-harder/*.

430   Warrell.

431   Karen Wright, "How to Take Feedback: Learn to give and get criticism." Posted Mar. 15, 2011 on *Psychology Today* website. *http://www.psychologytoday.com/articles/201103/how-take-feedback*.

432   Danielle LaPorte, quote posted on the *Goodreads* website. *https://www.goodreads.com/quotes /817248-you-will-always-be-too-much-of-something-for-someone*.

433   Winston Churchill, quoted in Saviuc, "9 Reasons Why You Should No Longer Care About People's Approval."

434   Albert Einstein, quoted in Saviuc, "9 Reasons Why You Should No Longer Care About People's Approval."

435   Acuff.

436   Mary Anne Radmacher, quote posted on Mary Ann Radmacher's home page on August 13, 2013, *http://www.maryanneradmacher.net*.

437   Wright, referring to work by organizational psychologist Robert Sutton.

438   Not long after, I was visiting a preschool and overheard one of the kids making fun of a little girl's hair. The girl just shrugged and said, "You're not in charge of my hair." I learned a great lesson from a confident 3-year-old that day.

439   Acuff.

440   My thanks to my friend and colleague, Peggy Bielen, for this suggestion. I've used this sentence (as well as "Thank you for sharing" or "No kidding") to avoid getting sucked into arguments or defensiveness on numerous occasions.

441   Wright.

442   Sauvic, "15 Things You Should Give Up to Be Happy."

443   Fucarino.

444   Regina Brett, "Regina Brett's 45 Life Lessons and 5 to Grow On." Posted May 28, 2006 on the *Cleveland Plain Dealer* website. *http://www.cleveland.com/brett/blog/index.ssf/2006/05/regina_bretts _45_life_lessons.html*.

445   Ryan Ferreras, quoted on the *Board of Wisdom* website. *http://boardofwisdom.com/togo/Quotes/Show Quote/?msgid=428714#.VTM5byk310A*.

446   Parrott, 33.

447   Rechtschaffen.

448   Annie Lennox, posted March 7, 2015, on the BBC 4 Facebook page. *https://www.facebook. com/BBCRadio4/photos/a.10155218400895459.1073741833.401538510458/10155229866815459/?t ype=1&theater*. Note: Time has become increasingly precious and I frankly don't care about many of the things that rattled me in years past. I have neither the energy nor the memory to hold grudges for long, and many experiences that once caused me to cringe carry little of the charge they once held. This may not be true for everyone, but I'm finding age to be one of the best therapies I've yet to encounter.

449   Umar Ibn Al-Khattaab, quote posted on *The Authentic Base* website. *http://theauthenticbase. wordpress.com/2011/03/08/umar-ibn-al-khattaab-no-amount-of-guilt-can-change-the-past/*.

450   Elicia Brown.

451   Calvin Coolidge, quoted on the *Success Vibe* website. *http://www.successvibe.com/forum/threads/ calvin-coolidge-persistence-quote.3044/*.

452   Marilyn vos Savant, quoted on the *Positively Positive* website. *http://www.positivelypositive.com/ quotes/being-defeated-is-often-a-temporary-condition-giving-up-is-what-makes-it-permanent/*.

453   Jason Selk, "Your New Mantra: Done Is Better Than Perfect." Posted Mar. 3, 2015, on the *Inc.* website. *http://www.inc.com/jason-selk/done-is-better-than-perfect.html?cid=sf01002*.

454   Georgia O'Keeffe. Posted May 18, 2015, on the *A Mighty Girl* Facebook page. *https://www. facebook.com/amightygirl/photos/a.360833590619627.72897.316489315054055/849604395075875/? type=1&theater*.

455   Diana Reid, "15 Ways to Bring Meaning Back into Your Life." Blog on *PurposeFairy* website. Posted Mar. 28, 2013, *http://www.purposefairy.com/10482/15-ways-to-bring-meaning-back-into- your-life/*.

456   KT Witten, quote posted on the *Tiny Buddha* website. *http://tinybuddha.com/wisdom-quotes/ your-dream-doesnt-have-an-expiration-date-take-a-deep-breath-and-try-again/*.

457   Henrik Edberg, "Give Yourself a Break and Choose Percentages Instead of Perfection." Translation posted on Dec. 16, 2013, at *http://blog.daum.net/_blog/BlogTypeView.do?blogid=oL1 ZK&articleno=8748972&categoryId=509825&regdt=20131216110441*.

458   Fuller.

459   Pyryt.

460   Excerpted from a quote by Neale Donald Walsch, posted on Facebook, Feb. 16, 2015. *https://www.facebook.com/NealeDonaldWalsch/photos/a.400017592343.181782.40638047343/10152 620073877344/?type=1&fref=nf*.

461   Amit Amin, "The 31 Benefits of Gratitude You Didn't Know About: How Gratitude Can Change Your Life." Posted on the *Happier Human* website. *http://happierhuman.com/benefits-of- gratitude/*; also Jane Bluestein, Judy Lawrence, and SJ Sanchez, *Magic, Miracles and Synchronic- ity: A Journal of Awareness and Gratitude* (Albuquerque, NM: I.S.S. Publications, 2009).

462   Oprah Winfrey, quote posted on *The Quote Yard* website. *http://www.quoteyard.com/the-more- you-praise-and-celebrate-your-life-the-more-there-is-in-life-to-celebrate/*.

463   Author unknown. Quote posted on *Emily's Quotes* website. *http://emilysquotes.com/if-we-do-not- feel-grateful-for-what-we-already-have-what-makes-us-think-wed-be-happy-with-more/*.

464   Robert Holden, quote posted on *Spiritual Quotes to Live By* website, *http://www.spiritual-quotes- to-live-by.com/robert-holden-quotes.html*.

465   Mizuta Masahide, quoted in Martin Pigg, "Masahide's Barn and the Meaning of Life." Posted March 23, 2014 on the *Medium* website. *https://medium.com/@martinpigg/masahides-barn- and-the-meaning-of-life-d881c8d7a7c9*.

466   Pigg.

467   Adapted from Jane Bluestein, "Gratitude: More than Just an Attitude." Posted Nov. 25, 2013, on Jane Bluestein's website. *http://janebluestein.com/2013/gratitude-more-than-just-an-atti- tude/*. This list includes one activity from each of the 12 chapters from original manuscript of *Magic, Miracles and Synchronicity*.

Chapter 17: In Connection with Others

468 Tiziana Casciano and Miguel Sousa Lobo. "Fool vs. Jerk: Whom Would You Hire?" Posted July 25, 2005, on the *Harvard Business School* website. *http://hbswk.hbs.edu/item/4916.html*.

469 Greenspon.

470 Eleanor Roosevelt, quoted on the *Site2Quotes* website. *http://site2quotes.com/friendship-quotes/friendship-with-ones-self-is-all-eleanor-roosevelt*.

471 Brené Brown, *The Gifts of Imperfection*, 25.

472 Courtney Walsh, excerpted from post, "Mirror, Mirror," shared in e-mail correspondence. Used with permission. Note: Like much of the material I discovered for this book that is addressed exclusively to women, I would like to confirm my belief that these words could resonate with many men as well.

473 Karen Salmansohn, Quote posted on Phuckyquote's Instagram page on the *Websta Instagram Web Viewer* page (no date). *http://websta.me/p/783535766193480656_216824519;* also posted to Facebook, August 12, 2014. *https://www.facebook.com/Ludacris/photos/a.10150257898620513.340076.49581355512/10152618230510513/?type=1&theater*.

474 Bryant McGill, posted on Bryant McGill's website. *http://bryantmcgill.com/excerpts/dont-waste-time-everyone-deserves-love.html*.

475 Charles F. Glassman, "6 Ways to Find a Soulmate." Blog posted Jan. 8, 2015, on Charles Glassman's website. *http://www.charlesglassmanmd.com/finding-your-soul-mate/blog-26/*.

476 Fred Rogers, quote excerpted from *The World According to Mister Rogers: Important Things to Remember* and posted on the *Deseret News* website. *http://www.deseretnews.com/top/1924/9/Love-isnt-a-state-20-life-lessons-from-Mister-Rogers.html*

477 Adapted from the introduction to Jane Bluestein, "What's So Hard About Win-Win?" a blog based on an article written for the Sept. 2011 issue of Educational Leadership magazine. Posted Jan. 8, 2013. *http://janebluestein.com/2013/whats-so-hard-about-win-win/*.

478 Diane Rheos, "The System Is Aggressive—We Are Love." Posted Mar. 3, 2015 on Diane Rheos's website. *http://www.dianerheos.com/the-system-is-aggressive-we-are-love/*.

479 Elizabeth Gilbert, posted on Feb. 10, 2015, on Elizabeth Gilbert's Facebook page; also posted Nov. 11, 2014, on Gilbert's website. *http://www.elizabethgilbert.com/know-where-you-have-power-and-where-you-do-not-have-power-dear-ones-duri/*.

480 Diane Rheos, "The System Is Aggressive—We Are Love."

481 Adapted from Jane Bluestein, "The Challenge of Setting Boundaries." Posted Aug. 10, 2012, on Jane Bluestein's website. *http://janebluestein.com/2012/the-challenge-of-setting-boundaries/*.

482 Leon F. Seltzer, "How—and How Not—to Stand Up for Yourself." Posted Sept. 5, 2012, on the *Psychology Today* website. *https://www.psychologytoday.com/blog/evolution-the-self/201209/how-and-how-not-stand-yourself*.

483 Seltzer.

484 Brosh.

485 Brosh.

486 Bluestein, "What's Wrong with I-Messages?"

487 Bluestein, "The Challenge of Setting Boundaries."

488 Brosh.

489 Scher.

490 Teversham, 57.

491 Brosh.

492 Author unknown, attributed to Mastin Kipp. Quote posted on *Emily's Quotes* website. *http:// emilysquotes.com/dont-change-so-people-will-like-you-be-yourself-and-the-right-people-will-love-the-real- you/*; also Jane Bluestein, "Dealing with Difficult Colleagues: What You Can Do About It." Posted Aug. 11, 2012 on Jane Bluestein's website. *http://janebluestein.com/2012/dealing-with- difficult-colleagues/*.

493 This is true even when I'm asleep: the foot of our bed is about four feet from where I've researched and written the bulk of this book. I do *not* recommend this arrangement, but it happens to be the quietest and most comfortable place inside the house for writing.

494 Shauna Springer, "How Perfectionism Hurts Relationships." Posted Sept. 29, 2012, on the *Psychology Today* website. *http://www.psychologytoday.com/blog/the-joint-adventures-well-educated- couples/201209/how-perfectionism-hurts-relationships*.

495 Diane Rheos, "BE— Perfectly Imperfect." Posted April 3, 2013, on Diane Rheos's website. *http://www.dianerheos.com/be-perfectly-imperfect/*.

496 Fucarino.

497 Edberg, "Let Go of Perfectionism: 7 Powerful Tips That Will Help You."

498 Staak.

499 Schoen, "Is Perfection Worth Striving For?"

500 Peter Shankman, quoted in Rosalie Rayburn, "Kill Them (with Kindness)." Published in the *Albuquerque Journal* (Apr. 2, 2015, B2).

501 Although this quote was recently attributed to Harry S. Truman, a similar version appeared as early as the mid-nineteenth century (with no evidence of any connection to Truman). "A Man May Do an Immense Deal of Good, If He Does Not Care Who Gets the Credit." Posted on the *Quote Investigator* website. *http://quoteinvestigator.com/2010/12/21/ doing-good-selfless/*.

502 Sauvic, "15 Things You Should Give Up to Be Happy."

503 Dodinsky, quote posted on the *Goodreads* website. *https://www.goodreads.com/quotes/837882-be- there-for-others-but-never-leave-yourself-behind*. This quote is from Dodinsky's book, *In the Garden of Thoughts* (Naperville, IL: Sourcebooks, 2013).

504 Dodinsky, quote posted on the *Raw for Beauty* website. *http://rawforbeauty.com/blog/when-faced- with-senseless-drama-spiteful-criticisms-and-misguided-opinions-walking-away-is-the-best-way-to-stand- up-for-yourself-to-respond-with-anger-is-an-endorsement-of-their-attitude-dodi.html*.

505 Adapted from Bluestein, *The Win-Win Classroom*, 256–7.

506 Rhonda Britten, posted on the *Inspiration Stories* website. *http://www.inspirationalstories.com/ quotes/t/rhonda-britten-on-forgiveness/*.

507 Jerose (Jerusalem P. Fermasis), quote on *Tumblr* website. *https://www.tumblr.com/search/jerose*.

508 Jane Bluestein, "Dealing with Difficult Colleagues."

509 Fucarino.

510 Adapted from material on healthy and unhealthy friendships: Jane Bluestein and Eric Katz, *High School's Not Forever* (Deerfield Beach, FL: Health Communications, Inc., 2007), 63–64.

511a *Deepak Chopra. Fire in the Heart: A Spiritual Guide for Teens* (New York: Simon and Schuster Books for Young Readers, 2004), 187.

Chapter 18: Moving Forward: Mind and Body

512 Robin Sharma, "30 Robin Sharma Inspirational Quotes to Live By." Posted on the *Addicted 2 Success* website. *http://addicted2success.com/quotes/30-inspirational-robin-sharma-quotes-to-live-by/*.

513 Burns, "The Perfectionist's Script for Self-Defeat," 46.

514 Sam Watts, "Disintegration and Reintegration: The Path of Awakening from Beginning to End." Posted Dec. 4, 2011, on the *Freestyle Awakening* website. *https://freestyleawakening.word press.com/2011/12/04/disintegration-and-reintegration-the-path-of-awakening-from-beginning-to-end/*.

515 Eckhart Tolle, "Eckhart on the Dark Night of the Soul," posted Oct. 2011 on Eckhart Tolle's website. *https://www.eckharttolle.com/newsletter/october-2011*. I would also see this as a potential for what we might call a breakdown—the falling apart before coming back together in a new, more functional state.

516 Tolle.

517 Robin Amos Kahn, "The Only Way Out Is Through." Posted Oct. 19, 2012 on the *Huffington Post* website. *http://www.huffingtonpost.com/robin-amos-kahn/emotional-health_b_1971749.html*.

518 Watts.

519 Cynthia Occe, quote posted on the *Quotes Pictures* website. *http://quotespictures.net/quotes-pictures-pics/2014/07/for-a-seed-to-achieve-cynthia-occe.png*.

520 Kahn.

521 Watts.

522 I offer this statement with caution. Alfano notes that treatment in mental health facilities may be dictated by the insurance companies, with an emphasis on "stabilizing" patients and releasing them as quickly as possible. "The most cost-effective treatment plan, of course, involves drugs," he says, cautioning that some of the drugs can be addictive or cause harmful side effects. He recommends programs that offer human interaction and enough time to allow healing to occur instead of the quick-fix approach he has seen based more on cost savings, speed, and results that, with "real therapy," are harder to quantify.

523 Springer.

524 Anne Lamott, quoted in Hepola.

525 Tolle.

526 A similar version of this quote, "If you're going through hell, don't stop," is attributed to Douglas Bloch. "If You're Going Through Hell, Keep Going." Posted on the *Quote Investigator* website. *http://quoteinvestigator.com/2014/09/14/keep-going/*. Note: This quote as used is often attributed to Winston Churchill, although according to this site, there is no evidence that Churchill ever expressed this thought in either version.

527 Josie Pickens, "Depression and the Black Superwoman Syndrome." Posted Apr. 15, 2014, on the *Ebony* website. *http://www.ebony.com/wellness-empowerment/depression-and-the-black-super woman-syndrome-777#axzz3WYRRlqi2*.

528 Spencer.

529 Pickens. Note: Pickens's article addresses the cost Black women pay for "doing the work to uplift others" and "masking up as superwomen;" however, many of her observations would apply to nearly every woman I've ever met, and many men as well.

530 Alfano has found that people with good insurance or financial resources are likely to have more options and better services than those without, people who may need to rely on community or religious organizations that are often stretched pretty thin. Nancy Knickerbocker, who has worked as a medical social worker, agrees. She likewise noted that the priority of providing quality mental health care for patients has lost ground to the demand for "documenting the care correctly in our electronic health records so that we can get the highest possible reimbursement. We're not allowed to have mental health issues that take a long time to heal," she adds. That said, we can also pay a lot of money for some pretty bad therapy, so it pays to look around—and *keep* looking until we find a good match with a group or therapist that fits our budget. Further, if money is an issue, Loretta Maase, a licensed certified counselor, recommends looking for highly rated or highly recommended practitioners. She says most busy therapists will still leave room on their calendars to see highly motivated, low-income patients at a reduced fee.

531 Smith, "The Never Enough Syndrome," 13.

532 Leman, Kevin. *Why Your Best Is Good Enough*, 17.

533 Alfano urges using what he calls "magic words," identifying yourself as a "danger to self (or others)" to get attention and help that might otherwise be put off or delayed.

534 Adderholdt and Goldberg.

535 Brené Brown, *The Gifts of Imperfection*, 10.

536 Jane Bluestein, "Non-Supportive Responses to Avoid."

537 Bryant McGill, quote posted on Bryant McGill's website. *http://bryantmcgill.com/excerpts/difference-between-giving-disengagement-know-difference.html*.

538 Toni Morrison, quote posted Apr. 24, 2013, on *The Tao of Dana* website. *http://www.fengshuidana.com/2013/04/24/if-you-want-to-fly/*.

539 Polona Somrak, "Soul Journey and Journaling." Blog on the *Ascension Pioneers* website. Posted May 4, 2013, *http://ascension-pioneers.org/articles/576-soul-journey-a-journaling.html*.

540 With thanks to Rudolf Alfano, Nancy Knickerbocker, and Loretta Maase. Also, "About AA Meetings." Posted © 2015 on the *Alcoholics Anonymous Australia* website. *http://www.aa.org.au/new-to-aa/about-aa-meetings.php*; also "Patterns and Characteristics of Codependence. Posted © 2015 on the *Co-dependents Anonymous* (CoDA) website. *http://coda.org/index.cfm/meeting-documents/patterns-and-characteristics-2011/*; "Welcome to Workaholics Anonymous." Posted © 2015 on the *Workaholics Anonymous* website. *http://www.workaholics-anonymous.org*; also "Finding Therapy," posted on the *Mental Health America* website. *http://www.mentalhealthamerica.net/finding-therapy*.

541 Rechtschaffen.

542 Somrak, "Soul Journey and Journaling."

543 Cameron, *The Artist's Way*, 96.

544 Anne Lamott, posted Apr. 8, 2015, on Anne Lamott's Facebook page. *https://www.facebook.com/AnneLamott/posts/662177577245222?fref=nf*.

545   I have always recommended journaling by hand because for me, the combination of the movement, the touch of the pen on the paper, and watching the ink flow into words and paragraphs is a great match for my visual-kinesthetic processing preferences. These days, physical pain prevents me from writing my thoughts and feelings out by hand, but I am still maintaining my journal with my laptop. It's not exactly the same, but it's close enough to still work well for me.

546   Miriam Adderholdt, "Perfectionism and the Gifted Adolescent." Chapter in *Understanding the Gifted Adolescent: Educational, Developmental, and Multicultural Issues*, edited by Marlene Bireley and Judy Genshaft. (New York: Teachers College Press, 1991).

547   Bradley Dowden, "Fallacies." Posted on the *Internet Encyclopedia of Philosophy* website. *http:// www.iep.utm.edu/fallacy/*.

548   "Psychotherapy." Post last modified Apr. 11, 2015, on the *Wikipedia* website. *http://en.wiki pedia.org/wiki/Psychotherapy*. Note: The practitioner in talk therapy could include a wide range of certifications including psychiatrist, psychologist, counselor, clinical social worker, clergy person, or alternative practitioner. Not all groups (such as 12-step programs) will involve a trained practitioner.

549   Includes material from Reid; also Polona Somrak, "The Soul Navigator;" also Burns, "The Perfectionist's Script for Self-Defeat," 46; also Brosh; also Beck, "Silencing the Voice That Says You're a Fraud."

550   These examples of therapeutic strategies include material from individual contributors, plus Antony and Swinson, 120–145; also Beck, "Inside the Minds of the Perfectionists;" also Webb; also Springer; also Ann Smith, "The Never Enough Syndrome," 13; also "Bibliotherapy." Definition from ODLIS, Online Dictionary for Library and Information Science, posted on the *American Library Association* website. *http://www.ala.org/tools/bibliotherapy*; also Bluestein and Katz; also Beck, "Silencing the Voice That Says You're a Fraud;" also professional licensed counselor Loretta Maase, who shared information about Dialectical Behavior Therapy. Note: Some treatments that are typically used with disorders other than perfectionism, such as depression, addiction, or obsessive-compulsive disorder, are likewise effective for treating perfectionism.

551   Bruce E. Wampold, "How Psychotherapy Works." Posted Dec. 22, 2009, on the *American Psychological Association's* website. *http://www.apa.org/news/press/releases/2009/12/wampold.aspx*; also "Psychotherapy." Post last modified Apr. 11, 2015, on the *Wikipedia* website. *http://en .wikipedia.org/wiki/Psychotherapy*

552   Among the most frequently mentioned were Eye Movement Desensitization and Reprocessing (EMDR) to help the brain reprocess information (especially traumatic events and memories), and Emotional Freedom Technique (EFT), a "psychological acupressure" technique designed to release energy blockages to alleviate emotional intensity and discomfort. Acupuncture and 12-step programs were also mentioned, along with other modalities, and a recent correspondence led to some interesting research on a Biocognitive Science approach. For more information: "How Does EMDR Work?" posted on the *EMDR International Association* website. *https://emdria.site-ym.com/?119*; also "What is EFT? The Origins and Background," posted 2015 on the *Energy Therapy Centre* website. *http://www. theenergytherapycentre.co.uk/eft-explained.htm*; also Tim Brown, "Body Psychotherapy: A Short Guide to the Art and Science of Bodylistening." Posted 2011 on the *Body Works* website. *http://www.bodyworks.org.uk/body_psychotherapy.htm*; also "12 Step Groups," last updated

March 2015 on the *Addictions and Recovery* website. *http://www.addictionsandrecovery.org/12-step-groups.htm*; also "Glossary: Types of Massage and Bodywork Defined." Posted 2003 on the *Massage Therapy* website. *http://www.massagetherapy.com/glossary/*; also "Philosophy (Mario Martinez, Biocognitive Science)." Posted on the *Biocognitive Science Institute* website. *http://www.biocognitive.com.*

553   Anonymous, "It All Began in Gym Class: Exercise Avoidance." Posted Nov. 24, 2007, on the *Overactive Fork* website. *https://overactivefork.wordpress.com/2007/11/24/it-began-in-gym-class-exercise-avoidance/*

554   Jane Alexander, "Brain Gym: Simple Exercises for a Better Mind and Body." Posted July 5, 2011, on the *Brutally Frank* website. *https://brutallyfrank.wordpress.com/2011/07/05/brain-gym-simple-exercises-for-a-better-mind-and-body/*. Also see "Edu-Kinesthetics: Brain Gym." Resources posted on the *Brain Gym/Edu-Kinesthetics* website. *http://www.braingym.com*; also "What is Brain Gym?" Information and resources posted on the *Brain Gym International* website. *http://www.braingym.org/about*. Brain Gym exercises offer a range of simple movements and positions that can change levels of alertness, including positions, usually referred to as "hook-ups," that can calm and center us, offering increased access to more rational parts of the brain.

555   Reid.

556   I am often the oldest and least fit (translate: largest) person in this class and although I hope to stop noticing that one day, I have gotten to the point where that really doesn't matter and has never kept me from participating. In fact, one of the highlights (and strongest reframing events) of my life was actually getting to *lead* a class a couple years ago.

557   Andrew Tate, "Steve Jobs Took Long Walks and Why You Should, Too." Posted March 6, 2015, on the *Design School Canva* website. *https://designschool.canva.com/blog/taking-long-walks/*.

558   Bluestein, Lawrence, and Sanchez. Activities excerpted from Chapter 2, "Wonder All Around."

559   June King, "Effects of Yoga on Children with Behavioural Problems," posted June 8, 2008, on the *Yoga Magazine* website. *http://www.yogamag.net/archives/2008/fjune08/behav.shtml*; also Elaine Gavalas, "Yoga May Help Relieve ADHD," updated Nov. 11, 2013, on the *Huffington Post* website. *http://www.huffingtonpost.com/elaine-gavalas/yoga-for-adhd_b_3849766.html*; also Emily Wax-Thibodeaux, "Warrior Pose: Yoga Catching on as Therapy for Veterans' PTSD," posted Apr. 13, 2015, on the *Stars and Stripes* website. *http://www.stripes.com/news/veterans/warrior-pose-yoga-catching-on-as-therapy-for-veterans-ptsd-1.339978* Note: Savasana, or "corpse pose," is an incredibly important yoga pose (or asana), which involves breath and body awareness, integration, and completion. The pose itself, lying on the floor, just happens to be one I can do.

560   Fucarino.

561   "Peter," contributor quoted in Bluestein and Katz, 155–156.

562   Bluestein and Katz, chapter 7.

563   Note: Selected music interventions can also be used therapeutically "to address physical, emotional, cognitive and social needs" and can help individuals in crisis "learn and use positive coping skills and express difficult feelings and emotions." From "Music Therapy in Response to Crisis and Trauma." Posted on the *American Music Therapy Association* website. *http://www.musictherapy.org/assets/1/7/MT_Crisis_2006.pdf*

564 Reid.

565 Taitetsu Unno, "Three Grapefruits: One Small Act of Giving Can Have Enormous Repercussions in an Interconnected World." Posted 2003 on the *Tricycle* website. *http://www.tricycle.com/practice/three-grapefruits*

566 Susanne Sagmeister, posted Mar. 17, 2015, on Suzanne Sagmeister's Facebook page. *https://www.facebook.com/sagmeisterphotography/photos/a.10151648205246849.1073741839.19661091848/10152799347666849/?type=1&theater.*

567 Mario Martinez, "Dr. Mario Martinez Discusses The Mind Body Code." Published May 28, 2013, on the *YouTube* website. *https://www.youtube.com/watch?v=f9KOQs5eS10.*

568 Courtney Walsh, from e-mail correspondence, July 3, 2013.

569 Erin Hanson, poem posted on *The Poetic Underground* website. *http://thepoeticunderground.com/post/55391927424/not-july-14th.* Used with permission.

The complete resource list and
bibliography for this book is available at:

http://janebluestein.com/2015/bibliography-for-the-perfection-deception/.